To Advance the Gospel

To Advance the Gospel

SELECTIONS FROM THE WRITINGS OF RUFUS ANDERSON

Edited with an Introduction

by

R. PIERCE BEAVER

WILLIAM B. EERDMANS PUBLISHING COMPANY
GRAND RAPIDS, MICHIGAN

FOREWORD

This is the second sourcebook on the rise and development of American missions in which the editor has endeavored to make available to students and readers important, and now rare, material which reveals the motives, aims, goals, principles, and methods of the earlier stages of the enterprise. Both have been published by William B. Eerdmans Publishing Company, a publisher performing a notable service in making Christian classics and historical sources currently available as well as publishing a wide range of religious books. The first in the series is *Pioneers in Mission: the Early American Missionary Ordination Sermons, Charges, and Instructions,* which closes with the ordination of the first overseas missionaries in 1812. This second volume gives the reader access to the thought of the grand architect of American foreign mission theory, Rufus Anderson.

It is strange that no full-scale scholarly study has been made with respect to either of the two greatest Protestant missionary thinkers and administrators of the nineteenth century, whose influence lasted until the middle of the twentieth, — Henry Venn, General Secretary of the Church Missionary Society of London, and Rufus Anderson, Corresponding (Foreign) Secretary of the American Board of Commissioners for Foreign Missions of Boston. Even the writings of these important missionary strategists are generally unavailable. The editor of this volume intends to make a further study of the life, thought, ministry, and influence of Dr. Anderson. Meanwhile he makes available this selection from his writings, introduced by an interpretative essay.

Published biographical material is scanty, mostly obituary notices, resolutions, and a slight volume published by the American Board:

Missionary Herald, vol. LXXVI, 1880, pp. 242, 247-251, 419.
ABCFM, *Annual Report, 1880,* p. xii.
Obituary by A. C. Thompson in *New York Observer,* June 3, 1880; reprinted.

Bradford Academy, *Memorials of Rufus Anderson, D.D., Mrs. Harriet Newell, and Mrs. Ann H. Judson;* Haverhill, Mass.: C. C. Morse & Son, 1884; pp. 3-8.

Thompson, A. C., and N. G. Clark, *Discourse Commemorative of Rev. Rufus Anderson, D.D., LL.D., late corresponding secretary of the American Board of Commissioners for Foreign Missions. Together with Addresses at the Funeral.* Boston: ABCFM, 1880. Commemorative discourse by Thompson and funeral addresses by Thompson and Clark.

There are three short treatments of Anderson's thought. The first is Study Six in Robert E. Speer's *Studies in Missionary Leadership;* Phila.: Westminster Press, 1914; pp. 237-238, entitled "Rufus Anderson, the Foremost American Missionary Administrator." Ten pages are devoted to Anderson by Peter Beyerhaus in *Die Selbstandigkeit der junger Kirchen als missionarisches Problem;* Wuppertal-Barmen: Verlag der Rheinischen Missions-Gesellschaft, 1956; pp. 45-56. Even less space is given in the English version, *The Responsible Church and the Foreign Mission,* by Peter Beyerhaus and Henry Lefever, Grand Rapids: Eerdmans, 1964. A third is an essay by the present editor, "Rufus Anderson's Missionary Principles," in *Christusprediking in de Wereld: Studiën op het Terrein van de Zendingswetenschap Gewijd aan de Nagedachtenis van Professor Dr. Johan Herman Bavinck;* Kampen: J. H. Kok N.V., 1965; pp. 43-62. The Werkcomité gave permission for publication of this essay also in some form in the United States. Some paragraphs of it have been incorporated into the introductory essay.

This collection of material excludes Dr. Anderson's historical works, which are the largest in size of his publications. It is hoped that the selections are sufficient to present the reader with the main features of his mission theory. Most of this material was originally published by the American Board, and it is now made available in this volume with the approval, encouragement, and permission of the officers of the successor agency, the United Church Board for Overseas Ministries.

The volume has grown too large for the inclusion of a highly desirable final item, the document in which the American Board officially incorporated Rufus Anderson's principles into stated policy. This is the famous *Outline of Missionary Policy,* written for the Prudential Committee by Secretary S. B. Treat, and adopted in 1856 as the ultimate and lasting result of the discussions which followed the presentation of the *Report of the Deputation* to India. Here theory is spelled out concretely in terms of policy.

TABLE OF CONTENTS

INTRODUCTION

Rufus Anderson,
Grand Strategist of American Missions

Rufus Anderson was described by Robert E. Speer as "the most original, the most constructive, and the most courageous student of missionary policy whom this country has produced, and one of the two most aggressive and creative administrators of missionary work."[1] Actually, in the judgment of the present writer, no other administrator has been his peer, and he combined original thought and decisive action to a degree unequalled by any other executive secretary in the entire course of the American overseas mission.[2] After ten years of "apprenticeship" as assistant secretary of the American Board of Commissioners for Foreign Missions, Dr. Anderson was for the next third of a century in office and then for another fourteen years in retirement the acknowledged theoretician of the American missionary enterprise. All the missionary agencies of the United States and Canada adopted most of the fundamental points of his policy. Robert E. Speer most closely resembles Anderson in interdenominational leadership in the subsequent period. He was Anderson's posthumous pupil and drew copiously from the master's ideas and principles. These he restated in numerous books and addresses and applied in his own administrative work. Andersonian principles, with this assist from Speer, continued to provide the basis

[1] Speer, Robert E., *Studies of Missionary Leadership;* Phila.: Westminster Press, 1914; p. 237.
[2] American missionary executives have been primarily administrators. The Church Missionary Society of London has been unique among Anglo-American agencies in expecting its general secretary to be first of all an original thinker and also an administrator, a tradition inaugurated by Anderson's contemporary and friend, Henry Venn.

9

of American missions through the decades of the 1930's. These boards and societies until the end of World War II generally stated the aim and goal of their ministry in terms of Rufus Anderson's "three-self" formula, — the planting and fostering of churches which would become "self-governing," "self-supporting," and "self-propagating."

ANDERSON'S MISSIONARY MINISTRY

Executive responsibility at the home base was to Rufus Anderson genuine missionary service. He discharged his missionary vocation in this manner, and not overseas, because the American Board of Commissioners for Foreign Missions requested this obedience of him. Born at North Yarmouth, Maine, on August 17, 1796, Rufus was the son of a distinguished pastor of the same name. Since his father belonged to the Hopkinsian school of New England theology, there was assured a missionary concern in the theological atmosphere of the home. Moreover, the father took his young son to the ordination service of the first band of overseas missionaries at the Tabernacle in Salem in 1812, and from that time forward the lad felt a strong sense of missionary vocation. The journal which he kept irregularly during student days contains numerous entries expressing his desire to be a missionary to India along with a conflicting sense of unworthiness.[3] After graduation at Bradford Academy, the young man entered Bowdoin College, of which his uncle was president, and took his A.B. degree in 1818. The next year he enrolled in Andover Theological Seminary, where he graduated in 1822. Despite the persistent feeling of unworthiness, Rufus presented himself to the American Board as a candidate for overseas service, and was accepted. However, for some time before graduation he had been assisting Jeremiah Evarts in the Board office with secretarial duties; and now, the volume of duties too much for one man, he was kept for the next year at these urgent duties. The Prudential Committee reported to the Board in 1823: "Mr. Anderson is ready to embark on a foreign mission. It will remain for the Board to decide whether his services will not be required at home."[4] By the spring of that year the decision was final, and the young man was named assistant secretary.

It was the practice of the New England Congregational churches to ordain a man only when he had received and accepted a call to a church. Beginning in 1812 ordination was extended to missionaries going into foreign service. It was a rare event when Rufus Anderson

[3] ABCFM Archives, ABC: 30.1., *Journal,* vols. 1-8; see entries for July 19, Aug. 17, Oct. 28, Nov. 24, Nov. 12, Dec. 31, 1815, for example.
[4] ABCFM, *Annual Report, 1823,* p. 137.

was ordained as an evangelist to be assistant secretary of the American Board along with four missionaries on May 10, 1826, at Springfield. This is probably the first instance when an American churchman was ordained to the ministry for denominational or interdenominational administration, and the office was properly regarded not as primarily administrative, but as missionary or evangelistic. As a missionary his salary was fixed in relation to missionary salaries rather than in comparison with the incomes of pastors and ecclesiastical dignitaries. No pastor in Boston received so small a stipend.[5] Dr. Elias Cornelius was elected corresponding secretary following the death of Jeremiah Evarts in 1831, but lived and served less than a year. Thereupon in 1832 Mr. Anderson was elected one of three corresponding secretaries and made a member of the Board.[6] Soon he became a member of the Prudential Committee and its chief guide. He was from the outset "the foreign secretary," while others handled the home base responsibilities. After a few years he was usually called "the senior secretary." He refused re-election in 1866, and his resignation was regretfully accepted.[7]

Retirement was from the duties of a specific office, but not from missionary service. Dr. Anderson remained a member of the Prudential Committee of his Board until 1875, when he was honored with emeritus status. Moreover, he was given an office in the headquarters, and there devoted himself to writing three histories of the missions and carrying on an extensive correspondence. He lectured at seminaries and colleges for a few years. Refraining entirely from administrative matters and leaving his successor a completely free hand, he gave of himself generously in consultation and writing past his eightieth year. Then increasing feebleness gradually restricted his activities until his death on May 30, 1880. He died acclaimed as the restorer of the apostolic model for mission, and all North American overseas missionary agencies professed to follow his teaching and to act on his principles.

Rufus Anderson never sought to impose his views on other boards and societies than his own. They spontaneously followed him on most points, taking American Board policy as their model. However, the senior secretary was sometimes accused of tyrannical domination of the American Board and its Prudential Committee. But according to his colleagues the Board and Committee members always found his reasoning irrefutable and adopted his views only after long and serious consideration, never giving mere "rubber stamp" approval. Some persons

---

[5] Thompson, A. G., *Discourse Commemorative of Rev. Rufus Anderson, D. D., LL.D.;* Boston: ABCFM, 1880; pp. 14-15.

[6] ABCFM, *Annual Report, 1823,* pp. 22-23.

[7] *Ibid., 1866,* pp. 39-46.

made similar charges of autocratic treatment of missionaries, especially in connection with the deputations to India and the Turkish Empire, when radical changes in program were effected. The missionaries declared that all decisions had been reached freely and democratically in open mission meeting, and although there were usually tremendous differences of opinion in the beginning, the secretary's careful and quiet presentation of a subject usually won the support of the great majority. Dr. Anderson was always pastor, as well as superintendent, to the missionaries. When he retired more than twelve hundred missionaries were serving under the American Board, and only six had not been appointed under him and upon his recommendation.[8]

PUBLICATIONS

Dr. Anderson wrote extensively, but his large works appeared mostly towards the end of his career. His publications on theoretical questions, excepting the book, *Foreign Missions: Their Relations and Claims,* are pamphlets, tracts, articles, and administrative documents, generally anonymous or simply signed "by a Secretary" or "by one of the Secretaries." He states in a footnote in the *Memorial Volume* that publications of the Board so signed are from his pen.[9] There is one exception, however, an important tract signed in this manner, which the present writer previously ascribed to Dr. Anderson. It is *The Grand Motive to Missionary Effort,* written by another of the secretaries, Dr. Swan L. Pomroy. These essays by Anderson were frequently reprinted, in a number of instances as items in the Board's series of *Missionary Tracts.* But pamphlets, tracts, and leaflets are fugitive and the location of articles is forgotten. Already by the time of his death much of this material was out-of-print and difficult to find. Not even the volume, *Foreign Missions: Their Relations and Claims,* a collection of lectures, brought Anderson's ideas into systematic presentation. The unavailability of much of the literature caused later generations of mission board directors, secretaries, and missionaries, to forget the origin of much of their basic policy and practice. The common pattern to which the American agencies had all come under Rufus Anderson's guidance through fifty years was passed on to following generations as the living, working tradition of the boards and societies although there was considerable modification in details.

---

[8] *Dr. Anderson's Farewell Letter to the Missionaries, July 5, 1866;* Boston: printed by the ABCFM for strictly private use, 1866.

[9] [Anderson, Rufus, ed. and major author], *Memorial Volume of the First Fifty Years of the American Board of Commissioners for Foreign Missions;* Boston: The Board, 1861; p. 192.

A list of Dr. Anderson's publications follows this introductory essay. It should be noted that many of them appear in the form of statements submitted to the annual meeting of the ABCFM by the Prudential Committee. Dr. Anderson's method was to prepare in advance full and often lengthy statements on important issues and problems, to present them to the Prudential Committee for study and discussion, and when adopted or commended to present them to the full meeting of the Board along with the Prudential Committee's recommendation. Quite often such statements were then both printed as part of the report of the annual meeting and as a separate pamphlet.

REACTION AGAINST THE EMPHASIS ON CIVILIZATION

The chief literary activity of the young assistant secretary for the decade after his appointment in 1823 was the editorship of *The Missionary Herald*. He wrote a *Memoir of Catherine Brown* and a few other compositions, but it was not until after the deaths of Evarts and Cornelius and his election to the office of corresponding secretary in 1832 that Mr. Anderson began to use pen and voice with vigor in an effort to shape the policy of the American Board and to influence American missions in general. He began by reacting sharply against what he thought to be wrong aims, methods, and emphases which had been inherited from the earlier missions to the American Indians and which prevailed in the overseas work. "Evangelization" and "civilization" had been the key words in American mission methods, — and in Protestant missions on the whole. There was argument about which should have priority, but it was generally held that the two were supplementary and complementary. It was believed that acceptance of the gospel through "evangelization" always brought to non-European peoples the desire and incentive to attain "Christian," i.e., *European* civilization; while if "civilization" were stressed in initial contacts with such people it produced understanding and acceptance of the gospel. Consequently, "civilization" was emphasized especially as fostered through schools.

Rufus Anderson believed it a grave mistake to make the transformation of civilization the aim of the mission. He had no doubt that "the civilization which the gospel has conferred upon our own New England is the highest and best, in a religious point of view, the world has yet seen,"[10] and that given plenty of time Christian faith would transform any society. But this would be a by-product of the mission, not its aim.

[10] *The Theory of Missions to the Heathen*, p. 73 below. Note that page references to selections in this book are to pages in this book, while references to those not here included are to pages in the edition used.

The very perfection of the European-American religious and social state tended to be a formidable hindrance to the prosecution of purely spiritual missions because missionaries and their supporters identify the Christian religion itself with "the almost universal diffusion among its professors of the blessings of education, industry, civil liberty, family government, social order, the means of a respectable livelihood, and a well-ordered community."[11] They erroneously expect the piety of new converts to be manifested in the forms familiar in England and New England, and the propagation of the faith is regarded as "the creation among heathen tribes and nations of a highly improved state of society, such as we ourselves enjoy."[12] Although this transformation of society took ages to achieve in the West, yet British and American Christians seem now to think that it should happen almost simultaneously with conversion of the first small group of neophytes. If this result is not speedily attained, then there seems to be a tendency to doubt both the genuineness of conversion and the faithfulness of the missionaries. The fatal consequence is that

> Unless this influence is guarded against by missionaries and their directors, the result is that missions have a twofold object of pursuit; the one, that simple and sublime spiritual object of the ambassador of Christ mentioned in the text, "persuading men to be reconciled to God," the other, the reorganizing, by various direct means, of the structure of that social system, of which the converts form a part. Thus the object of missions becomes more or less complicated, leading to a complex, burdensome, and perhaps expensive course of measurements for its attainment.[13]

Therefore, Anderson sounded a clarion call to move forward in a different direction, to a simple spiritual mission of proclamation of the gospel so as to win souls, gather them into churches, and enlist them in the same mission.

The Pauline Model

It was in the New Testament, and particularly in the work of Saint Paul, that Rufus Anderson found the lasting norm and model for Christian missions. The Apostles were missionaries in the ordinary sense, even though they were given inspiration, authority, and miraculous powers peculiar to them alone. Despite their unique equipment they profited by experience, and that experience later missionaries will find helpful for their own instruction and encouragement. It puzzled An-

[11] *Ibid.*
[12] *Ibid.*
[13] *Ibid.*, pp. 74-75.

derson that the Apostles were so slow in discharging their missionary responsibility. They had to be taught by Paul that the Church was for the whole world. Even the commissioning of Paul and Barnabas by the Church of Antioch did not inaugurate the real foreign mission. It was only when the constitution of the Gentile churches had been settled by apostolic authority in the meeting at Jerusalem and when Paul embarked on his second tour that he began his uninterrupted career as a foreign missionary. All this time apparently was necessary to develop the understanding of the pure spiritual character of the Church and of missionary work. There is no reliable evidence about the missionary activity among the Gentiles by the other Apostles, and so it is to Saint Paul that one must look for illuminating principles.

There are nine observations to be made about Paul as a missionary.[14] First, as Christ's ambassador, authorized to speak in His name, Paul sustained an intimate relationship to our Lord, which gave him courage and spiritual strength. Secondly, his responsibility under the Great Commission was "to plant and water," that is, in the general publication of the gospel he was to gather converts into churches. Thirdly, and this seems to be the most important point, his "grand means as a missionary" was the gathering and forming of local churches, each placed under its own presbyters for pastoral care. When thus organized, the Apostle would leave the local church safely to itself under the supervising grace of God. Anderson comments: "Had not the apostolic idea of self-governing, self-supporting, self-propagating churches dropped out of the Christian mind soon after the age of the Apostles, not to be fully regained until modern times, how very different had been the history of Christendom and of the world!" The fourth observation is that despite their special inspiration and miraculous powers, the Apostles did not appear to their contemporaries to be extraordinary individuals, and outside the household of faith they were accorded no more reverence and esteem than modern missionaries. Fifthly, there were no missionary societies. The poor churches of Judaea even looked to the Gentile churches for relief. Peter and the others "lived by the Gospel" in preaching to the Jews, while Paul among the Gentiles relied mostly upon his own labor for support. He and Barnabas probably used their private property for the work, and Paul did allow the Church of Philippi to provide for his support. He enjoyed the hospitality of converts, but did not depend upon his mission churches for his maintenance. In the sixth place, the apostolic strategy was to work from the bottom of society upward, not from the top down. Next the influence of "pious females" in the mission is noted. Eighthly, the apostolic

[14] *Foreign Missions: Their Relations and Claims*, pp. 44ff.

churches do not excel the modern churches in perfection, and grave
defects coexisted with great excellencies. "We come to this result as to
the character of the apostolic churches: that while the primitive converts were remarkable as a class for the high tone of their religious
feelings, and the simplicity and strength of their faith, they were deficient in a clear, practical apprehension of the *ethical code* of the
Gospel. Considering all things, this was not strange; and we should
always remember this, when we consider the character of modern
mission churches. The situation of the young churches is parallel to that
of the apostolic churches, not to those of Europe and America." Finally, the Apostles had no great large-scale successes. They did see
self-governing, self-supporting, self-propagating local churches planted
in all the principal cities of the Roman Empire. They were lights
shining amid deep spiritual gloom, and each was extending its illumination.

The pioneer theoretician of American missions summed up the
distinctive characteristics of apostolic missions in these words:

> Such were the apostolic missions. Such were the efforts made for
> propagating the Gospel among the heathen by missionaries under a
> special divine guidance. It was by gathering converts into churches at
> the centers of influence, and putting them under native pastoral in-
> spection and care. The means employed were spiritual; namely, the
> Gospel of Christ. The power relied upon for giving efficacy to these
> means was divine; namely, the promised aid of the Holy Spirit. The
> main success was among the middle and lower classes of society; and
> the responsibilities for self-government, self-support, and self-propa-
> gation were thrown at once upon the several churches.[15]

This, then, was the picture of apostolic missions which Rufus Anderson drew, and he brought emotional as well as intellectual understanding to it. It was by this ideal that he judged the contemporary
mission. It was in accord with this model that he sought to reconstruct
American Board missions, and on this foundation he erected his theoretical system. He did not find in apostolic missions an exact blueprint for
the conduct of all subsequent missionary activities until the end of time;
but he did find here a set of principles and a norm which he believed
always to be valid. If this were recognized, then changing situations
and circumstances in the course of history and in any particular place
or culture could properly be taken into account. Above all, young
churches were to be *churches* from the outset, and not colonial outposts
of Western churches nor carbon copies of them.

[15] *Ibid.,* p. 61; see also p. 109.

CHRISTIAN OBEDIENCE

The major motive in American missions from the seventeenth century until the rise of overseas missions was *gloria Dei*.[16] But, most strangely, the giving of glory to God then lost influence and was replaced by the motives of obedience and pity for the perishing souls of the heathen. Only two sermons out of one hundred twenty-six dated between 1825 and 1850 mention it. Rufus Anderson, despite the Hopkinsian background of his youth, is typical of his contemporaries in ignoring it. For him Christian obedience is the prime motive and mission is the fundamental and central function of the Church of Christ. Seeking the salvation of souls because of love of Christ is his second motive, and the opportunity of meeting the greatest need of mankind is the third.

Mission, to Anderson, is "the great thing" for which the Church exists and for which the Christian lives.[17] The Great Commission "of our Lord presents, and was intended to present, the great standing work of the Christian Church for all ages of the world."[18] The Church has been lazy and disobedient with respect to its missionary obligation.[19] To be sure, it was not until the nineteenth century that providence actually opened the way for evangelical Christians to evangelize the world, but in a second "fullness of time" — comparable to the first at the advent of our Lord — the door had now been fully opened, heathen nations rendered accessible, communications made easy, and voluntary associations for missions organized.[20] This situation summoned the Church to missionary obedience with a new urgency.[21] "One grand end of the organization of the church is, that it may distribute to every kindred, and tongue, and people, and nation under the whole heavens, the bread of eternal life."[22]

Dr. Anderson through half a century urged upon the church in America its "standing task," but it was primarily individual disciples whom he challenged. The obligation rests upon the individual Christian rather than upon the Church collectively, and obedience is primarily a personal matter. Study of the New Testament convinced Anderson that the preaching of the gospel to the world and the discipling of the

---

[16] Beaver, R. Pierce, *Pioneers in Mission;* Grand Rapids: Eerdmans, 1966; pp. 17-19.

[17] *The Promised Advent of the Spirit*, p. 47.

[18] *The Time for the World's Conversion Come*, p. 61.

[19] *The Promised Advent of the Spirit*, pp. 49, 57.

[20] *The Time for the World's Conversion Come*, pp. 60, 63ff., 68; *Theory of Missions to the Heathen*, p. 73.

[21] *Time for the World's Conversion Come*, pp. 68ff.

[22] *Ought I to Become a Missionary to the Heathen?*, pp. 182-183.

nations was first and always committed by our Lord to individual believers rather than to the Church, because the Great Commission was
given prior to the emergence of the Church.[23] Each Christian is to
decide under the guidance of the Holy Spirit whether he is to offer
himself for overseas service or whether he is to support those sent
abroad.[24] None other than the Holy Spirit can tell him. He who goes
abroad goes primarily in discharge of his own personal obligation.

> It is a fundamental principle, that the missionary goes on his mis-
> sion in the discharge of his own personal duty; not as a servant of
> the churches, and not as a servant of the missionary society. The
> churches and the missionary society are his helpers, to carry out his
> own benevolent purpose. The missionary is indebted to the churches
> just as the churches are indebted to him; and he does their work in
> the same sense in which they do his by supporting him.[25]

Undoubtedly the senior secretary of the greatest interdenominational
voluntary society was confirmed in his view of the New Testament teaching by the peculiar necessities of Congregational polity and the practical
issues involved in interdenominational cooperation, on the one hand,
and the attacks of Old School Presbyterians on the legitimacy of voluntary associations, on the other. The Old School leaders, who resented
Presbyterian participation in union home and foreign missionary societies, insisted that the missionary obligation and function belong to
the Church, and not to individuals either in their personal obedience
or their voluntary association as a group in organizations outside an
ecclesiastical structure. Nevertheless, Dr. Anderson sincerely believed
that the New Testament evidence puts the obligation and duty squarely
on each individual Christian and especially upon ministers, whose call
to preach the gospel is a universal one.

Two tracts on this subject are addressed to ministers and theological
students and were tremendously influential in stimulating missionary
vocation. Robert E. Speer many decades later took the essential points
of both and incorporated them into his tract, *What Constitutes a Missionary Call?*, which was reprinted in innumerable editions and helped
thousands of Student Volunteers to make their decisions. They are:
Ought I to Become a Missionary to the Heathen?[26] and *On Decid-*

[23] Yet Anderson always presented the mission as the Church's mission. The
missionary movement "is the Christian Church going forth, under its Great Captain, for the subjugation of the world" (*Foreign Missions*, p. 307).
[24] The assumption is that the call is to foreign service unless it can clearly be
known to be to the domestic field. See Selection 10, *passim*.
[25] *Foreign Missions: Their Relations and Claims*, Chapter IX, "Missionary Life
Illustrated," p. 197. See also p. 132.
[26] Pp. 175-184. See also *Foreign Missions*, Ch. XIII.

ing Early to Become a Missionary to the Heathen.[27] Since the duty
is binding on all Christians, an extraordinary call of the Holy Spirit
seldom occurs. Careful study of the situation of mankind and of Christ's
provision for the world's salvation should, by the illumination of the
Spirit, convince one of his duty and awaken interest. Our own feelings
and desires may never be taken as a test of duty, and a strong bias in
favor of home keeps many from obedience. Ardent desire for foreign
work will come after thorough, impartial, and prayerful examination,
for then usually the wants of that field will be seen to be more urgent
than those of the domestic field and the call will be louder.

> But what Christian, in these circumstances, would not have this desire?
> It is nothing mysterious or uncommon — nothing but the feelings com-
> mon to every pious heart, directed by a judgment under the influence
> of truth, and the Spirit of God, strongly drawn out toward the heathen
> by their wretched, helpless, perishing condition. This is the true, much
> talked of, but much mistaken, *missionary spirit.*[28]

"The foreign and domestic are but departments of the same grand
field."[29] No special call is needed then to Burma or India. Let each
decide what portion of the field opens the widest prospect of usefulness
and the most urgent demand for his labors. That "unconditional commission," the command of Christ, bids us to go, if we can, and the
example of the Apostles seconds it. They were required to begin at
Jerusalem but forbidden to remain there; and when they lingered too
long they were scattered abroad by a persecution. If it is argued that
the need at home for ministers is as great as abroad, then the utmost
that can be inferred is that an equal number should be distributed to
both fields. With our Savior's unconditional commission in our hand,
and the condition and destiny of the heathen before us, let us ponder
the question of our duty and obedience, admonishes Mr. Anderson.
There has been, there is, guilt somewhere. "Let us see to it, that it rest
not on our heads." Therefore, "every student, looking forward to the
sacred ministry, should decide EARLY, in view of existing circumstances, whether duty requires him to become a missionary to the
heathen."[30] Many advantages come from knowing early where is the
field to which the Holy Ghost calls a minister: studies can best be
utilized, one possesses a tranquil mind, influence for the cause can be
exerted on fellow students, later on in the field one is likely to be more

[27] Pp. 185-196.
[28] *Ought I to Become a Missionary to the Heathen?*, p. 178.
[29] *Ibid.*, p. 179.
[30] *On Deciding Early to Become a Missionary to the Heathen*, p. 185.

courageous, and cheerful, and useful. "The command to 'preach the gospel to every creature,' comes to us with a distinct specification of the unevangelized world as our field; and we rest in this decision, till unanticipated, unsought-for events change the grounds of our decision, and call for reconsideration, and perhaps a reversal."[31]

The Great Commission voices Christ's charge to both Church and disciple. It is his explicit and unlimited command, especially urgent now. "To us he says, 'Go!' — with an emphasis and a meaning such as the command never had to ministers and Christians in former ages."[32] Yet this obedience is not submission to power nor legalistic conformity to an authoritarian decree. It is rather the glad obedience of love to the heart's desire of the Beloved and to the prompting of his Holy Spirit. "It is a desire springing from supreme love to the Savior."[33] All the greater reason then that this is a commission to be obeyed. True Christian love of fellow men, genuine compassion for perishing souls, not the popular frantic, sentimental "plucking of brands from the burning" so common in that day, adds to this sense of duty, accenting Christ's loving command, because it is a love derived from his own. The present working of God's providence in preparing the way for mission underscores the duty imposed by both loves.

> Should we take the wings of the morning, and fly millions of leagues beyond our globe, we could by no means thus escape from the responsibility that has come upon us; for we know our duty, and we can never be as though we had not known it. We should be held and treated, wherever found by ministering angels, as deserters from the army of the Lord of hosts. God's Word, and Spirit, and Providence now all concur in the command to publish the gospel to all the nations; and if we refuse, the blood of perishing nations will cry against us. This is the age for the work, and we are the people to do it. From this warfare Christ will give us no discharge.[34]

> Let us get the full impress of our duty. Let us awake to its great reality. Nothing is more truly binding upon us than the obligation to impart the gospel to those whom we can reach, and who will perish if they do not receive it. That surely is the most destructive immorality which withholds from immortal man the only gospel of salvation. The most pernicious infidelity is surely that which cares not for a world perishing in sin. And that must be the most high-handed disregard of Heaven's authority, and must reflect most dishonor upon the Son of God, which refuses, in the face of his most explicit command, to publish the gospel to every creature. Let us remember, that

[31] *Ibid.,* pp. 186-187.
[32] *The Time for the World's Conversion Come,* p. 69.
[33] *Ought I to Become a Missionary to the Heathen?,* p. 178.
[34] *The Time for the World's Conversion Come,* p. 69.

He who requires this is our God, in whose hands are our possessions, our lives, and our immortal souls, and that our opportunities are rushing by us, and fast passing away forever.[35]

THE HOLY SPIRIT

The Holy Spirit is the ever-present prompter of Church and disciple to missionary obedience, the opener of the door of opportunity, and the power for witness. He is evidently God himself in missionary action. Dr. Anderson was first impressed with the missionary activity of the Spirit in the contemporary world scene which was then so urgently summoning Christians to missionary dedication. One hears echoes of Jonathan Edwards here. After two centuries of American missions to the Indians on the frontier and a quarter-century of sending missionaries overseas, it was evident that human disobedience and weakness within the Church so inhibited evangelism that the Church on its own would never convert the world, although this is its "standing work." The majority of Christians persist in regarding missions as a "charity" and not the great thing for which the Church exists and the Christian lives.[36]

Yet it must confidently be expected that the world will be converted by human instrumentality, because, as the Prophet Joel foretold, both Church and world would receive a transforming visitation from on high. "There is to be an advent of the Spirit, so to speak — a grand putting forth of his influence, a mighty effort of his power, that shall insure both the publication and the triumph of the gospel over all the world."[37] Only the divine power can accomplish so great a work; it is not only prophesied but is the inevitable consequence of Christ's work of reconciliation. The foretold results of the reign of the Messiah are still to come. The expected outpouring of the Spirit is even now indicated by remarkable preparatory measures of a providential nature in the world and of renewal within the Church, even in young churches in heathen lands, such as the Sandwich Islands' "Great Awakening" of 1836-1839. When this outpouring reaches flood tide, no Christian will hold back from world evangelism and the needed resources for mission will be brought forth. The Spirit will move the Church, but meanwhile the Church is required to go before the Spirit and prepare for his advent. In fact, evidence multiplies that the fullness of the time

[35] *Ibid.,* p. 70.
[36] *The Promised Advent of the Spirit,* p. 47.
[37] *Ibid.,* p. 48.

has come, the Spirit is pouring out upon the Church, and the time for the world's conversion has come.[38]

It is the same Holy Spirit who leads the individual disciple to his missionary vocation. This he does not by an extraordinary special call, but by guiding and illuminating him in a quiet, serious, prayerful study of the gospel, of the provision for its extension, of the present state of mankind, of one's own abilities and situation, and of God's intended place for that person in his service.[39] It is the Spirit who determines the real nature of mission and gives power for its accomplishment, — the purely spiritual work of reconciling men to God in Christ.[40] The Spirit in modern times as in the days of the Apostles seems to "restrict his converting influences among the heathen chiefly to this species of agency, and to this grand theme," i. e., the ministry of reconciliation and the preaching of the cross of Christ.[41] "Conversion is the prerogative and work of the Holy Spirit."[42] The missionary may not usurp his role, and "the conversion of the world, strictly speaking, is made no part of our duty." The Spirit, the ultimate Converter, may effect conversion by other means, but he usually effects it through "the living preacher." If this is the heart of mission work, then the missionary and the society may look for the aid of the Holy Spirit.[43] The mission churches are subject to the same laws of spiritual growth and development as any individual disciple.[44] "And when the unevangelized world shall be dotted over with such churches, so that all men have it within their power to learn what they must do to be saved, then we may expect the promised advent of the Spirit, and the conversion of the world."[45]

The Purpose and Goal of Mission

The true and only office and work of missions to the heathen is the beseeching of men to be reconciled to God in Jesus Christ.[46] The object of the mission then, from one point of view, may be said to be the saving of souls, which is a work of faith designed to manifest the great-

[38] *The Time for the World's Conversion Come*, pp. 59-60.

[39] *Ought I to Become a Missionary to the Heathen?* and *On Deciding Early to Become a Missionary to the Heathen, passim*, pp. 175-184; 185-196.

[40] *The Theory of Missions to the Heathen, passim*, pp. 73-88.

[41] *Ibid.*, p. 78.

[42] American Board Archives, Personal Papers of Rufus Anderson, "Manuscript of an Address to Students," n.d., c. 1836; ABC:30, v. 23.

[43] *The Theory of Missions to the Heathen, passim*, p. 85.

[44] *Memorial Volume*, Section: The Missions, Ch. III, "Development of the Missions," pp. 90ff.

[45] *Foreign Missions: Their Relations and Claims*, Ch. VII, p. 101 below.

[46] *The Theory of Missions to the Heathen*, p. 75.

ness and power of God.[47] However, the winning of souls to Christ is not merely a matter of seeking individual conversions. Converts are to be gathered into churches which will, on the one hand, nourish the disciples, and, on the other, take up the task of evangelism. "The great object of foreign missions is to persuade men to be reconciled to God, as their rightful and only Sovereign; and the organization of churches is as really a means to this great end, as the preaching of the gospel, or the printing of the Holy Scriptures."[48] "The chief work of evangelical Christendom for the conversion of the heathen world, is to plant churches, instinct with gospel life, in all the central and influential districts of the unevangelized land."[49] "The grand object is to plant and multiply self-reliant, efficient churches, composed wholly of native converts, each church complete in itself, with pastors of the same race with people."[50] While such churches should be self-governing and self-supporting, the fundamental hope is that "they should also be self-propagating from the very first."[51] Such churches are the "life, strength, and glory of missions." Located in strategic places they then undertake the evangelization of their countrymen throughout the whole land while the missionaries go on to other frontiers, but their duty is as universal as that of the churches which have planted them through missionaries. They are to undertake their own part in the world mission and become sending churches also. Self-propagation is not simply local evangelism. Dr. Anderson asserted, having cited the Hawaiian Church as an example, that "it is impossible for mission churches to reach their highest and truest state, without the aid of what is to them virtually a foreign mission, — without some outside field of labor for them, resembling the 'hole of the pit' from which they had themselves been digged."[52]

As the result of discussion following the Report on the Deputation to India in 1856, the American Board of Commissioners for Foreign Missions adopted its celebrated *Outline of Missionary Policy*, in which Dr. Anderson's principles were formulated into official policy.[53] It

[47] *Report of the Deputation to the India Missions;* Boston: The Board, 1856; pp. 66-67.

[48] *The Control to Be Exercised over Missionaries and Mission Churches,* p. 138.

[49] *Foreign Missions: Their Relations and Claims,* Ch. VIII, "The Value of Native Churches," p. 113.

[50] *Ibid.,* Ch. VII, "Principles and Methods of Modern Missions," p. 101.

[51] *Ibid.,* pp. 98-99.

[52] *Ibid.,* Ch. VI, "Historical Development of Modern Missions," p. 107 (not in this collection, p. ref. to original text).

[53] *Outline of Missionary Policy;* Boston: The Board, 1856; Missionary Tract No. 15. Drafted by Dr. S. B. Treat.

opens with the Andersonian affirmation: "Missions are instituted *for the spread of a scriptural, self-propagating Christianity. This is their only aim.*"[54] This aim of missions includes four elements: "(1) the conversion of lost men, (2) organizing them into churches, (3) giving those churches a competent native ministry, and (4) conducting them to the stage of independence and (in most cases) of self-propagation."[55]

Simplicity of administration and methods and avoidance of secular complications are in accord with such an object. Rufus Anderson never ceased to be impressed with the magnitude of the task of world evangelization and the paucity of resources for it. It is imperative that every society and board, along with every missionary, practice good stewardship. Since multitudes are perishing without knowledge of the gospel, speed is urgent. Therefore, considerations of time and economy in personnel and funds demand cooperation among missionary societies in a united evangelistic approach to the entire globe, agreeing upon assignment of responsibility in particular regions to particular agencies and establishing comity in every locality. The American Board's foreign secretary was one of the chief architects of the pan-Protestant system of comity.[56]

The mission board or society in the process of attaining this goal is not a denominational or confessional empire builder but merely a functional agency for associating Christians and congregations for sending missionaries who will plant and foster churches which will take up their part in the same universal task. The means which its missionaries employ in seeking this end are not prescribed, excepting preaching, and they may vary according to conditions. The test is pragmatic, not theological. "Whatever assists in imparting efficiency to the gospel comes fairly within the meaning of our great commission."[57] Preaching is the most important, and it is most effective in the regular stated worship services and other more informal meetings of a gathered congregation.[58] All other methods, including providing the Bible in the vernacular, which is an extension of preaching,[59] are directed to building up the local church for its mission. "Education, schools, the press, and whatever else goes to make up the working system, are held in strict

[54] *Ibid.,* p. 3.
[55] *Ibid.,* p. 5.
[56] See especially relevant sections in the ABCFM *Annual Report, 1836, 1837, 1838,* and for a review and documentation, R. Pierce Beaver, *Ecumenical Beginnings in Protestant World Mission;* N. Y.: Thomas Nelson and Sons, 1962; pp. 47-59.
[57] *Outline of Missionary Policy,* p. 6.
[58] *Memorial Volume,* Ch. III, "Development of the Missions," pp. 89-90.
[59] *Ibid.,* p. 90.

subordination to the planting and building up of effective working churches."[60]

School and press and all other activities are only auxiliaries, giving greater power to the preacher's voice. Since oral preaching is ever the grand means for the proclamation of the gospel, the ordained missionary and the native pastor are the key agents.[61] There are two considerations to be kept in mind in the use of all means and methods. One is to remain free from the old error which holds that civilization is the end of mission work. "Civilization, as an *end,* missions never attempt; still they are the most successful of all civilizing agencies, because (1) a certain degree of general improvement is involved in a self-propagating Christianity, and must be fostered as a *means* thereto; and (2) a rapid change in the intellectual and social life is a sure outgrowth therefrom."[62] Social progress is the inevitable by-product of missions, but only a by-product. "The proper test of success in missions, is not the progress of civilization, but the evidence of a religious life."[63] The other consideration is that all such auxiliaries be principally aids to oral preaching and the growth of local self-propagating churches. "The governing object to be always aimed at, is self-reliant, effective churches, — churches that are purely native. . . . The use of schools and the press comes under the question, how far are they subservient to the great end, namely, the rapid and perfect development of churches."[64]

Rufus Anderson was regarded by many British and some American missionaries and mission directors as being anti-education. They looked upon him as the prime foe of Alexander Duff and Scottish mission methods. He was not. From the very beginning of his ministry he insisted upon the necessity of schools and of education. The tract of 1838 on *Missionary Schools*[65] is the chief American apology for missionary education. This pamphlet, the second tract of the same title of 1861, Chapter VII of the *Memorial Volume,* and numerous passages in many of his works refute the erroneous notion. The state of culture and religion, the prevalence of superstition in every non-Christian land, even in the old societies of Asia, hold the mind in thraldom. Converts need enlightenment so that they may become self-responsible,

---

[60] *Foreign Missions: Their Relations and Claims,* Ch. VII, "Principles and Methods of Modern Missions," p. 99.

[61] *Outline of Missionary Policy,* p. 5.

[62] *Ibid.,* pp. 7-8.

[63] *Foreign Missions: Their Relations and Claims,* Ch. VII, "Principles and Methods of Modern Missions," p. 102.

[64] *Ibid.,* p. 99.

[65] Pp. 147-167.

Bible reading, practicing Christians; and national teachers, evangelists, and pastors simply have to be educated to fulfill their offices.[66] When we both give the people the Bible and then teach them to read it, we are obeying the Great Commission.[67] Schools

> are not designed to open and smooth the way for the gospel. They
> are not *preparatory* work. They are the very work itself — as much
> so as the conferring of miraculous gifts or prophecy and teaching, or
> the writing of the Gospels, or the inspired Epistles anciently were.
> The schools are — if they are what they ought to be — nurseries of
> piety, places and means for the direct inculcation of gospel truth in
> youthful minds and hearts. They are folds where the lambs of the
> flock are to be fed.[68]

Missions cannot educate the whole body of youth of a nation. They are to be particularly for training laity and educating national workers in the Church, but they can also be model schools and nurseries for teachers.[69] The system may eventually be extensive, but: "The rule is this; — *That the system of education, in all its parts, so far as it is supported by the funds of the mission, should have a direct reference to the training up of native teachers and preachers.*"[70] Thirty years later in retirement Dr. Anderson could confidently affirm: "Without education, it is not possible for mission churches to be in any proper sense self-governed; nor, without it, will they be self-supported, and much less self-propagating."[71]

The issue with Anderson was never that of schools or no schools, but, first, one of schools for nourishing the churches versus schools for cultivating public favor and providing supposed evangelistic opportunity and, second, of vernacular over against English instruction. The senior secretary went to India in 1854-1855 with the intent of breaking up the great concentrated, central mission stations, organizing village churches, and ordaining national pastors of those rural churches. He went also to challenge the growing tendency to conduct higher schools using the English language. He questioned in these schools the employment of non-Christians. "The heathen schoolmaster is a questionable agent for inculcating gospel truth." As he saw it, the English language schools neither trained pastors nor produced conversions, but only provided the government and commercial firms with English-

---

[66] *Missionary Schools,* p. 156; *Theory of Missions to the Heathen,* pp. 79-80.
[67] *Ibid.,* p. 161.
[68] *Ibid.,* pp. 161-162.
[69] *Ibid.,* p. 163.
[70] *Ibid.,* p. 164.
[71] *Foreign Missions: Their Relations and Claims,* Ch. VII, "Principles and Methods of Modern Missions," p. 99.

speaking clerks and minor officers. The Marathi Mission by 1855 had not one convert among 10,000 pupils and the Ceylon Mission could point to only about thirty out of 30,000.[72] The conclusion was: "Schools, regarded as *converting* instrumentalities, have almost wholly disappointed us; regarded as *preparatory* means, they have not answered expectations; and as *auxiliaries,* they have been expensive."[73] Such schools received government grants, and that could lead to undesirable control. There might, indeed, be some place for some such schools in great cities but not in the rural areas of India or other countries. They might be an approach to the elite of Indian society. They might be the exception, but not the rule. As Dr. Anderson told his critic, the Scottish Free Church secretary, Dr. Robert S. Candlish: "Decidedly Christian schools, adapted to the condition of the people, following in the train of the preached gospel, and purely auxiliary to its ministrations, we all regard, and have long regarded, as an essential element in a well-conducted mission."[74]

THE OFFICE OF MISSIONARY

The missionary goes abroad with the same design as that on which Paul and his associates were sent, — to be an ambassador for Christ, beseeching men to be reconciled to God. "They are ambassadors sent on the same general errand that brought the Lord Jesus from heaven, and their commission is to proclaim abroad the fact, history, design, and effect of his atonement, and bring its renovating power to bear as widely as possible upon the human race."[75] The missionary preaches the cross of Christ.[76] His business is not with Christian believers, but with the unconverted.[77] He is an evangelist, not a pastor or ruler.[78] His office, like that of the Apostles, the first evangelists, is very different from that of the pastor, and his function is to proclaim the gospel and plant its institutions.[79] The missionary's first duty is to gather a local church.[80] He should then not be its pastor, but having planted

[72] *Report of the Deputation to the India Missions;* Boston: The Board, 1856; p. 28.

[73] *Ibid.*

[74] *Letter to the Rev. Robert S. Candlish, D. D.;* Boston: T. R. Marvin and Son, 1862; portion reproduced here as Selection 10, p. 172.

[75] *Theory of Missions to the Heathen,* p. 75.

[76] *Ibid.,* p. 78.

[77] *Ibid.,* p. 76.

[78] *The Control to Be Exercised over Missionaries and Mission Churches,* p. 123.

[79] *Theory of Missions to the Heathen,* pp. 75-76.

[80] *Foreign Missions: Their Relations and Claims,* Ch. VII, "Principles and Methods of Modern Missions," p. 97.

it and others he will be to them a father in God and a spiritual ad-
visor.[81] The missionary prepares new fields for pastors, and when they
have been prepared and he can turn them over to competent pastors,
then "he ought himself to move onwards, — the pioneer of Christian
institutions, and in effect of a Christian civilization — but in office,
work, and spirit, an ambassador for Christ, to preach the gospel where
it has not been preached."[82]

The sole exception to the rule on pastoral service is at the time of
the organization of the church, if then there is no competent national
pastor available. But this is to be a temporary expedient only. As
quickly as possible the missionary is expected to raise up indigenous
leadership to take charge. He should not even be a member of the
national ecclesiastical body when it is formed, because he is a foreigner,
he is temporary, and because without the missionary's interference —
even his presence — the independence of the "native element" will be
more sure and the power of self-government best developed.[83] The missionary ought not be slow to permit the people to take initiative and
responsibilities. "The native churches and ministers must have responsibilities to bear, before they can learn to bear them."[84] The presence
of too many missionaries in any given region can retard the development of the churches.[85]

There is no doubt that to Dr. Anderson *the missionary* is the ordained missionary engaged in evangelism. Farmers, mechanics, and
other lay craftsmen were no longer in the employment of the American
Board, and its secretary considered their use by other agencies to be
the consequence of a wrong emphasis on "civilization."[86] "The honest
aim in sending these secular helpers was to aid the preaching missionaries."[87] The only laymen in Anderson's mind at the time of most
of his writing were physicians, printers, wives, and single women
teachers. The printers were engaged in a form of the preaching of
the Word and were indispensable assistants to the ordained men.
Physicians were principally needed to give medical care to families of
married missionaries and were not sent where adequate medical service

[81] *Ibid.,* p. 99.

[82] *Theory of Missions to the Heathen,* p. 76.

[83] *Outline of Missionary Policy,* p. 17.

[84] *Ibid.,* p. 18.

[85] *Memorial Volume,* Ch. III, "Development of the Missions," Selection 4, p.
95.

[86] *Foreign Missions: Their Relations and Claims,* pp. 96-98; *Memorial Volume,*
pp. 276-277.

[87] *Ibid.,* p. 97.

was available. Always they "were all expected to be missionary physicians; that is, to make their medical practice subservient to the grand object of the missions." In other words, in the second place, "they are expected to exert a conciliating influence among the natives by the kindly offices of their profession."[88] A few single women and the wives were needed as teachers in educating the girls and women of the churches and in training up suitable wives for pastors. This, too, is a service auxiliary to the evangelistic task.

However, the wives have an especially important function in supporting their husbands so that these men can fulfill their responsibilities. A few single men missionaries are needed for the initial exploration of pioneer areas and in extended itinerant supervision of the work, but even they need the loving care provided by the homes of married colleagues when they return from their travels.[89] All other men should normally be married.

> The experience of the Board favors the marriage of missionaries, as a general rule, and always when they are going to a barbarous people. Wives are a protection among savages, and men cannot long there make a tolerable home without them. When well selected with respect to health, education, and piety, wives endure "hardness" quite as well as their husbands, and sometimes with more faith and patience.[90]

It is not good for a man to be alone. "In a word, woman was made for man, and as a general thing man cannot long be placed where he can long do without her assistance."[91] "Regarding the wife as a friend, counsellor, companion, the repository of her husband's thoughts and feelings, the partaker of his joys, the sharer of his cares and sorrows, and one who is to lighten his toils, and become his nurse in sickness; the missionary needs such a helper far more than the minister [in America]."[92]

Marriage is a resource for the mission and the wife performs genuine missionary service for other reasons also. The heathen should have the opportunity of seeing Christian families, and the missionary home illustrates the duties of the family state. A model is provided. Almost invariably the wife has educational responsibilities: an infant school

---

[88] *Memorial Volume*, p. 276.

[89] Introductory essay to *Memoir of Mrs. Mary Mercy Ellis*, Selection 14, pp. 209-210.

[90] *Memorial Volume*, p. 272.

[91] Selection 14, p. 211.

[92] *Ibid.*, p. 210.

of her founding or direction, all female schools, and direct approach to secluded women.[93]

Missionary service is wholly voluntary, and in it the man discharges his own personal obligation.[94] His freedom of responsible action matches the freedom of his vocational choice. Initiative lies with him and his colleagues. His liberty is equal to that of pastors in the homeland.[95] He is as carefully educated and selected as homeland ministers, and like them has been judged qualified. His board does not treat him like a hired man.[96] The Scriptures are his sufficient rule for faith and practice.[97] When the board or society has accepted him, the missionary engages to conform to its rules and regulations, and if he decides to depart far from them the board can withdraw its support.[98] That is the only control which the sending agency may actually exercise over him, other than its general superintendence and concern. Proper and effective "control" of missionaries is effected by their own consciences and by the brethren's mutual watchfulness over each other.[99]

Dr. Anderson never sentimentalized missionaries and did not regard them as a special brand of spiritual heroes. They are simply men and women dutifully obeying Christ. The missionary does encounter severe trials due to the conditions and place of his service, and he is required to renounce the world to a degree not asked of the pastor at home.[100] Only those persons with a strong desire for the work should enter upon it, inspired with an ardent love to the Savior and a burning zeal for the salvation of sinners.[101] The missionary needs patience, perseverance, and a spirit of self-denial.[102] Generally speaking, his qualifications are the same as those of all Christian ministers. Relying on the doctrine of a future life, the missionary makes "a deliberate sacrifice of time for eternity, and of earth for heaven."[103] Only by looking to Jesus can he be able with patience to run the race set before him.[104]

---

[93] *Ibid.,* pp. 212ff.; ABCFM, *Annual Report, 1842,* pp. 42-44.
[94] *Control to Be Exercised over Missionaries and Mission Churches,* Selection 8, pp. 132-133.
[95] *Ibid.,* p. 122.
[96] *Ibid.,* pp. 126-127.
[97] *Ibid.,* p. 129.
[98] *Ibid.,* p. 128.
[99] *Ibid.,* pp. 134-135.
[100] *Theory of Missions to the Heathen,* pp. 77, 79.
[101] *Ought I to Become a Missionary to the Heathen?,* p. 178.
[102] *Ibid.,* p. 179.
[103] *Theory of Missions to the Heathen,* p. 78.
[104] *Ibid.,* p. 87.

The Native Church and Ministry

Rufus Anderson is a pioneer founder of the indigenous church principle. However, one must be careful not to read into his statements later ideas about "sending" and "receiving" in the relationship between churches nor to confound self-government with self-interest and self-sufficiency. The three-self formula was originally devoid of many of the connotations later supposedly derived from it. A church which lived to itself for itself would be abhorrent to Anderson. Mission is, moreover, not a matter of geography and chronology, but of process and development. The sequence is not sending, conversions, churches, but rather sending, conversions, churches, evangelism and further sending *ad infinitum* or more truly until the whole world has been converted. Churches are never to be ends in themselves, but means to enlargement and extension of the mission. The great concern is for "a scriptural, self-propagating Christianity."

Just as education and other auxiliaries to preaching are intended, according to Rufus Anderson, to serve the growth and development of local churches, even so self-government and self-support contribute to the maturity and vigor of churches and their ability to make witness. A church which is self-governing and self-supporting from the beginning will be self-propagating. The apostolic model reveals the relationship of these three factors. The people should build their own churches according to their own style, and not after Western models, at almost all their own expense.[105] As quickly as possible each congregation should have its own native minister, and only in the rare instance when such a native guide is not available at the organization of the church, should a missionary assume pastoral oversight. Any financial aid given at the beginning should be very short term help. Schools, too, should quickly move to support by the Christian community.

> As soon as possible every church should have its own native pastor, the members on their part, contributing for his support according to their ability, and he, on his part, adapting himself in reasonable degree thereto. Such aid as the mission may render should be considered as *supplemental* and *temporary*. And not only should the pecuniary burden be thrown upon the church, as fast as possible; the responsibility of government should also be assumed at the proper time.[106]

Such a responsible local church is "the divinely appointed illuminating power for its district. It is the great power in missions. It is leaven,

---

[105] *Foreign Missions: Their Relations and Claims,* pp. 210-211.
[106] *Outline of Missionary Policy,* p. 15.

which may be expected in time to leaven the whole lump."[107] How-ever, these new churches do not exhaust their responsibility in local evangelism. They, too, are to send, and to engage in foreign mission, that activity being required for their full maturity.[108] "And when the unevangelized world shall be dotted over with such churches, so that all men have it within their power to learn what they must do to be saved, then may we expect the proclaimed advent of the Spirit, and the conversion of the world."[109]

Missionaries and their home constituency are too prone to delay overlong the organization of local churches. They expect new converts immediately to manifest all the marks of Christian life and practice that characterize Western Christian communities. However, the quality of their Christian life is not to be measured in terms of such con-formity, but rather by the degree of difference from their heathen neighbors. They are just like the infant churches of the apostolic age when they had come out of paganism and they, for all their imper-fections, possessed as much genuine piety as modern Christians in the West. Irregularities, imperfections, disorders, and even immoralities are to be expected in newly gathered churches. Let all remember that: "The fact is, that the fair moral face of our community, in the church and out of it, is not wholly attributable to existing piety in the hearts of individuals, but is the result of that cultivation, intellectual, moral, and social, which has been gradually effected by the long-continued inculcation of Christian truth, the prevalence of general knowledge, progress in the arts and refinements of life, and the enlightening and sustaining influences of God's Spirit."[110] Both older and younger churches are under the same rule, that of the Bible, but in judging that rule, circumstances must be taken into account. There may be more "docility and active Christian principles" in the new mission churches, despite outward appearances, than in European and American churches. A real crucifying of the old man, a fierce struggle with principalities and powers, a growth in Christlikeness may well be there.[111] The new Christian may appear imperfect but actually have been raised far above

[107] *Memorial Volume,* Ch. III, "Development of the Missions," Selection 4, p. 96.

[108] *Foreign Missions: Their Relations and Claims,* p. 107.

[109] *Ibid.,* Ch. VII, "Principles and Methods of Modern Missions," Selection 5, p. 101.

[110] *Labors and Hindrances of the Missionary;* Boston: ABCFM, n.d.; pp. 9-10; *Memorial Volume,* Ch. III, "Development of the Missions," pp. 93ff.

[111] *Ibid.,* pp. 8-10.

his former state. "That such churches should live, thrive, and ever reach the self-sustaining point, is a miracle of grace."[112]

Even though it may be difficult for a missionary to decide when a church is to be organized, that day dare not long be delayed. "The first duty of a missionary is to gather such a church."[113] Initially he may establish any order of polity which he believes consistent with the New Testament, but he usually follows the pattern of his own sending church and society. Yet it is to be understood that the members have the right to alter that form at their discretion.[114] Local churches should be

> composed only of hopeful converts; and should have, as soon as possible, a native pastor, and of the same race, who has been trained cheerfully to take oversight of what will generally be a small, poor, ignorant people, and mingle with them familiarly and sympathetically. And by a native pastor, I mean one recognized as having the pastoral care of a local church, with the right to administer the ordinances of baptism and the Lord's Supper.

> As soon as the mission church has a native pastor, the responsibilities of self-government should devolve upon it. Mistakes, perplexities, and sometimes scandals, there will be; but it is often thus that useful experience is to be gained, even in churches here at home. The salary of the native pastor should be based on the Christianized ideas of living acquired by his people; and the church should become self-supporting at the very earliest possible day. It should also be self-propagating from the very first. Such churches, and only such, are the life, strength, and glory of missions.[115]

The bearing of responsibilities alone makes for growth. Local churches, the field mission, and the work of the board are subject to the same laws of growth as individuals, — advancement is the condition of health. There is no standing still; there must be development.[116]

How the churches should be related to one another is also to be left "to the good sense and piety of the missionaries on the ground,"[117] and the native Christians are to be free to modify the initial arrangement later. Experience has shown that with respect both to local and

[112] *Memorial Volume*, Ch. III, "Development of the Missions," p. 93.
[113] *Foreign Missions: Their Relations and Claims*, Ch. VII, "Principles and Methods of Modern Missions," p. 97.
[114] *Memorial Volume*, p. 282.
[115] *Foreign Missions: Their Relations and Claims*, Ch. VII, "Principles and Methods," pp. 98-99.
[116] *Memorial Volume*, Ch. III, "Development of the Missions," pp. 90-91.
[117] *Foreign Missions: Their Relations and Claims*, Ch. VII, "Principles and Methods," p. 98.

regional polity it is not wise "to attempt to transfer the religious denominations of Christendom, full-grown with all their peculiarities, into heathen lands."[118]. Young churches possess the same ecclesiastical freedom claimed by the older sending churches, and they do not come properly under the control of any board, society, or church in Europe or America.[119] A board or society can only exert influence on such churches through the counsel of its missionaries.[120] "The religious liberty which we ourselves enjoy, is equally the birthright of Christian converts in every part of the heathen world, on coming into the spiritual kingdom of Jesus Christ."[121] Anderson asked for practice consistent with principle:

> Nor may we expect to require of the mission churches, as the condition for giving them the gospel and its institutions, that they shall always think, judge, and act just as we do. We ought cheerfully to abide the consequences of the full assertion of our principles; and have patience, and bear long, and not give over, till it is evident that our moral means are exhausted, and that our enterprise has failed.[122]

Unfortunately an opportunity for missionary paternalism was opened in Anderson's scheme by a temporary concession to apparent practicality. A missionary might deny the church's freedom and delay development by his control. This opening for paternalism is provided by giving the missionary responsibility to decide when a church is to be organized, to determine how it shall be organized and associated with other churches, and to exercise pastoral rule if a native minister is not available. Moreover, the secretary acknowledges that the missionary has a powerful means of control over the churches, since "a wise disbursement of funds will provide all the checks which are necessary or proper."[123] However, Dr. Anderson expected the missionary to act on scriptural principles fitted to make the most of every member of the church,[124] and attainment of self-support would liberate a church from control by even the most paternalistic missionary.

The same perplexing questions arise with regard to the time and manner of missionary withdrawal as in the determination of when to

[118] *The Control to Be Exercised over Missionaries and Mission Churches,* p. 139.

[119] *Ibid.,* p. 138.

[120] *Ibid.,* pp. 143-145.

[121] *Ibid.,* p. 139.

[122] *Ibid.,* p. 140.

[123] *Outline of Missionary Policy,* pp. 15-16. However, S. B. Treat drafted this statement which implements Anderson's policy, and it may not be proper to impute this idea to Anderson himself.

[124] *The Control to Be Exercised over Missionaries and Mission Churches,* p. 139.

organize a local church.[125] It is not easy to close down a mission and to turn everything over to an indigenous church. The American Board did this in the Hawaiian Islands in 1863, near the close of Dr. Anderson's tenure of office.

The native pastor is the key to the development of the indigenous church. The use which the Apostles made of native pastors is one of the grand principles of their missions and provides a continuing principle for mission theory and practice, — "simple, economical, practical, scriptural, mighty through God."[126] It is the pastor who makes the native church a power for mission, and he should have ample scope for preaching and for all ministerial and pastoral abilities and duties. The missionary should not stand in his way.[127] Neither should missionaries stationed in any area be so numerous as to deny "the free growth and action of a numerous native ministry, and for devolving upon that ministry the heaviest responsibility it will bear."[128] Seminaries are essential for the education of pastors and female boarding schools for the training of wives for them.[129]   While the students are in seminary a careful selection can be made among them for the various grades and types of church work, of which the pastorate is the highest. There ought to be no undue delay in ordaining suitable men to the ministry, and this delay should not result from the missionary requiring too much from the candidates. The hope of realizing the goal of the mission rests in native pastors, because the mission agency can hope that the cost of support will be infinitesimal in comparison with the cost of maintaining a missionary and they can be stationed far and wide in great numbers over churches engaged in evangelism. Native pastors overcome the obstacles of distance, expense, and climate inherent in a foreign mission.[130]

Rufus Anderson provided the young church with a charter and a bill of rights for its existence, work, and liberty. In his insistence on its wholeness from the outset, the right and necessity of its being actually the Church of Christ from the very beginning, its commitment to evangelism, and its freedom to alter patterns introduced by missionaries, Anderson gave the young church the chance to be itself, that is, to be the universal Church of Christ manifest in a given locality in a particular cultural and social setting. He had no respect for Oriental,

[125] *Memorial Volume,* Ch. III, "Development of the Missions," pp. 93ff.
[126] *On Raising Up a Native Ministry,* p. 103.
[127] *Foreign Missions: Their Relations and Claims,* Ch. III, "Development of the Missions," p. 96.
[128] *Ibid.,* p. 95.
[129] *On Raising Up a Native Ministry,* p. 104.
[130] *Ibid.,* pp. 105-106.

Pacific, and African cultures and religions, and he provided for adaptation only in polity and church building. Nevertheless, he would not doubt the genuineness of conversion and of spiritual life in Christ when one discovers

> that converts under the torrid zone go but half clothed, that they are idle on a soil where a small amount of labor will supply their wants, that they sometimes forget the apostle's cautions to his converts, not to lie to one another, and to steal no more, in communities where the grossest vice scarcely affects the reputation, and that they are slow to adopt our ideas of the rights of man.[131]

Few of Anderson's contemporaries in the mission held so liberal a view. It is evident that within his doctrine of the liberty, responsibility, and self-sufficiency of the native church there is room even for possible cultural adaptation. His views were not accepted without resistance, and he sought to prove his points by appeal to actual achievements by young churches and ministers. Selection 7, "The Value of Native Churches," being a chapter from *Foreign Missions,* illustrates this.

Anderson and Venn

The mutual influence of Rufus Anderson and Henry Venn on each other is a subject needing further investigation. This mutual influence is obvious. The two men were exact contemporaries, born within the same year, and there were a number of corresponding factors in their lives. Dr. A. C. Thompson added this interesting footnote to his reference to Venn in the *Discourse* which he gave at the commemorative service for Dr. Anderson.

> [Born] at Clapham, February 10, 1796. And in their lives there are other coincidences; parentage determined the peculiar type of character in each; each was the eldest son; each lost his mother at seven; each lost his father at seventeen; they both graduated from college in the same year, Mr. Venn from Queen's College, Cambridge; the atmosphere of home gave coloring and direction to the career of each; both became foreign corresponding secretaries, Dr. Anderson of the largest society in America, Mr. Venn of the largest Protestant society in Europe, the Church Missionary Society in England; and both were acknowledged to be, in the positions they filled, men unsurpassed in their day by any who belonged to their respective countries.[132]

---

[131] *Theory of Missions to the Heathen,* p. 74.
[132] *Discourse Commemorative of Rev. Rufus Anderson, D. D., LL. D.;* Boston: ABCFM, 1880; p. 39.

The American Board secretary had long read the publications of the Church Missionary Society and had knowledge of Henry Venn's views, but personal friendship and discussion of mission principles and problems began with his visit to London in August, 1854, when the C. M. S. secretary received him most cordially. After a number of conversations, Anderson left with Venn a list of practical questions, which were answered in a letter of September 6, 1854.[133] Such correspondence continued until Anderson's retirement, but the letters of the last years up to Venn's death are mostly letters of introduction of American visitors to Venn. Anderson had clearly come to his full position before establishing his personal relationship with Venn, but doubtless the give and take discussion helped him in the final formulation of his system of principles. Anderson, in speaking of the importance of the native pastor in *Foreign Missions: Their Relations and Claims,* states that a number of persons came to this discovery about the same time out of common experience, and quotes a letter of Venn on the subject, dated January, 1867. He says in the footnote concerning Venn: "No one is better informed on missionary subjects."[134] Venn and Anderson approached the question of the native church from quite different Anglican and Congregationalist positions, but arrived at much the same conclusions about self-government, self-support, and the general character and function of such churches. Venn probably came to the additional stress on self-propagation through Anderson's influence. The two men are jointly to be regarded as authors of the three-self aim in the planting of young churches.[135]

THE INFLUENCE OF RUFUS ANDERSON

Dr. Anderson's teaching on the principles and methods of missions can be criticized in numerous respects from the vantage point of the common experience accumulated by the seventh decade of the twentieth century. Nevertheless, he provided a remarkably sound basis for the development of American missions, and nearly all American.boards and societies professed to follow him, although not putting all his principles fully into practice. As late as 1914 Robert E. Speer could describe him as "the most original, the most constructive, and the most courageous student of missionary policy whom this country has produced, and one of the two most aggressive and creative administrators

---

[133] American Board Archives, ABC: 14, vol. 3, no. 506.

[134] See Selection 5, p. 98, footnote.

[135] The reader may learn something of Venn's views and of the relationship of them to Anderson's in Beyerhaus, Peter, and Henry Lefever, *The Responsible Church and the Foreign Mission;* Grand Rapids: Wm. B. Eerdmans Publishing Co., 1964; pp. 25-33.

of missionary work."[136] The fact that Roland Allen, apparently without knowledge of his writings, comes to very similar views attests to Anderson's soundness. Dr. N. G. Clark, who succeeded Anderson as foreign secretary, declared at his funeral: "There can be no hesitation in saying that the world owes to Dr. Anderson the reviving of the true method of missionary effort as illustrated most fully in the Acts of the Apostles by the Apostle Paul. . . . This method and the principles involved are now the common possession of all missionary societies the world over. They are recognized in the plans adopted and in the tributes paid to Dr. Anderson in this country, in Great Britain, in Germany, and wherever missions are known."[137]

Until at least the 1950's no American mission agencies or missionaries ever openly questioned Dr. Anderson's aim for the mission, namely, the fostering of self-propagating, self-governing, self-supporting churches, but within ten years of his death Americans along with British and continental European missionaries had caught the "colonial mind" by contagion from colonists and officials in many a land, and a new emphasis on denominationalism combined with that outlook to stimulate missionary paternalism and imperialism. There was a general tendency to make the young churches into ecclesiastical colonial copies of the planting churches. It required the surveys and studies of the Edinburgh Conference of 1910 to challenge the practice and awaken the missionaries again to the reality of the national church. American missions had soon also departed from Anderson's limitations on higher education and on English language schools. They sought the expansion of the Kingdom of God through institutions, and tended to confuse that Kingdom with modern "progress." Anderson approached every people in evangelism at the bottom of the social scale, among the masses, and would work up towards the elite. Alexander Duff took the opposite approach, hoping to win the elite and through them eventually capture the masses. Both actually had similar hopes and goals for the young churches. American agencies increasingly added Duff's emphasis to that of Anderson, and gave institutions a place which the latter would have thought unwise. However, American boards continued in theory to keep the young churches central in their policies and program and to expect the eventual conversion of the world through them.

[136] Speer, Robert E., *Studies of Missionary Leadership;* Phila.: Westminster Press, 1914; p. 237.

[137] Funeral sermon included with *Discourse Commemorative of Rev. Rufus Anderson,* pp. 57-58. See p. 2, note.

The Literary Works of Rufus Anderson

The official papers of Rufus Anderson are in the Archives of the American Board of Commissioners for Foreign Missions at Harvard University, deposited in Houghton Library. There are also some personal papers of much less value, catalogued as ABC: 30; vols. 1-23.

The *Missionary Herald* was edited by Mr. Anderson during the first ten years of his secretarial service, and the issues of that period contain many unsigned items written by him, as is true also of later volumes.

Tracts, pamphlets, and articles are indicated by an asterisk (*) in the following list.

HISTORY AND BIOGRAPHY

* *Bartimeus, The Blind Preacher of Maui.* n.p., n.d.

* *The Church in Past Ages Unable to Propagate the Gospel throughout the World.* n.p., n.d.

The Gospel in Bible Lands. See *History of the Missions of the A.B.C.F.M. to the Oriental Churches*

The Hawaiian Islands: Their Progress and Condition under Missionary Labors. Boston: Gould & Lincoln; N.Y.: Sheldon & Co., 1864; 2nd ed., 1864; 3rd ed., 1865

A Heathen Nation Evangelized. History of the Sandwich Islands Mission. Boston: Congregational Publishing Society, 1870; also London: Hodder & Stoughton, 1872.

> revised ed. entitled:
> *History of the Mission of the American Board of Commissioners for Foreign Missions to the Sandwich Islands.* Rev. ed., Boston: Congregational Publication Board, 1872; reprinted 1874. At head: A Heathen Nation Evangelized.

History of the Missions of the American Board of Commissioners for Foreign Missions in India. Boston: Congregational Publishing Society, 1874; reprinted 1875, 1884

History of the Missions of the American Board of Commissioners for Foreign Missions to the Oriental Churches, 2 vols. Boston: Congregational Publishing Society, 1872-73; 2nd ed., 1875

* *History of the Missions of the Nestorian Christians in Central and Eastern Asia.* Reprinted from *Missionary Herald,* vol. XXXIV, no. 8, 1838, pp. 289-298

* *The Irish Missions in the Early Ages.* Reprinted from *Missionary Herald,* April, 1868

* *Kapiolani, the Heroine of Hawaii, or, a Triumph of Grace at the Sand-wich Islands.* N.Y.: Charles Scribner, 1866. Reprinted from *Hours at Home,* May, 1866

   Memoir of Catherine Brown, a Christian Indian of the Cherokee Nation. Boston: Crocker & Brewster; N.Y.: J. P. Haven, 1824; 2nd ed., 1825; re-published Phila.: American Sunday School Union, 1832

* *Memoir of John Arch, a Cherokee Young Man.* Boston: Massachusetts Sunday School Union, 1832; 2nd ed. same year

   Memorial Volume of the First Fifty Years of the American Board of Com-missioners for Foreign Missions, ed. by Rufus Anderson and almost all written by him. Boston: The Board, 1861. At least 5 editions through 1862.

* *The Morning Star and Micronesia,* by Rufus Anderson and S. L. Pomroy. Boston: The Missionary House, 1856

* *Results of a Statistical History of Benevolent Contributions.* In ABCFM, *43rd Annual Report, 1852,* pp. 15-19; tables for the same, pp. 213-217

* *Statistical History of Benevolent Contributions in the Past Sixteen Years.* For use of the ABCFM, September, 1852. 2nd ed., rev.; Boston: T. R. Marvin, 1853

* *Statistics Relating to Charitable Contributions.* In ABCFM, *31st Annual Report, 1840,* pp. 45-47

PRINCIPLES, METHODS, PROBLEMS OF MISSIONS

* *Claims of the Missionary Work on Pious Physicians.* Reprinted from *Missionary Herald,* February, 1866

* *The Control to Be Exercised over Missionaries and Mission Churches.* Boston: ABCFM, 1948. The work of Rufus Anderson principally, but signed by Anderson, David Green, and S. B. Treat. Tract, reprinted from ABCFM, *Annual Report, 1848,* pp. 62-80

* *Control of Missionaries and Mission Churches.* In ABCFM, *Annual Re-port, 1849.* In further reference to the preceding document.

* *The Essentially Progressive Nature of Missions to the Heathen.* In ABCFM, *Proceedings . . . at the Special Meeting held in New York, Jan. 18, 19, and 20th, 1842,* pp. 17-22. Rarely seen also as a tract.

   Foreign Missions: Their Relations and Claims. N.Y.: Scribner, 1869. 3rd ed. rev., 1870

* *Interference of Different Missionary Societies with Each Other's Proceed-ings.* In ABCFM, *Annual Report, 1838,* pp. 32-34

* *Leading Object of the Missions to the Oriental Churches.* In ABCFM, *Annual Report, 1842,* pp. 54-57

* *Letter to the Rev. Robert S. Candlish, D.D.* Boston: T. R. Marvin: 1862. On schools

* *Marriage of Missionaries.* In ABCFM, *Annual Report, 1842,* pp. 42-44

* *The Marriage of Missionaries, — An Introductory Essay on.* In Ellis, William, *Memoir of Mrs. Mary Mercy Ellis.* . . . Boston: Crocker & Brewster, 1836; pp. vii-xxii

* *The Missionary Age: A Half-Century Discourse.* See *The Time for the World's Conversion Come.*

* *Missionary Schools.* Boston: 1838; reprinted from *The Biblical Repository.* Issued also as *Missionary Schools,* ABCFM Missionary Tract No. 10, n.d.

* *Missionary Schools.* Boston: ABCFM, 1861. A tract reproducing much of the contents of Ch. VII, "Schools," of the *Memorial Volume,* with some slight differences.

* *The Native Pastorate an Essential Means of Procuring a Native Ministry.* In ABCFM, *Annual Report, 1862,* pp. 17-22

* *On Deciding Early to Become a Missionary to the Heathen.* Boston: ABCFM, 1834. Reprinted under same title as Missionary Tract No. 7; Boston: ABCFM, 1851

* *On Missions to the Jews.* Boston: ABCFM, 1849

* *Proposals for Raising Up a Native Ministry.* [Boston: The Board, 1841]; reprint of *On Raising Up a Native Ministry among the Heathen* in ABCFM, *Annual Report, 1841,* pp. 44-47

* *A Sermon on the Promised Advent of the Spirit.* Boston: Crocker & Brewster, 1841. Reprinted as *The Promised Advent of the Spirit,* ABCFM Missionary Tract No. 6, n.d.

* *Synopsis of Lectures on Foreign Missions,* n.p., n.d. [c. 1867-68]. Outline of about 70% of contents of *Foreign Missions.*

* *The Theory of Missions to the Heathen. A Sermon at the Ordination of Mr. Edward Webb, as a Missionary to the Heathen. Ware, Mass., Oct. 23, 1845.* Boston: Crocker & Brewster, 1845. Reprinted as *The Office and Work of the Missionary to the Heathen,* ABCFM Missionary Tract No. 1 [c. 1846]

* *The Time for the World's Conversion Come.* Missionary Tract No. 10; Boston: ABCFM, n.d. Also published as *The Missionary Age: A Half-Century Discourse;* Boston: T. R. Marvin, 1851; and originally published as an article in *The Religious Magazine,* Boston, in its final year of publication, 1837-1838.

Instructions to Missionaries

It was the custom for a considerable period to read Instructions and hand them to missionaries at their ordination or commissioning, and these were often printed in the *Missionary Herald* or in some other manner. Many of them, probably most, are the compositions of Rufus Anderson. The following are examples.

* *Extracts from Instructions of the Prudential Committee to the Rev. Benjamin W. Parker and the Rev. Lowell Smith, Missionaries, and Mr. Lemuel Fuller, Printer, destined to the Sandwich Islands, Nov. 6, 1832.* In ABCFM, *Annual Report, 1832,* pp. 157-163.

* *Instructions of the Prudential Committee, delivered in Park Street Church, Boston, on the Evening of Oct. 24, 1832, to the Rev. William Thompson, Rev. Elias Riggs, and Doct. Asa Dodge, about to Embark as Missionaries to the Mediterranean.* In ABCFM, *Annual Report, 1832,* pp. 152-157

* *Instructions of the Prudential Committee to the Rev. William Gottlieb Schauffler, Missionary of the A.B.C.F.M. to the Jews of Turkey.* In Stuart, Moses, *A Sermon at the Ordination of the Rev. William G. Schauffler, a Missionary to the Jews, . . . Nov. 14, 1831.* Boston: 1831; 3rd ed., 1845

* *Objects of the Missions to the Oriental Churches and the Means of Prosecuting Them. Instructions of the Prudential Committee to the Rev. Cyrus Hamlin. . . .* In *Missionary Herald,* Jan. 1839, pp. 39-44.

ADMINISTRATION, INFORMATION, PROMOTION

* *Ability of the Board to Conduct Missions on a More Extended Scale.* In ABCFM, *Annual Report, 1850,* pp. 70-79. Published also as first part of Missionary Tract No. 9, which includes also articles by Pomroy and Beman.

* *Building Church Edifices at Mission Stations.* In ABCFM, *Annual Report, 1865,* pp. 22-26

* *Can the Board Be Kept out of Debt, and in What Manner?* In *Annual Report, 1859,* pp. 11-14; also published as Missionary Tract No. 16; Boston: The Board, 1859

* *Citizenship of Missionaries and Their Children.* In ABCFM, *Annual Report, 1841,* pp. 36-38

* *Connection with the Reformed Dutch Church.* In ABCFM, *Annual Report, 1857,* pp. 20-22

* *Economy and Curtailments in Missions.* In ABCFM, *Annual Report, 1861,* pp. 10-13

* *How Far the Amount of the Board's Indebtedness Is under Control of the Prudential Committee.* In ABCFM, *Annual Report, 1843,* pp. 52-54

* *Intercourse with the Greek Government on the Subject of Education in Greece.* Reprinted from *Missionary Herald,* February, 1830

* *Letter to Mr. Barnes on the Armenian Converts in Constantinople.* In *American Presbyterian,* New ser., vol. I, no. 14, p. 105. Reply on pp. 105, 108.

* *Letters on the Constitution of the Board.* Boston: ABCFM, 1836

* *Limiting the Expenses of the Missions.* In ABCFM, *Annual Report, 1839,* pp. 31-33

* *Mr.* [i.e., Bishop] *Southgate and the Missions at Constantinople.* Boston: The Board, 1844

* *Oahu College.* Boston: The Board, 1856

* *Organization of the Missions of the Board.* In ABCFM, *Annual Report, 1838,* pp. 28-29

* *The Recent Interference with Our Work at the Sandwich Islands.* In ABCFM, *Annual Report, 1864,* pp. 17-22

* *The Reformed Catholics and the Sandwich Islands Mission.* In ABCFM, *Annual Report, 1866,* pp. 26-37

* *Return of Missionaries.* In ABCFM, *Annual Report, 1838,* pp. 29-30

* *Returned and Disabled Missionaries.* In ABCFM, *Annual Report, 1839,* p. 30

* *Returned Children of Missionaries.* In ABCFM, *Annual Report, 1840,* p. 51

* *Systematic View of the Responsibilities Involved in the Prosecuting of the Work of Missions.* In ABCFM, *Annual Report, 1843,* pp. 61-64

* *Use of Missionary Maps at the Monthly Concert for Prayer.* In ABCFM, *Annual Report, 1841,* pp. 56-58

* *Urgent Claims of the Armenian Reformation.* In ABCFM, *Annual Report, 1851,* pp. 19-23

* *The Work of Missions to Be Progressive; a Sermon on the Present Crisis in the Missionary Operations of the A.B.C.F.M.* In Boston: The Board, 1840

DEPUTATION REPORTS

* *Report of the Deputation to India.* In ABCFM, *Annual Report, 1856, with Minutes of the Special Meeting, March 4-6, 1856,* pp. 7-11. Also separately printed for limited use; Boston: T. R. Marvin, for the Board, 1855.

Report of the Deputation to India: Related Documents
  Reports and Letters Connected with Special Meetings of the Mahratta and and Tamil Missions of the A.B.C.F.M. in February, March, April, May and June, 1855, also, Reports of the Syrian Mission, and of a Conference at Constantinople. For use of the Prudential Committee. India documents printed in India, Syrian and Constantinople portion printed by T. R. Marvin, Boston, 1856. Bound together at Boston with a general preface and index by Rufus Anderson and A. G. Thompson.

* Special Committee of Thirteen on the Deputation to India, *Report,* in ABCFM, *Annual Report, 1856,* pp. 29-67. Includes the *Outline of Missionary Policy.* Also separately printed as a pamphlet.

* ABCFM, *Outline of Missionary Policy.* Drafted by S. B. Treat. Missionary Tract No. 15. Boston: The Board, 1856. Reprinted from the foregoing item, pp. 51-58

Report to the Prudential Committee of a Visit to the Missions in the Levant. By Rufus Anderson. *Also a Letter to the Committee from the Rev. Dr. Hawes.* Boston: Printed for the Board by T. R. Marvin, 1844

* *Report of Visit to the Sandwich Islands: Portions of a Report in Preparation.* In ABCFM, *Annual Report, 1863,* pp. 17-23

MISCELLANEOUS

* *An Address, Delivered in South Hadley, Mass., July 24, 1839, at the Second Anniversary of Mount Holyoke Female Seminary.* Boston: Perkins & Marvin, 1839

* *Address to the Hawaiian Mission Children's Society, Delivered June 20, 1863.* n.p., n.d.

* *The Christian Missionary Desiring to Be with Christ. A Sermon Preached at Westborough, Ms., June 30, 1840, at the Funeral of Rev. Ephraim Spaulding, a Missionary of the A.B.C.F.M.* Boston: Crocker & Brewster, 1840

Observations upon the Peloponnesus and Greek Islands, Made in 1829. Boston: Crocker & Brewster; N.Y.: J. Leavitt, 1830

* *Remarks on the Island of Cuba.* Reprinted from the *Missionary Herald.*

PERSONAL

* *Dr. Anderson's Farewell Letter to the Missionaries.* Dated July 5, 1866. Boston: ABCFM, printed for strictly private use, 1866

* *Dr. Anderson's Letter to the President of the A.B.C.F.M.* n.p., n.d. Letter of resignation of Sept. 20, 1866, addressed to Rev. Dr. Mark Hopkins. Included also in item: "Dr. Anderson Declines Reelection," in ABCFM, *Annual Report, 1866,* pp. 39-46

* *Letter Declining Reelection as a Member of the Prudential Committee of the A.B.C.F.M., 1875.* n.p., n.d.

PART I

THE CALL TO MISSION

Selection 1

THE PROMISED ADVENT OF THE SPIRIT[1]

And it shall come to pass afterward, that I will pour out my Spirit upon all flesh; and your sons and your daughters shall prophesy, your old men shall dream dreams, your young men shall see visions; and also upon the servants and upon the handmaids, in those days, will I pour out my Spirit. And I will show wonders in the heavens and in the earth, blood, and fire, and pillars of smoke. The sun shall be turned into darkness, and the moon into blood, before the great and terrible day of the Lord come. And it shall come to pass, that whosoever shall call on the name of the Lord shall be delivered. —The Prophet Joel.

How evident it is that more is wanting than we now have to bring about the conversion of the world — both to multiply the means, and to give them success! Not that the churches of Christ are unable to publish the gospel every where. Not that there is a lack of opportunity. Not that the experiments already made have been without ample encouragement. Not that a sufficient motive is wanting to go into all the world and preach the gospel to every creature. But who does not know, that the churches are slow to engage in this work? — that the work itself is regarded in the light of a *charity,* which one is at liberty to perform, or not, as he pleases, instead of being the *great thing,* for which the church exists, and for which the Christian lives? — and that it is hard to obtain the men to go as missionaries to heathen nations, and still harder to obtain the means of supporting the small number that go; while the results of missionary labor, though equal, and in fact superior, to those of pastoral labor at home, and greater than is gen-

[1] Boston: Crocker and Brewster, 1841; reprinted as Missionary Tract No. 10, n. d. Originally a sermon.

erally supposed, are still such as would require ages to complete the earth's spiritual renovation?

Does it follow, that the conversion of the world by means of human instrumentality, is a hopeless or even doubtful work? By no means. On the contrary, the enterprise is full of hope, full of certainty. And it is so for a reason which is gloriously set forth by the prophet Joel. The piety of the professed people of God is not always to remain in its present low condition. The church is to have a transforming visitation from on high, and the world is to have a similar visitation. The Spirit is to be poured out upon all flesh. There is to be an *advent* of the Spirit, so to speak — a grand putting forth of his influence, a mighty effort of his power, that shall insure both the publication and the triumph of the gospel over all the world.

A time is coming, when divine power is to be exerted, in connection with the preached gospel, at home and abroad, so as to render the gospel triumphant every where beyond all former experience.

1. Such an exercise of divine power is necessary, if the world is to be converted.

Look at the greatness of the work. The field is the world, with scarcely less than a thousand millions of inhabitants. Three fourths of these are Mohammedans and Pagans. Estimating the population of China at three hundred and fifty millions, at least eight hundred millions are yet to be made acquainted with the gospel. Whether we regard this part of the great field numerically, or geographically, its magnitude is truly overwhelming. And all the missions we discover in our survey of it, seem only a few bright points on a boundless region of darkness. We may contemplate the magnitude of the work in a twofold aspect; first, as so many hundred millions of minds, to be approached in all the extent of their wide dispersion, and then interested, enlightened, and won over to the kingdom of Jesus Christ; involving the overthrow of numerous ancient systems of philosophy and superstition, and an almost entire revolution in the social state of mankind; and secondly, as an endeavor to enlist the whole Christian community in this work, and to an extent of self-consecration and devotedness very far beyond any thing yet seen in any considerable portion of that community. How many thousands of the best and ablest members of the church must engage personally as missionaries! and how many millions of money must be contributed annually, to furnish them and their native helpers with the means of living and usefulness!

Now, who does not see, in this view, the necessity of such an agency of the Spirit? In vain without it shall we expect so universal a movement, so vast a spiritual revolution, either in the church or in the world. Indeed, it must be confessed, that the zeal and enterprise of the church are almost as much behind this result, as is the spiritual condition of pagan nations. There is even more difficulty in perceiving how we are to obtain the means for the great moral conflict, than how, if we had them, they could be successfully employed. We feel more inclined to despair, when looking on the worldliness and apathy of the church, than by all we can see of opposition and difficulty elsewhere. Wo to the world, if the church is not to be blessed with such an outpouring of the Spirit! And alas for mankind, if that Almighty Agent does not soon accompany his truth every where with far more of the energy of his power divine!

2. Such a result is not only necessary, but highly probable, irrespective of all direct prophecy or promise on the subject.

Who can believe that a world embraced within the range of the influence of Christ's atoning blood, is always to remain covered with the ruins of the fall? Who, after learning that the Son of God made a sacrifice of his own life in order to destroy the works and power of the devil, can believe that the god of this world is always to hold his usurped dominions? Who, that has reflected on the object, plan, and history of redemption, does not expect that work to proceed onward till its influence embraces the earth? It is not prophecy and promise alone, that awaken expectations of this sort. Such expectations arise also from just views of the gospel as a system of mercy; they are the spontaneous breathings of every heart that is filled with the love of Christ. The true follower of Christ rejoices to anticipate the triumphs of his King, the universal extension of his reign, and the clearing off from the face of the whole earth of the ruins of the fall. And though this result be connected with ever so great an amount of human instumentality, he spontaneously refers it to divine power as the only effective cause. And the more pains you take to make him acquainted with the greatness of the enterprise, the more does he feel the necessity of divine interposition for its accomplishment, and the more probable does it seem to him that his almighty and gracious King will grant such an interposition. Yes, it is an animating truth, that what the world needs, there is the highest probability, under the government of God, it will sooner or later have. And what does it need so much as a gracious visitation of the Holy Spirit, such as is predicted and promised in the Scriptures?

3. The Scriptures foretell and promise a great and general outpouring of the Spirit in the latter days.

The following is, perhaps, the most remarkable passage, bearing on this subject, in the word of God: "And it shall come to pass afterward, that I will pour out my Spirit upon all flesh; and your sons and your daughters shall prophesy, your old men shall dream dreams, your young men shall see visions; and also upon the servants and upon the handmaids, in those days, will I pour out my Spirit. And I will show wonders in the heavens and in the earth, blood, and fire, and pillars of smoke. The sun shall be turned into darkness, and the moon into blood, before the great and terrible day of the Lord come. And it shall come to pass, that whosoever shall call on the name of the Lord shall be delivered." The apostle Peter, in his sermon on the day of Pentecost, declares this passage to be a prediction of events which were to happen under the Christian dispensation. Referring his hearers to the outpouring of the Spirit and the wonderful events they then saw, he says, "This is that which was spoken by the prophet Joel;" and then he quotes the whole passage. He means that the time on which they were then entering was the time referred to by the prophet, that the events they then saw were the kind of events foretold, and that this remarkable prophecy began then to receive its fulfilment. *Then commenced the* DISPENSATION OF THE SPIRIT. It was, however, only the commencement of that dispensation. The grand progress, the glorious consummation, was reserved for other days. The pouring out of the Spirit on all flesh, with that universal, overwhelming influence described by the inspired bard in figurative language drawn from prophetic raptures and Oriental warfare, is a blessing the world is yet waiting for. It is to be an all-subduing agency of the Almighty Spirit. Coming in its power and fulness, it will be to the whole church, with the exception of miraculous gifts, what it was to the small company of disciples assembled in the upper room; and it will be to the whole world, what it was to the three thousand that wept and repented under the preaching of Peter. Then was seen, though on a small scale, what is yet to be seen on the broad scale of the universal church and the entire earth. Then was seen the beginning of the fulfilment of a prediction, that looks mainly at that last great shock in the mighty conflict, which is to be followed by voices in heaven, saying, "The kingdoms of this world are become the kingdoms of our Lord and of his Christ, and he shall reign forever and ever!"

But there is another source of proof, still more convincing, in the *results* foretold as to follow from the reign of the Messiah and the publication of his gospel, every one of which presupposes an extraordinary putting forth of divine power. We quote only a very few of the many predictions. "Thy watchmen shall lift up the voice, with the voice together shall they sing; for they shall see eye to eye, when the Lord shall bring again Zion." (Isa. lii. 8.) "And they shall beat their swords into ploughshares, and their spears into pruning-hooks; nation shall not lift up sword against nation, neither shall they learn war any more." (Isa. ii. 4.) "The wolf also shall dwell with the lamb, and the leopard shall lie down with the kid, and the calf and the young lion and the fatling together, and a little child shall lead them. And the cow and the bear shall feed, their young ones shall lie down together, and the lion shall eat straw like the ox. And the sucking child shall play on the hole of the asp, and the weaned child shall put his hand on the cockatrice's den. They shall not hurt nor destroy in all my holy mountain; for the earth shall be full of the knowledge of the Lord, as the waters cover the sea. The envy also of Ephraim shall depart, and the adversaries also of Judah shall be cut off; Ephraim shall not envy Judah, and Judah shall not vex Ephraim." (Isa. xi. 6-9, 13.) "In his days shall the righteous flourish, and abundance of peace so long as the moon endureth." (Ps. lxxii. 7.) "For thus saith the Lord, Behold, I will extend peace to her like a river, and the glory of the Gentiles like a flowing stream." (Isa. lxvi. 12.) "The kingdoms of the world [shall] become the kingdoms of our Lord and of his Christ, and he shall reign forever and ever." (Rev. xi. 15.) "And so all Israel shall be saved; as it is written, There shall come out of Zion the Deliverer, and shall turn away ungodliness from Jacob." (Rom. xi. 26.)

Now, these results are to happen on the earth, under the reign of the Messiah; and who does not perceive that they are what has never been? Yet, making due allowance for figurative language, they are what would certainly follow from such an outpouring of the Spirit as is foretold by the prophet. But in vain shall we look for them, without such a visitation, either in the church or the world. All that we now see, and all that we read of since the apostolic times, whether in the church or out of it, are scarcely the dawn of the glorious day predicted in the passages just quoted. In the church, Ephraim is then no more to vex Judah, nor is Judah to vex Ephraim, because the spirit of sect will then cease to exist, if not its very form and reality, under the almighty influence of the Spirit of truth and love. The world, too, is to become thoroughly pacific, and to be filled with the knowledge of the Lord. On the most moderate supposition, its inhabitants will then be generally blessed with a religious education, and the prevalence of piety. There are said to be as many as ninety-five thousand teachers of schools in the United States, at the present time, and not less than fifteen thousand preachers of the gospel. To supply the world with means of instruction no better than our own country possesses, would require (to say nothing of books) that in some way, but chiefly from inhabitants of the several countries, a million of preachers be furnished, every twenty years, for the pulpit, and more than six millions of teachers, every five years, for the school-room. And to bring the world under such a holy and blessed influence as the word of God predicts, even within the space of a century, the church must hear of not less than twenty millions of souls brought into the kingdom of Christ every year, or what on an average shall be equivalent to that. All this and far more would take place, if the Spirit were to be poured out upon all flesh; for the great body of these teachers, both for the school-room and the pulpit, are not to be sent from Christian lands; they are to be raised up on the spot; they are to be of native growth. But without such an outpouring, the greatest possible array of means could be regarded with no feeling of hope. Nor must we for one moment forget the lamentable truth, that the very same outpouring of the Spirit is as necessary to procure the means, as it is to make them effectual.

With the same unwavering confidence, therefore, with which we do actually look forward to the universal triumph of the gospel on the earth, do we anticipate this universal outpouring of the Spirit. This certainly is yet to come. All that has been seen of his agency in the world hitherto, has been in the first instance to plant, and then to *preserve,* a church upon the earth, rather than to make that church universal. His presence has been, as it were, local and occasional, rather than general and constant. The church has looked to this grandly decisive outpouring as yet to come, rather than rejoiced in it as already happened. As, under the old dispensation, the church waited, and waited long, for the promised Messiah to make redemption for the world, so now, under the new dispensation, the church waits, and has waited long too, for the promised Spirit to come and appropriate to the world the blessings of that redemption. Yes, *we* now stand in the interesting attitude of waiting for the coming of the Spirit, just as the saints of old did for the advent of the Saviour. And let us wait with prayer, with earnest hope, with joyful expectation. For he will surely come. We are disposed to believe he will come suddenly — it may not be every where at once, but wherever there are the due preparations for his operating on the minds of men. It may be that he will come first into his church, his spiritual temple, and cast out thence the spirit of the world, and fill it (blessed day!) with the beauty and glory of his celestial influence.

4. This advent of the Spirit is even now indicated by certain remarkable preparatory measures.

Some of these preparatory measures result from direct efforts of the church, and others — and those as yet the most important — from great providential movements in human society.

The unprecedented efforts made by the church to multiply the number of preachers of the gospel in Christian lands, to plant new churches, and to extend the benefits of a Christian education, are all so many preparations for the Divine Spirit to exert his power. The Spirit operates on the minds of men *by means* of the truth, and therefore whatever is done to increase the amount of religious knowledge, prepares the way for his coming and agency. This is the object of the Christian ministry; and, we need not say, this is the object of Christian missions to the heathen. Missionaries go as the forerunners of the Spirit, as pioneers, as heralds. Their whole prescribed duty is to make proclamation of the truth. They are answerable only for making this proclamation faithfully. He who sends them forth says to each of them, as he does indeed to every preacher of the gospel, "Son of man, if thou warn the wicked, and he turn not from his wickedness, nor from his wicked ways, he shall die in his iniquity, but thou hast delivered thy soul." Christian missionaries have executed their commission when they have made all possible efforts to bring the gospel in contact with the minds of men. They can do no more. The hearing ear, the awakened conscience, the understanding heart, the willing obedience, are all the appropriate work of the Holy Spirit.

Now there has been a commencement of preparations of this sort in very many of the benighted nations and tribes of men. In hundreds of dark places the truth begins to shine, in most very feebly; nevertheless it shines, and there is a gradual and constant increase of the light of life. Some millions of immortal minds are no longer in the total darkness they once were; and all that is necessary to make full preparation for the Spirit among the heathen, is to have these lights multiplied and increased in brightness, so as to throw the rays of truth over all nations.

The other preparations, resulting from providential movements in society, are on a far more extended scale. God, by means of a thousand causes, is fast throwing the world open to his people, and is even bringing large portions of it either under the government or the controlling influence of Christian nations. He is furnishing his people with means for bringing the gospel to bear on the minds of men, far more powerful than he saw fit to bestow on his people in former ages; and he is taking away the impediments to travelling, and making access easy to almost all parts of the world. In a word, who can look over the earth and not believe that providential preparations are in progress on a vast scale for the coming of the Spirit? While the preparatory agency of good men is beheld only here and there, providential preparations are going on throughout the earth. And doubtless there are preparatory influences of the Spirit himself on the minds of men, even where the gospel is not known, and where there is no truth except a few rays of the light of nature.

5. Some recent events in heathen lands seem like forerunners to this advent of the Spirit.

Perhaps the most remarkable of these events is the outpouring of the Spirit at the Sandwich Islands.[2] Such an outpouring as that, in connection with all the other Protestant missions now in the heathen world, would bring millions of souls into the visible church in a single year. And it is well known that many of the islands in the South Pacific Ocean, where English missionaries are laboring, have been blessed with similar gracious visitations.[3] In Tinnevelly, also, a district in Southern India, there was an awakening, a few years since, which, extending with like power over all India, would subvert the great Brahminic system of idolatry, and make Christianity the nominal religion, at least, of a hundred and thirty millions.[4] There have been outpourings of the Spirit in South Africa, which, if generally diffused, would have Christianized the entire Hottentot and Caffre races.[5] The same remark may be made respecting the Karens of Burmah, the Greenlanders, the North American Indians, the Armenians, Nestorians, etc.[6]

Now, these several agencies of the Spirit, viewed in connection with the preparatory measures already mentioned, seem like forerunners of that universal outpouring, which is to change the moral aspect of the world. They encourage the hope of such a blessing, and they may perhaps be regarded as the first fruits of it.

We have gone through with the argument; and may we not yield our faith to the delightful anticipation that there is yet to be a great and universal outpouring of the Spirit upon the church and the world? Believing that we may, let us take a brief survey of the effects of this heavenly visitation.

[2] "The Great Awakening" in Hawaii, 1836-1839. In the years 1839-1841 alone there were 22,297 accessions to church membership, despite rigorous screening and training of candidates. See Anderson, *History of the Sandwich Islands Mission*, pp. 121-156, and Strong, *Story of the American Board*, pp. 71-73. —Ed.

[3] Mass movements brought practically all the inhabitants into the Christian faith in many of the islands of the South Pacific, but here the reference is probably to great revival movements such as that in Tonga in 1834. Findlay, G. G., and W. W. Holdsworth, *History of the Wesleyan Methodist Missionary Society*, vol. II, pp. 287-309. —Ed.

[4] Characterized by a mass movement in the 1840's. Pascoe, C. F., *Two Hundred Years of the S. P. G.*, pp. 533ff. —Ed.

[5] This could refer to numerous developments. The date of the pamphlet brings to mind especially the work of the French mission in Basutoland, begun in 1833. Groves, C. P., *The Planting of Christianity in Africa*, vol. II, p. 147. —Ed.

[6] The early rapid growth of Christianity among the Karens, marked by tremendous spiritual vigor, was a cause of great encouragement to American missions. Torbet, Robert G., *Venture of Faith, The Story of the American Baptist Foreign Mission Society*, pp. 63ff. —Ed.

And first, in the CHURCH. The real people of God will be induced to enlist fully in the work of preparing the way of the Lord in every part of the earth. No longer will there be any reserve, any holding back. This mighty result is one which the Holy Spirit can effect with infinite ease. He has only to touch the powers of discernment and feeling in the soul, and the work is done. The spiritual world opens and spreads out in glorious prospect, as Canaan did to Moses on the top of Pisgah. The whole heart, the whole man yields, voluntarily, joyfully. Where now is the fascinating, bewildering power of riches, or of the honors and pleasures of the world? Gone! Fled before the presence of Him, whose prerogative it is to proclaim liberty to spiritual captives. Ambition, pride, vanity let go their avaricious hold upon millions of wealth. God's people are made willing, and there is a liberal hand and a full treasury. Men feel their duty to be a privilege. What the amount will be of individual prayer and labor, and what the proportion will be of individual contribution to help onward the cause of Christ in that day, we pretend not to determine. But who believes that the men and women now constituting the visible church are doing all they would rejoice to do, were the Spirit to make them this visitation? Ye, who dwell in your ceiled houses, who recline on your couches of ease, whose tables are loaded with the bounties of Providence, and who have all that heart can desire, may ye feel this melting, all-subduing influence. And may all of us be anointed with this holy anointing, baptized with this heavenly baptism, created anew in Christ Jesus by this spiritual regeneration. Even so it will yet be throughout the church. The state of benevolence, now scarcely any where above the lowest standard of Christian self-denial, is not always to continue thus. The true members of Christ's church are to become the subjects of a wonder-working divine energy. They are to feel the powerful influence of the grace of Christ, who became poor for our sakes that we might be rich. The abundance of their joy in their unreserved consecration of themselves to their Lord and Master, will abound in the riches of their liberality; yea, and abound too in prayer, flowing out of a full spirit, that will not cease its importunities for this very blessing from on high.

What an admirable object will the Christian then be and what an admirable object the Christian church. Zion will arise and shine, her light being come, and the glory of the Lord being risen upon her. The church will exist for the good of the world. No talents will be deemed too great for the missionary work, no learning too profound, no eloquence too fervid, no standing too elevated. What armies will be sent by the church into the empire of darkness, and what means will it put in requisition for the holy warfare!

We must here guard, however, against a serious misapprehension.

Nothing in the leading sentiment of this discussion can excuse the church for delaying to enter fully upon the prosecution of this work. We have indeed stated our belief, that, in point of fact, the church will not enter upon this work as it ought to do, until the Holy Spirit is poured out upon it in more copious measure. But this belief is founded only on the fact, that the love and zeal of the church are at present wholly inadequate. Let no one urge this as forming any excuse for the church to delay the work. It can be no reason why the work should not be prosecuted to its full extent. How can the church be excusable in waiting for the grand advent of the Spirit, when the very thing it is required to do is to go before the Spirit, and prepare the way for his advent? — and when, too, it now has all the learning, all the wealth, all the power of speech, all the facilities for travelling, that it would have, if the Spirit were thus poured out? — and when it has the most abundant favoring indications of Providence, and all it ever will have that is imperative in the command of its Savior, and all it ever *can* have that is affecting and overpowering in motive? How can this be a valid excuse, when all that the church needs, more than it now has, to cause it speedily to publish the gospel through the world, is more willingness, more inclination to do what is confessedly its duty? In view of this lamentable backwardness, we do indeed rejoice in the promised great outpouring of the Holy Spirit upon the Christian church; — but then, ye people of God, ye surely can have no right to *wait* till ye are thus visited. If really converted men and women, how can ye have the face to demand more grace before performing the very work for which ye were called into the kingdom?

We must also make one other remark, before proceeding to illustrate the effects of this visitation upon the world at large. In speaking of this outpouring of the Spirit, we would by no means deny that it will be attended, for a time, by such divisions and heresies in the church, and by such fearful convulsions in and among the nations, — owing to the vastly excited and as yet unsubdued state of men's minds, — as almost to realize the prophet's figurative description of wonders in the heavens and in the earth, blood and fire and vapors of smoke, the sun turned into darkness, and the moon into blood. Such a thing is not improbable. It may even be an indirect consequence of the first onset of the mighty Agent for the overthrow of iniquity. And what observing, thoughtful mind does not now perceive indications of a future war of opinion, in which religion shall be a predominant element, a war of religions as it were, more extended and more terrible than any thing of the kind yet seen, and which may at length fearfully threaten even the very existence of the true church? And it may be — and the Scriptures give countenance to the idea — that just in this emergency, God the Holy Spirit will come forth in the transcendent power and majesty of his grace, as he came forth at the formation of the earth, with his creative power upon the dark, tumultuous waters of the chaotic deep.

Secondly, the WORLD will feel a renovating spiritual influence throughout the vast extent of its population. Far more than we have seen on any of the more favored spots that have been mentioned, will then be witnessed wherever the gospel is proclaimed. The progress of the heralds of the cross will be one of light, and every where their message will be armed with power. At the sound of the gospel trumpet, every Jericho shall come down; and at the call of the minister of Christ, the sun shall stay his progress. And then, as we believe, will Satan be bound, that he deceive the nations no more, and satanic power and influence be withdrawn from the earth. What a change will there be in the policy of the nations, when he, who has swayed his wicked sceptre over them for ages, is hurled from his impious and bloody throne! What a change in the civil and social condition of mankind! What rapid and wonderful change will there be daily, all over the world! Men will yield themselves in masses to the divine influence. Nations will be born in a day. Idols, idol-worship, and superstition in its thousand forms, will come to an end. The day of mercy for the world has come. Bramha, Vishnu, Boodh, the False Prophet, the Man of Sin, and every other spiritual abomination, fly before the Almighty Spirit, like the shades of night before the rising sun, and the messengers of the gospel have free course throughout the earth. Soon every island and continent is effectually subdued, the prophetic visions and paintings of the latter day are realized, and Jesus reigns over a redeemed, sanctified, and happy world.

What hinders this work from advancing among heathen nations far more rapidly than at present? What except the worldliness and apathy of the Christian church? To the church is given the work of preparing the way for the Spirit to bless the world with his influences, and the church has not done it. The gospel has not been every where preached, and comparatively few among the heathen have yet been trained to take the oversight of converts, when greatly multiplied in every land. Should the harvest wave over the field of the world, most of it would perish for want of reapers. Why has the church so long neglected this work, and why does she neglect it now?

Can *we* plead guiltless? Have we prayed as we should have done? Are we doing all that in us lies to awaken songs of praise to the Savior over the earth? The indifference of Christians to this great work is amazing. Who would believe that a child of God, an heir of glory, redeemed by the blood of Christ, and commanded to publish abroad the tidings of his love, could think and care so little whether they were proclaimed or not? How can we have the spirit of Christ, if it be so with us? How can we look forward with hope to the time when we shall stand before him in heaven, and see him face to face? Verily the church has neglected this work too long, and so have we its members. Let us arise, every one, in the strength of the Lord God, and do our duty, that our own souls, in holy fellowship with the Spirit, may have everlasting joy.

Selection 2

THE TIME FOR THE WORLD'S CONVERSION COME[1]

When the fullness of the time was come, God sent forth his son.

—Galatians iv. 4.

The "time" was that appointed for the advent of the Messiah. When the preliminaries and preparations were completed, and every thing was ready in the world and in the Jewish church, and all indicated the period for the coming of the Messiah, then he came, and made the long-promised atonement for the sins of mankind. The time was fully come.

This was the most important of three grand prophetic epochs. The liberation of the enslaved church from Egypt was one. The return of the captive church from Babylon was another. But the coming of the Messiah formed an epoch of far greater interest. All the ceremonial institutions, types and shadows looked to his advent and death, and there found their meaning and termination; and so did the whole Levitical priesthood. The old dispensation of the law ended, and the new dispensation of the gospel commenced. And it was this grand epoch, this "fullness of the time," that prophets and kings so earnestly desired to see.

But there is another predicted epoch, another "fullness of the time," yet to come, of the highest possible interest, when the Spirit shall be poured out upon all flesh, with a universal and overpowering influence, and "the kingdoms of this world" shall become "the kingdoms of our

[1] First published in *The Religious Magazine*, Boston, in its final year, 1837-38; republished as *The Missionary Age: A Half-Century Discourse;* Boston: T. R. Marvin, 1851; and finally as *The Time for the World's Conversion Come*, No. 10 of *Missionary Tracts;* Boston: The Board, n.d.

Lord and of his Christ, and he shall reign forever and ever." To this
fourth grand epoch the Christian church is now looking forward with
the same earnest desire and expectation that the ancient church did to the
coming of the Messiah. As there was a *"fullness* of the time" for the
one, so is there for the other; and the latter has its preliminaries, preparations, and appropriate signs, equally with the former. The probable
ends, moreover, to be answered by a delay during so many centuries,
would be found remarkably alike in both cases; and we should come
to the conclusion that if there were signs to justify that general expectation of the Messiah which seems to have pervaded the civilized
world just before his advent, then the Christian world is now justified
in expecting the universal extension of the gospel, as an event near at
hand.

Instead, however, of tracing this analogy through eighteen hundred
years, (which would require a volume,) I shall confine myself to the
half of the present century lately completed.

At the opening of the present century, our nation was mourning
the death of Washington, and Europe was entering that terrible tempest
of fire and blood, in which the genius of Napoleon was so conspicuous.
The spirit of infidelity was every where abroad, creating alarm; and little
did good men, even of the strongest faith, imagine what was really to
be the grand characteristic of the century.

But it often happens, that the stirring up and agitation of men's
minds by such causes, though fearful at the time, is the providential
preparation for spiritual reformation, intellectual progress, and great
social improvement. It was so in the early part of the present century.
An impulse was given to the human mind, that has been greatly felt in
all the departments of science and art, in all the forms and conditions
of social life, and perhaps most of all in the Christian church. Is it not
remarkable what an influence this has had in stimulating and organizing
the churches for religious effort? At all events, it is certain that a great
change has come over the spirit and habits of God's people as a body.
Practical piety is now a very different thing from what it once was, —
more comprehensive in its views and feelings, more active, more benevolent and aggressive, more alive to its individual and social responsibilities, and a thousand times more influential, in the aggregate, than it
was fifty years ago. Somehow, the denominational and social conscience can no longer sleep amid the groans of a perishing world. Somehow, the churches have been led into extensive systematic organizations for propagating the gospel at home and abroad, and these are
gaining strength and momentum in every free Protestant community;
and somehow, missionary institutions have been planted over a large

portion of the heathen world, with the declared purpose of taking possession of the whole for Christ.

Such facts as these may well awaken our curiosity to look more deeply into the matter, and to learn more of the position in which we, as Christians, and the churches of our day, are placed by God's providence and grace; and my object is to illustrate this point, and to bring it out distinctly to view.

THE WAY NOT OPENED FOR THE UNIVERSAL PROPAGATION OF THE GOSPEL UNTIL NOW

I. *It was not until the present century that the way was actually opened, by God's providence, for Christians to reach and evangelize all nations.*

This truth, if it be one, has of course a momentous bearing on the responsibilities of the present generation. Christ's command to "go into all the world, and preach the gospel to every creature," does not prove that his immediate disciples, or the whole body of Christians in their day, were able themselves actually to publish the gospel to all mankind. In fact they did not. They did what they could. They are not open to reproach. They were faithful. Theirs was preëminently an enterprising, missionary age. It may well be presumed that they proclaimed the gospel as far as they could. Though their number was so small, they preached it through a considerable portion of the then civilized world. But it is almost certain that they went scarcely beyond. Our Lord intended his injunction not merely for them nor merely for their age, but for the whole church, in all ages, till the gospel should be literally preached to every creature, — nay, till the end of the world; for in the millennium the gospel will need to be preached every where, as really as now. It will then be, as it is now, the duty of the Christian church to see that it is so preached; and this injunction of our Lord presents, and was intended to present, *the great standing work* of the Christian church for all ages of the world.

As the apostolic missions were nearly all within the limits of the civilized world, so were they doubtless restrained by the most formidable obstacles to their going farther. We have certain knowledge, indeed, that at that time the Romans had almost no acquaintance with countries beyond their own empire. India was to them the farthest east, and the British Isles the farthest west. The immense regions of Northern and Eastern Asia had scarcely more existence in their minds than the continents and islands of this western hemisphere. This ignorance, and much more the nature of its causes, made it impossible, as the primitive churches were situated, and as society and navigation then were, for the apostles and their associates to publish the gospel to all the world.

This profound ignorance of the existence and condition of distant nations continued for many centuries, and was to a great extent invincible. And so far as it was invincible, it was an insuperable obstacle to the universal preaching of the gospel. If not so, how came *commerce,* the insatiable greediness of commerce, to be restricted, all the while, within precisely the same limits? How came the reckless, indomitable *avarice* of the world not to break forth over all the earth, as it has done in our age even in advance of the gospel? It did not, only because it could not. Its progress was barred, in respect to the greater portion of the world, as it now is in respect to the kingdom of Japan; only the obstacles were far more numerous and insuperable.

It was, indeed, most obviously the divine will, — for all-wise reasons not fully revealed to us, — that the nations of the world should long remain in great measure isolated in respect to each other; and that the visible Christian church should pass, meanwhile, through a period of trial, and through a series of great errors, apostasies, and reformations, before it spread itself and the religion it professed over all the earth. These were probably needful to the full working out of the great plan of redemption, and to the full preparation of the church for this great work.

I by no means intend to affirm that the true church of Christ has not, in every age since the apostles, been culpable for not having done more than it actually did for extending the gospel. I speak, however, of the *true spiritual church,* and not of the mere nominal church, which early began to apostatize from the spirit and truth of the gospel, and the more as it rose in power and influence. And the question I raise concerning the *true* church, is not whether it could have done more in the way of missions than it did, but whether it could have diffused the gospel, in past ages, through the entire world.

There is the strongest historical proof that the ignorance of the true Christian church in past ages, with respect to the great portion of the heathen world, admitted of but a partial removal. For many ages, the whole frontier of pagan Africa and Asia was occupied by Saracens and Turks, then forming together the most powerful of all the nations, in armed and fierce defiance of Christian Europe. Goths, Huns, Vandals, and Saracens also disturbed for centuries the security and peace of Christendom. So did the Crusaders. Moreover, the true church of Christ necessarily participated in the ignorance, mental imbecility, and superstition of Christendom from the seventh century onward, which rendered impossible any such rational, scriptural, and extended missions as are necessary to evangelize the whole heathen world. The pope and his cardinals were also in great power, and arrogated to themselves all the functions and privileges of the church of God, and allowed no religious freedom of mind, speech, or action; and the few scattered and feeble disciples of the Lord Jesus had more than they could do to stay the progress of superstition in the visible church. And ofttimes they were compelled to wander in deserts and mountains, and in dens and caves of the earth, and to purchase a mere existence by silence and obscurity. In such circumstances, which in fact lasted for ages, down even to the Reformation, the true church *could* do but little for the benefit of remote countries. Then what scanty facilities were there for traveling! For twelve centuries after the apostles, men continued to regard the earth as an extended plain, and to sail by the stars and cling to the shores; and not till long after that did the mariner boldly venture across the ocean. Mind, too, had no such mighty instruments to work with as now, for exerting influence on mind near or remote. The invention of the printing press preceded but a few years the discovery of America; and the use of machinery in working the press, or that wonderful machine called the power press, which can print fifteen hundred or two thousand copies of the New Testament in a day, is a device of our own age. I need not add, that associations on a large scale for propagating the gospel, except in the form of monkish institutions, are all of recent date — the result of that intelligence and large intercommunity of thought, and feeling, and freedom of action, which belong to the age of printing, and distinguish the Protestant world of modern times. So far as the apostolical and later ancient churches were able to act together for the propagating of the gospel, it was by platoons and companies, while the evangelical churches of our day act by divisions and armies, with the momentum of great masses.

THE WAY NOW OPENED

But nothing is more certain than that *now* almost every heathen nation is entirely accessible, and that this amazing result has been brought about chiefly within the past half century, — in that silent, scarcely observed manner which characterizes the great operations of God's providential government. Those who remember (as some of us do) the embarrassments with which our own Board of Foreign Missions commenced its operations, forty years ago, will bear witness that I do not exaggerate. It was then thought difficult to find a field of labor even for four or five missionaries. Little did our pious fathers think what God purposed to do for this work, even before some of them should have gone to their everlasting rest. Little did they imagine, for instance, how soon the world would be explored, and its condition made

known to God's people; — how soon the intolerant secular power of
idolatry would be overthrown in India; — how soon the gates of China
would be forced open; — how soon Protestant governments, then all
indifferent and some even hostile to missions, would find it for their
interest, as they have, to act the part of protectors; — how soon rail-
roads would bind the earth together, and send men over it by day and
night with the swiftness of the winds; — how soon thought would dart
across continents and oceans with lightning's speed; — and how soon
the currents of all the rivers and the storms of all the oceans would be
overcome by steam, and commerce fill and pervade every sea; thus
giving to the people of God a free and easy access to every land.

These astonishing events have all become so familiar as scarcely to
excite our wonder. But they are all events of our own age. They belong
to the nineteenth century. For the first time since the opening of the
Christian dispensation, for the first time since the dispersion at Babel,
God has made a large portion of the world to cease from the strange
isolation of its several parts, and to become known and accessible to
his people. With our railroads, our steamships, our telegraphic wires,
our power presses, our commerce and commercial exchanges, our
sciences and arts, our geography, our personal security; with no more
Gothic or Vandal invasions to drive back the tide of civilization; nor
False Prophet, nor Man of Sin, as we may hope, again to deceive on
the large scale of nations; — who can doubt, that the "fullness of the
time;" for blessing the earth with the gospel has come, and that this
great work forms the grand mission and business of the churches and
Christians of our day?

This conviction will be strengthened by the illustrations under our
second proposition.

THE CHURCHES NEVER BEFORE ORGANIZED FOR THE CONVERSION OF THE WORLD

II. *It was not until the present century that the evangelical churches
of Christendom were ever really organized with a view to the conversion of the world.*

What are called *voluntary associations* for religious purposes, in
distinction from local churches, are not indeed a new thing on the
earth. They have existed, in some form, from an early period of the
Christian church. It was probably through such that the gospel has ever
been propagated by the church beyond the voices of its own immediate
pastors. *Monasteries* were voluntary societies; and so were all the
different orders of *monks*. It was by means of associations such as
these that the gospel was originally propagated among our ancestors,

and over Europe. These are the *Papal* forms of missionary societies and missions.

The *Protestant* form is what we see in Missionary, Bible, Tract, and other kindred societies; not restricted to ecclesiastics, nor to any one profession, but combining all classes, embracing the masses of the people; and all free, open, and responsible. They are voluntary associations in reality, whether their executive officers be appointed by associations of Christians formed expressly for the purpose, or by means of particular ecclesiastical bodies; for it is *the contributors of the funds,* who are the real association; not the American Board, not the General Assembly's Board, nor any other, but the individuals, churches, congregations, who freely act together, *through such agencies,* for an object of common interest. The Board, or whatever be the executive body, is an agency, and stands so related to the donors on the one hand, and to the missionaries on the other. Those who employ it are all alike voluntary in so doing, in all the Protestant societies of benevolent organization. No compulsory taxation, no taxation whatever, is allowable in Christian benevolence. None are to be *taxed* for the *spread* of the gospel. All must needs be voluntary and free to give, and to determine what they shall give and for what objects, in order to be cheerful and accepted givers. Our age is singular and remarkable for its disposition to *associate* in action. It associates for the accomplishment of almost every object; and this disposition *may* be so extended, for an object of great interest, that the society shall embrace even thousands of churches, belonging to several kindred denominations. We see such wonders in our times, in Bible and Tract societies, and even in Missionary societies. The American Board of Commissioners for Foreign Missions is itself an instance. But whatever the name, constitution, or religious object of the association, the action put forth is as much that of *churches* as it can be on so large a scale, or perhaps as it ought to be when involving the receipt and disbursement of large sums of money.

This Protestant form of association — free, open, responsible, embracing all classes, both sexes, all ages, the masses of the people — is peculiar to modern times, and almost to our age. Like our own form of government, working with perfect freedom over a broad continent, it is among the great results of the progress of Christian civilization in this "fullness of the time" for the world's conversion. Such great and extended associations could not possibly have been worked, they could not have been created, or kept in existence, without the present degree of civil and religious liberty and social security, or without the present extended habits of reading and the consequent wide-spread intelligence among the people; nor could they exist on a sufficiently broad scale, nor act with sufficient energy for the conversion of the world, under despotic governments, or without the present amazing facilities for communication on the land, and the world-wide commerce on the seas. Never, until now, did the social condition of mankind render it possible to organize the armies requisite for the world's spiritual conquest.

The Churches Now Organizing for the Entire Work

Such new forms of association as have been described arose with the opening of the unevangelized world to the gospel, and with the consequent rise of the missionary spirit; and I believe that every evangelical denomination in Protestant America and Europe now has them. They belong almost exclusively to this century. In our own country indeed, fifty years ago, there was not one foreign Missionary society, properly so called; nor a Bible, Tract, Education, or Seamen's society; and the Home Missionary societies were mere local institutions working on the smallest scale. But *now* our system of organization for propagating the gospel, at home and abroad, receives contributions to the amount of a million and a half of dollars annually, besides half a million more for the sale of Bibles and other religious books at cost. In the evangelical churches of Great Britain and America, the aggregate of the receipts is about five millions of dollars; or at least *a hundred times* more than was contributed, by the same bodies of Christians, fifty years ago.

Foreign Missions Now Forming on the Broad Scale of the World

III. *Till the present century, the evangelical churches of Christendom had no commanding system of missions abroad, designed expressly for the conversion of the world.*

At the opening of the century, a few missions, most of them of recent origin, might be seen faintly twinkling out from the depths of pagan darkness. But they were feebly sustained, had gained no strong hold on the heathen world, and awakened no general interest among the churches. Never did any age, not even the apostolical, behold such a system of missions as we are now permitted to see. They are not indeed universal; for some portions of the world are as yet scarcely accessible. But the Christian traveler would find them on nearly all the more important points along two thousand miles of the African coast; in nearly every important centre of influence in Western Asia; on the upper waters of the Indus; along the Ganges; around nearly the whole sea-coast of India, and over nearly the length and breadth of its great peninsula. He would find them in Ceylon, in Assam, in Siam, in the

Indian Archipelago, and in the five chief ports of the Chinese empire. Launching abroad on the Pacific, he might venture to cast anchor in almost any of the groups of islands, in the confidence that missionaries of the cross are there to protect him from savage men; and already do Christian missions afford a more effectual and better protection to the mariner in that "Island World" than could be furnished by all the navies of Christendom. And along the great rivers of our western wilds, after crossing the Rocky Mountains, how often would the traveler be gladdened at evening by the songs of Zion, when fearing he should hear the war-cry of the savage!

Though all this be but the *beginning* of the enterprise for the world's conversion, (and it is nothing more,) yet how great is that beginning! — how wide! — in how many places! — how extended over the earth! You find the heralds of the cross alike in the burning and temperate zones, in every climate; encountering every form of barbarism, every language, every religion; and laboring, with equal cheerfulness, in every part of the unevangelized world.

No Other Great Enterprise More Successful

Nor are these missionaries laboring in vain. Theirs, through God's blessing, is one of the most successful great enterprises that was ever undertaken by man. Look at the Sandwich Islands. Look at the long line of island groups in the South Pacific. Look at New Zealand. Behold, in the Cherokee and Choctaw nations, the "wild Indian" both civilized and Christianized. Behold in Western Asia the two religious reformations now in progress, among the Armenians and the Nestorians. Behold in Africa, West and South, the many thousands gathered into churches. Behold the increasing number of Christian villages in India — germs of coming Christian provinces, and of a Christian empire. Behold the multitude of schools, the seminaries, the native preachers, the printing establishments. Behold the hundred and twenty languages of the pagan world lately reduced to writing, and beginning to be enriched with the Scriptures, and with school books and religious tracts. Behold at least a thousand churches, with two or three hundred thousand members, enjoying the ministrations of some fifteen hundred foreign missionaries and thousands of native Christian helpers. Behold, in Christian lands, thousands of feeble churches edified by nearly as many home missionaries. Behold near forty millions of Scriptures issued by Bible societies, — a greater number than ever before since the Law was given on Sinai; and thousands of millions of tracts and religious books issued by Tract and Sabbath school societies.

Did time permit, I might speak of the impulse that has thus been given to our religious education, to our religious literature, to our devotional and practical piety, to our churches and ecclesiastical bodies, and to all our evangelical denominations. I might show how this vastly-extended benevolent enterprise has raised the character of the Christian church, and secured for it a consideration among men such as it never had before. But there is not time, and what has been adduced is sufficient for my purpose. Enough for me that the world is so far opened, and that the churches are beginning in earnest to gird themselves for the great spiritual conflict in every land.

The Call of Providence

Now, how do you account for all this? What does it mean? Why, within the memory of many now living, has the world been thus strangely opened and made accessible, as by a stupendous miracle? And why has such a vast systematic organization grown up as in a day, of associations at home and missions abroad, with the specific and declared design of publishing the gospel to every creature? Was there ever such a thing before? *Why* has the great and blessed God crowded so many of such stupendous results into our day?

I am unable to answer these inquiries, except on the supposition that the *"fullness* of the time" has actually come for the predicted publication and spread of the gospel through the world. I am sure that they cannot be answered on any other supposition. There never has been an age like the present. Never did churches, or individual Christians, or any man with the gospel in his hands, stand in such a relation to the heathen world as we now do. Not only is that world accessible, but it even lies on our very borders. We cannot sympathize with Richard Baxter,[2] in his almost despairing hope that the time *might* come when the gospel should have access to the Orient; for *with us,* hope has given place to certainty, and every man, woman, and child may now operate, with the greatest ease, upon the most distant nations. Men sometimes complain of the frequency and urgency of the calls that are made on their religious benevolence. But do they not see, that the most urgent of these calls result necessarily from the character which God has impressed on our age, and from the relation we stand in to the surrounding world? Our fathers of the last century had no such calls upon them as we have from nations beyond the bounds of Christendom; and they had not, because those nations were then comparatively unknown, or unapproachable. But God has been pleased, in our day, to lift the pall of death from off the heathen world, and to bring it near, and to fill our eyes with the sight and our ears with

---

[2] Richard Baxter, 1615-1691, English Puritan divine. —Ed.

the cry of their distress. He has leveled the mountains and bridged the oceans which separated the benighted nations from us, and has made for us highways to every land. To us he says, "Go!" — with an emphasis and a meaning such as this command never had to ministers and Christians in former ages.

No Escaping from the Duty

Should we take the wings of the morning, and fly millions of leagues beyond our globe, we could by no means thus escape from the responsibility that has come upon us; for we know our duty, and we can never be as though we had not known it. We should be held and treated, wherever found by ministering angels, as deserters from the army of the Lord of hosts. God's Word, and Spirit, and Providence now all concur in the command to publish the gospel to all the nations; and if we refuse, the blood of perishing nations will cry against us. This is the age for the work, and we are the people to do it. From this warfare Christ will give us no discharge. It by no means follows, that *we* shall be saved in the neglect of this work, because our fathers were. Our circumstances differ wholly from theirs. Western Asia, India, China were shut to them, but are open to us. Neither had God been pleased to teach them, as he has us, to associate and combine their strength, and act in masses for the accomplishment of great religious enterprises.

The Work to Go on to Its Completion

Verily it is no transient opinion, nor mere popular sentiment, accidentally arisen and liable to pass away, that has put forth and sustains the missionary work. It is the onward, almost fearful progress of God's gracious providence. As long as there is liberty of thought, speech, and action, a free press, an advancing civilization, and an unshackled, universal commerce, we may be sure that the motives to prosecute the missionary work will continue to increase in their manifold power upon the hearts, consciences, and conduct of the Christian church. No one can doubt this, who knows the circumstances that marked the rise, progress, and decline of all past missions of the church, or who takes a comprehensive view of this "fullness of the time" for the grand spiritual renovation of the world. These mighty beginnings of the past half century will have glorious developments in the half century to come; and the children will have far more to do, and will do far more, than their fathers did or supposed they could do.

The idea that the ability of the churches to give is already fully tasked, comes from a profound ignorance of the statistics of our religious charities. Nearly one half of the three millions of professedly evangelical church members in our country are believed yet to give nothing at all for missions, foreign or domestic. Nearly a third, even in New England, are believed to give nothing; and very many, even in our own denomination, contribute not more than *half a dollar* a year for propagating the gospel; which is at the rate of *twenty-five dollars* in half a century! Or, if twice this sum, it would be but *fifty dollars* during a long, long lifetime! — and for the object that brought the Son of God on his mission from heaven to earth! Are these *faithful* stewards? Will *they* hear the heaven-creating words, *"Well done!"* addressed to them on the great day, by the Judge on the throne?

THE APPEAL

I am not pleading specially for any one missionary society, nor for any one class of missions, nor for the millions of any one nation or continent. I stand on higher, broader ground. I am pleading for the *general cause* of missions and of the gospel. I am pleading for the *world;* in view of the length, breadth, depth, and height of the love of Christ, and of our obligations to him. Is *this* a work we may do, or not do? Is it to be reckoned among mere human enterprises? *Can* we neglect it, and think calmly of our neglect in our dying day?

Let us get the full impress of our duty. Let us awake to its great reality. Nothing is more truly binding upon us than the obligation to impart the gospel to those whom we can reach, and who will perish if they do not receive it. That surely is the most destructive immorality which withholds from immortal man the only gospel of salvation. The most pernicious infidelity is surely that which cares not for a world perishing in sin. And that must be the most high-handed disregard of Heaven's authority, and must reflect most dishonor upon the Son of God, which refuses, in the face of his most explicit command, to publish his gospel to every creature. Let us remember, that He who requires this is our God, in whose hands are our possessions, our lives, and our immortal souls, and that our opportunities are rushing by us, and fast passing away forever.

NOTE — As a few readers may perceive a resemblance, in some portions of the foregoing discussion, to an anonymous article in the "Religious Magazine," published some years ago, it is proper to say that both originated from the same source.

PART II

PRINCIPLES OF MISSION

Selection 3

THE THEORY OF MISSIONS TO THE HEATHEN[1]

2 Corinthians v:20. *Now then we are ambassadors for Christ; as though God did beseech you by us, we pray you in Christ's stead, be ye reconciled to God.*

Comparing the present period of the church with the apostolical, we come to two very different results respecting our own age. One is, that the facilities enjoyed by us for propagating the gospel throughout the world, are vastly greater than those enjoyed by the apostles. The other is, that it is far more difficult now, than it was then, to impart a purely spiritual character to missions among the heathen.

As to facilities, we have the advantage of the apostles in all respects, except the gift of tongues. The world, as a whole, was never so open to the preacher of the gospel since the introduction of the Christian dispensation. The civilization, too, that is connected with modern science, is all connected also with Christianity in some of its forms. I should add, that the civilization which the gospel has conferred upon our New England is the highest and best, in a religious point of view, the world has yet seen.

But, on the other hand, this very perfection of our own social religious state becomes a formidable hindrance to establishing such purely spiritual missions among heathen nations, as were those of the apos-

[1] *The Theory of Missions to the Heathen, A Sermon at the Ordination of Mr. Edward Webb, as a Missionary to the Heathen. Ware, Mass., Oct. 23, 1845;* Boston: Crocker and Brewster, 1845. Reprinted as No. 1 of *Missionary Tracts* with the title, *The Office and Work of the Missionary to the Heathen;* Boston: The Board, n.d. [c. 1846]. The Rev. and Mrs. Edward Webb were members of the Madurai, South India, Mission of the American Board.

tolical times. Not that this is the only hindrance to this result; there are many others, but this is an important one. For, the Christian religion is identified, in all our conceptions of it from our earliest years, with the almost universal diffusion among its professors of the blessings of education, industry, civil liberty, family government, social order, the means of a respectable livelihood, and a well ordered community. Hence *our* idea of piety in converts among the heathen very generally involves the acquisition and possession, to a great extent, of these blessings; and *our* idea of the propagation of the gospel by means of missions, is, to an equal extent, *the creation among heathen tribes and nations of a highly improved state of society, such as we ourselves enjoy.* And for this vast intellectual, moral and social transformation we allow but a short time. We expect the first generation of converts to Christianity, even among savages, to come into all our fundamental ideas of morals, manners, political economy, social organization, right, justice, equity; although many of these are ideas which our own community has been ages in acquiring. If we discover that converts under the torrid zone go but half clothed, that they are idle on a soil where a small amount of labor will supply their wants, that they sometimes forget the apostle's cautions to his converts, not to lie one to another, and to steal no more, in communities where the grossest vice scarcely affects the reputation, and that they are slow to adopt our ideas of the rights of man; we at once doubt the genuineness of their conversion, and the faithfulness of their missionary instructors. Nor is it surprising that this feeling is strongest, as it appears to be, in the most enlightened and favored portions of our country; since it is among those whose privilege it is to dwell upon the heights of Zion, that we have the most reason to expect this feeling, until they shall have reflected maturely on the difference there is between their own circumstances and states of mind, and those of a heathen and barbarous people.

Now the prevalence of these sentiments at home has exerted an influence on all the missions. Nor is the influence new. You see it in the extent to which farmers and mechanics — pious but secular men — were sent, many years ago, along with the missionaries, to assist in reclaiming the savages of the wilderness from the chase and settling them in communities like our own — a practice now nearly discontinued, except where the expense is borne by the national government.

Unless this influence is guarded against by missionaries and their directors, the result is that the missions have *a two-fold object of pursuit*; the one, that simple and sublime spiritual object of the ambassador for Christ mentioned in the text, "persuading men to be reconciled to God;" the other, the reorganizing, by various direct means, of the structure of that social system, of which the converts form a part. Thus the object of the missions becomes more or less complicated, leading to a complicated, burdensome, and perhaps expensive course of measures for its attainment.

I may be allowed, therefore, to invite attention to what is conceived to be *our true and only office and work in missions to the heathen.* "Now then we are ambassadors for Christ; as though God did beseech you by us, we pray you, in Christ's stead, be ye reconciled to God." The ambassadors here spoken of were missionaries — missionaries to the heathen, for such were Paul and his associates; sent, instead of Christ the Mediator, on a ministry withheld from angels, to plead with rebellious men to become reconciled to God. They are ambassadors sent on the same general errand that brought the Lord Jesus from heaven, and their commission is to proclaim abroad the fact, history, design and effect of his atonement, and bring its renovating power to bear as widely as possible upon the human race.

It will be necessary to dwell a short time on the leading aspects of this enterprise. And,

1. The vocation of the missionary who is sent to the heathen, is not the same with that of the settled pastor.

The work of human salvation is one of vast extent, whether we regard the time it is to occupy, the objects upon which it operates, the agents it employs, or the results which are to be accomplished. And it is performed with that regard for order and gradual development, which generally characterizes the works of God. Upon the Lord Jesus it developed to make the atonement, thus preparing the way, as none else could do, for reconciling man to his Maker; and then he returned to the heaven whence he came. Upon his immediate disciples it then devolved to make proclamation of the atonement, and its kindred and dependent doctrines, throughout the world, the whole of which world, excepting Judea, was then heathen. This they were to do as his representatives and ambassadors; and to expedite the work, they were furnished with the gift of tongues, and an extraordinary divine influence attended their preaching. Their commission embraced only the proclamation of the gospel and planting its institutions. As soon as the gospel by their means had gained a footing in any one district of country, they left the work in charge to others, called elders and also bishops or overseers of the flock and church of God, whom they ordained for the purpose. Sometimes they did not remain even long enough to provide spiritual guides for the churches they had planted. "For this cause," says Paul to Titus, "left I thee in Crete, that thou shouldest set in order the things that are wanting, and ordain elders in every city, as I had appointed thee." The elders were the pastors of the new churches. Elsewhere the apostle speaks of different departments of labor and influence assigned to the ministers of Christ. He says that when Christ ascended up on high he gave gifts unto men; to some apostles, to some prophets, to some evangelists, to some pastors and teachers. Whatever was the peculiar office of 'prophets' and 'teachers,' none can doubt that 'evangelists' were fellow-laborers of the apostles in the missionary work, and that 'pastors' had the stated care and instruction of particular churches. Now missionaries are the true and proper successors of the apostles and evangelists, and their sphere of duty is not the same with that of pastors, who are successors, in their sacred functions, not so much of the apostles and evangelists, as of the elders and bishops. It enters into the nature of the pastor's relation, that he remain or be intended to remain long the spiritual instructor of some one people. It is indeed as really his business to call sinners to repentance, as it is that of the missionary; but, owing to his more permanent relations, and to the fact that he is constituted the religious guide and instructor of his converts during the whole period of their earthly pilgrimage, his range of duty in respect to them is more comprehensive than that of the missionary in respect to his converts. The pastor is charged, in common with the missionary, with reconciling men to God; and he has also an additional charge, arising from the peculiar circumstances of his relation, with respect to their growth in grace and sanctification. But the missionary's *great* business in his personal labors, is with the unconverted. His embassy is to the rebellious, to beseech them, in Christ's stead, to be reconciled to God. His vocation, as a soldier of the cross, is to make conquests, and to go on, in the name of his divine Master, 'conquering and to conquer;' committing the security and permanency of his conquests to another class of men created expressly for the purpose. The idea of *continued conquest* is fundamental in missions to the heathen, and is vital to their spiritual life and efficiency. It will doubtless be found on inquiry, that missions among the heathen have always ceased to be healthful and efficient, have ceased to evince the true missionary spirit in its strength, whenever they have ceased to be actively aggressive upon the kingdom of darkness.

In a word, the missionary prepares new fields for pastors; and when they are thus prepared, and competent pastors are upon the ground, he ought himself to move onward, — the pioneer in effect of a Christian civilization — but in office, work and spirit, an ambassador for Christ, to preach the gospel where it has not been preached. And, whatever may be said with respect to pastors, it is true of the missionary, that he is to keep himself as free as possible from entanglements with literature, science, and commerce, and with questions of church government, politics and social order. For,

2. The object and work of the missionary are preëminently spiritual.

His embassy and message are as really from the other world, as if he were an angel from heaven. He who devotes himself to the work of foreign missions, comes thereby under peculiar engagements and obligations. His situation is in some important respects peculiar, compared with that of all others. His sphere of action lies beyond the bounds of his native land, beyond the bounds of Christendom, where society and the family and human nature lie all in ruins. As the great Originator and Lord of the enterprise came from the realms of heavenly blessedness to this world when it was one universal moral waste, so his representatives and ambassadors have now to go from those portions of the earth that have been illuminated by his gospel to regions that are as yet unvisited by these benign influences. They are therefore required preëminently to renounce the world. From the nature of the case they make a greater sacrifice of worldly blessings, than their brethren at home can do, however much disposed. They forsake their native land and the loved scenes of their youthful days. Oceans separate them from their relatives and friends. They encounter torrid heats and strange diseases. They traverse pathless wilds, and are exposed to burning suns and chilling night-damps, to rain or snow. Yet these things, when in their most repulsive forms, are reckoned by missionaries as the least of the trials appertaining to their vocation. The foreign missionary's greatest sacrifices and trials are *social* and *religious*. It is here that he has a severity of trial, which even the domestic missionary ordinarily cannot have. Whatever the devoted servant of Christ upon the frontiers may endure for the present, he sees the waves of a christian civilization not far distant rolling onward, and knows that there will soon be all around him gospel institutions and a Christian community. But it is not so with the foreign missionary. It requires great strength of faith in Christ for him to look at his rising family, and then with unruffled feelings towards the future. True, he sees the gospel taking hold of minds and hearts in consequence of his ministry, and souls converted and reconciled to God; he gathers churches; he sees around him the germs of a future Christian civilization. But then, owing to the imperfect and disordered state of society in heathen communities, he dares not anticipate so much social advancement for two or three generations to come as would make it pleasant to think of leaving his children among the people for whose spiritual well-being he delights to spend his own strength and years. And then his heart yearns ofttimes to be braced and cheered by social Christian fellowship of a higher order than he finds among his converts from heathenism. It is not the 'flesh-pots of Egypt' he looks back upon, nor any of the pleasant things that used to gratify his *senses* in his native land; but he does sometimes think of the kindred spirits he would find in that land, and of the high intellectual and spiritual fellowship he would enjoy in their society, and how it would refresh and strengthen his own mind and heart. Often there is a feeling of weakness and faintness arising from the want of such fellowship, which is the most painful part of his sufferings. The foreign missionary is obliged, indeed, to act preëminently upon the doctrine of a future life, and of God's supreme and universal government, and to make a deliberate sacrifice of time for eternity, and of earth for heaven. And this he does as an act of duty to his Redeemer, for the sake of extending the influence of his redemption, and bringing its reconciling and saving power to bear upon the myriads of immortal souls dwelling beyond the utmost verge of the Christian church.

And thus the foreign missionary is driven, as it were, by the very circumstances of his position, as well as led by his commission and his convictions of duty, to concentrate his attention and energies upon the Soul, ruined though immortal. And truly it is a vast and mighty ruin he beholds — more affecting to look upon in the light of its own proper eternity, than would be the desolation of all the cities in the world. It is too vast a ruin for a feeble band to attempt the restoration of every part at once. As Nehemiah concentrated his energies upon re-building the walls of the city of his fathers, rightly concluding that if the walls were rebuilt and threw their encouraging protection around, the other portions of the city would rise of course; so the missionary, as a thoughtful and wise man, sets himself to reconcile the alienated heart to God, believing that that point being gained, and the principle of obedience implanted, and a highly spiritual religion introduced, a social renovation will be sure to follow. He considers not, therefore, so much the relations of man to man, as of man to God; not so much the relations and interests of time, as those of eternity; not so much the intellectual and social degradation and debasement, the result of barbarism or of iron-handed oppression, as the alienation and estrangement of the heart of man from his Maker, and the deadly influence of hateful and destroying passions upon his soul. As when a house is burning in the dead of night, our first and great concern is not for the house, but for the sleeping dwellers within; so the missionary's first and great concern is for the *soul,* to save it from impending wrath.

And the *means* he employs in this ministry of reconciliation, are as single and spiritual as the end he has in view. He *preaches the cross of Christ.* The apostle Paul declares that this was his grand theme. And it is remarkable how experience is bringing modern missionaries to the same result. Their grand agent is oral instruction; their grand theme is the cross. And now, perhaps not less than in the days of the apostles, the Holy Spirit appears to restrict his *converting* influences among the heathen chiefly to this species of agency, and to this grand theme. Excepting in the schools, the usefulness of books is chiefly with those whose hearts have been in some measure moved and roused by the preached word. It appears to be the will of the great Redeemer, who came in person to begin the work that his salvation shall every where be proclaimed in person by his ambassadors, and that his message of grace shall have all the impressiveness of look and voice and manner, which they are able to give it. After the manner of their illustrious predecessor, they must teach publicly, and from house to house, and warn every one night and day with tears. The necessity of this in order to reconcile rebellious men to God, has not been diminished by the multiplication of books through the press. Well-authenticated cases of *conversion* among pagans, by means of books alone, not excepting even the Scriptures, are exceedingly rare. By the divine appointment, there must also be the living preacher; and his preaching must not be "with the wisdom of words, lest the cross of Christ should be made of none effect."

You see, then, Brethren, the high spiritual calling of the missionary. At the very threshold of his work, he is required, in a preëminent degree, to renounce the world. His message, wherein lies his duty and all his hope of success, is concerning the cross of Christ; and the object of it is to restore the lost spiritual relation between man and God. The impression he is designing to make is directly upon the soul. And his work lies so altogether out of the common range of worldly ideas, and even of the ideas of many professed Christians, that multitudes have no faith in it; it is to them like a root out of a dry ground, and they see no form nor comeliness in it, and nothing that should lead them to desire it. Nor is it until the civilizing results come out, that these unsanctified or very partially sanctified persons can give the missionary work any degree of their respect.

The necessity of connecting a system of *education* with modern missions, is not inconsistent with the view we have taken of the true theory of missions to the heathen. The apostles had greatly the advantage of us in procuring elders, or pastors for their churches. In their day the most civilized portions of the world were heathen — as if to show the weakness of mere human learning and wisdom; and the missionary labors of the apostles and their associates, so far as we have authentic accounts of them, were in the best educated and in some respects highly educated portions of the earth. Wherever they went, therefore, they found mind in comparatively an erect, intelligent, reasoning posture; and it would seem that men could easily have been found among their converts, who, with some special but brief instruction concerning the gospel, would be fitted to take the pastoral care of churches. But it appears that, until schools expressly for training pastors were in operation, — as ere long they were at Alexandria, Caesarea, Antioch, Edessa, and elsewhere, — it pleased God essentially to aid in qualifying men for the office of pastors by a miraculous agency: the Holy Ghost exerting upon them a supernatural influence, by which their understandings were strengthened and spiritually illuminated, and they gifted with powers of utterance.

But, at the present time, the whole civilized world is at least nominally Christian, and modern missions must be prosecuted among uncivilized, or at least partially civilized tribes and nations, from which useful ideas have in great measure perished. Even in those heathen nations which make the greatest pretensions to learning, as in India, we find but little truth existing on any subject. Their history, chronology, geography, astronomy, their notions of matter and mind, and their views of creation and providence, religion and morals, are exceedingly destitute of truth. And yet it is not so much a *vacuity of mind* here that we have to contend with, as it is *plenitude of error* — the unrestrained accumulations and perversions of depraved intellect for three thousand years. But among savage heathens, it is *vacuity* of mind, and not a *plenitude,* we have to operate upon. For, the savage has few ideas, sees only the objects just about him, perceives nothing of the relations of things, and occupies his thoughts only about his physical experiences and wants. He knows nothing of geography, astronomy, history, nothing of his own spiritual nature and destiny, and nothing of God.

In these circumstances and without the power of conferring miraculous gifts, modern missionaries are constrained to resort to education in order to procure pastors for their churches. They select the most promising candidates, and take the usual methods to train them to stand alone and firm in the gospel ministry, and to be competent spiritual guides to others. This creates, it will be perceived, a necessity for a system of education of greater or less extent in each of the missions, embracing even a considerable number of elementary schools. The whole is designed to secure, through the divine blessing, a competent native ministry, who shall aid missionaries in their work, and at length take their places. The schools, moreover, of every grade, are, or ought to be so many preaching places, so many congregations of youth, to whom, often with parents and friends attending, the gospel is more or less formally proclaimed.

I have thus endeavored, my Brethren, to set before you the foreign missionary enterprise in what I conceive to be its true scriptural character; as an enterprise, the object of which, and the sole object, is the reconciling of rebellious men in heathen lands to God.

And what is true of the individual missionary, is of course equally true of the Missionary Society, which directs his labors and is the medium of his support. The Society sends forth men to be evangelists, rather than permanent pastors; and when pastors are required by the progress and success of the work, it seeks them among native converts on the ground. And herein it differs from the appropriate usages of the Home Missionary Society, which, operating on feeble churches within Christian communities, or in districts that are soon to be covered with a Christian civilization of some sort, sends forth its preachers all to become settled pastors as soon as possible. The foreign missionary work is in fact a vast *evangelism;* with conquest, in order to extend the bounds of the Redeemer's kingdom, for its object; having as little to do with the relations of this life and the things of the world and sense, and as few relations to the kingdoms of this world, as is consistent with the successful prosecution of its one grand object — the restoring, in the immortal soul of man, of that blessed attraction to the Centre of the Spiritual Universe which was lost at the fall.

This method of conducting foreign missions, besides its evident conformity to Scripture, is supported by various weighty considerations.

1. It is the only method that, as a system of measures, will commend itself strongly to the consciences and respect of mankind.

The first mission sent forth under the care of the American Board, was such a mission. And it was sent to the subjects of a nation, with which our country was then unhappily at war. But the missionaries were regarded on all hands as belonging preëminently to a kingdom not of this world, and having an object of a purely spiritual nature. And when, notwithstanding this, the policy of the East Indian government would have sent them away, it was this that gave convincing and overwhelming force to the following appeal made by our brethren to the governor of Bombay:

"We entreat you by the spiritual miseries of the heathen, who are daily perishing before your eyes, and under your Excellency's government, not to prevent us from preaching Christ to them. We entreat you by the blood of Jesus which he shed to redeem them, — as ministers of Him, who has all power in heaven and earth, and who with his farewell and ascending voice commanded his ministers to go and teach all nations, we entreat you not to prohibit us from teaching these heathens. By all the principles of our holy religion, by which you hope to be saved, we entreat you not to hinder us from preaching the same religion to these perishing idolaters. By all the solemnities of the judgment day, when your Excellency must meet your heathen subjects before God's tribunal, we entreat you not to hinder us from preaching to them that gospel, which is able to prepare them, as well as you, for that awful day."[2]

Nothing but a consciousness of the high spirituality of their object and the impossibility of connecting it with questions of a secular nature, imparted boldness to our brethren to make this appeal, and gave it favor and efficacy in the high places of power. And it is this, which lately preserved our brethren on Mount Lebanon harmless amid the fury and carnage of a civil war. And this it is that imparts a degree of inviolability to the persons and efforts of Protestant heralds of the cross among all the nations which respect their religion. It is the grand predominance of the *spiritual* in their characters and pursuits, showing that they really do belong to a kingdom not of this world, and are not to be involved in the conflicting relations and interests of earthly communities. English statesmen in India acknowledge, that the general prevalence of Christianity in that country would at length make it impossible for their nation to hold the country in subjection, and yet they encourage the labors of the missionary. This they do because the missionary's *object,* whatever be the known *tendency* of his labors, is not to change the civil relations of the people, but to give them the gospel and save their souls; and because these statesmen are convinced in their consciences, that this is an object of unquestionable benevolence and obligation, for which Christ died, for which the ministry was instituted, which at this day is to be countenanced and encouraged at all events by every man claiming the name of a Christian; and which, however humbling it shall prove in its results to avaricious and ambitious nations, cannot be otherwise than beneficial on the broad scale of the world and to the great family of man.

2. This method of conducting missions is the only one, on which missionaries can be obtained in large numbers, and kept cheerfully in the field.

For objects that are not spiritual and eternal, men will seldom

---

[2] Gordon Hall, Samuel Nott and his wife, joined soon by Samuel Newell, were under orders of deportation to England. This appeal was addressed to the Governor, Sir Evan Nepean, who was friendly to the cause of mission and delayed the deportation. Meanwhile a great battle had been going on in Great Britain aimed at forcing the Directors of the East India Company to open India to missionaries. This was achieved in the course of the renewal of the Company's charter by Parliament in 1813, and the Americans were allowed to remain. A state of war between the United States and Great Britain had further complicated the situation. —Ed.

renounce the world for themselves and their families, as missionaries must do. Mere philosophers have never gone as missionaries; and seldom do mere philanthropists go into the heathen world, nor would they remain long, should they happen to go. Nor will a merely impulsive, unreflecting piety ever bring about a steady, persevering, laborious, self-denying mission. It generally gives out before the day for embarkation, or retires from the field before the language is acquired and the battle fairly commenced. Nothing but the grand object of reconciling men to God, with a view to their eternal salvation, and the happiness and glory thus resulting to Christ's kingdom, will call any considerable number of missionaries into the foreign field, and keep them cheerfully there. And it is necessary that this object be made to stand out alone, in its greatness and majesty, towering above all other objects, as the hoary-headed monarch of the Alps towers above the inferior mountains around him. It is not fine conceptions of the beautiful and orderly in human society that will fire the zeal of a missionary; it is not rich and glowing conceptions of the life and duties of a pastor; it is not broad and elevated views of theological truth, nor precise and comprehensive views of the relations of that truth to moral subjects. It is something more than all this, often the result of a different cast of mind and combination of ideas. The true missionary character indeed is based upon a single sublime conception — that of *reconciling immortal souls to God*. To gain this with an effective practical power, the missionary needs himself to have passed from death unto life, and to have had deep experience of his own enmity to God and hell-desert, and of the vast transforming agency of the reconciling grace of God in Christ. As this conception has more of moral greatness and sublimity in it than any other that ever entered the mind of man, no missionary can attain to the highest elevation and dignity of his calling, unless he have strong mental power and a taste for the morally sublime. This the apostle Paul had. What conception of his office and work and of spiritual things animated the great soul of that apostle! "Now, then, we are ambassadors for Christ; as though God did beseech you by us, we pray you, in Christ's stead, be ye reconciled to God." — "Eye hath not seen, nor ear heard, neither have entered into the heart of man the things which God hath prepared for them that love him." — "Oh the depth of the riches both of the wisdom and knowledge of God." — "Able to comprehend with all saints what is the breadth and length and depth and height, and to know the love of Christ, which passeth knowledge."

To make persevering and useful missionaries, however, it is not necessary that the power of thought and of spiritual apprehension should come nearly up to that of the apostle Paul. But there should be a similar cast of mind, similar views and feelings, and a similar character. There should be a steady and sober, but real enthusiasm, sustained by a strongly spiritualized doctrinal experience, and by the "powers of the world to come," intent upon reconciling men to God from a conviction of its transcendant importance.

Such men must compose the great body of every mission, or it will not be worth supporting in the field; and the only way such men can be induced to engage in the work, is by having the idea of spiritual conquest, through the cross of Christ, the predominant and characteristic idea of the enterprise. That will attract their attention while they are preparing for the ministry; that will enlist their consciences and draw their hearts; that will constrain them to refuse every call to settle at home, however inviting; and if they have learning and eloquence, that will lead them the more to desire to go where Christ has not been preached, where useful talent of every kind will find the widest scope for exercise.

Nor will any other scheme of missions, that was ever devised, keep missionaries cheerfully in the field. It is only by having the eye intent on the relations the heathen sustain to God, and on their reconciliation to him, and by cultivating the spirit of dependence on God and the habit of looking to him for success, that the piety of a mission can be kept flourishing, its bond of union perfect, its active powers all in full, harmonious and happy exercise. And unless these results are secured, missionaries, like the soldiers of a disorganized army, will lose their courage, their energy and zeal, their serenity and health, and will leave the field. Alas for a mission, where the absorbing object of attention with any of its members is any thing else, than how Christ crucified shall be preached to the heathen so as most effectually to persuade them to be reconciled to God.

3. This method of conducting missions is the only one, that will subjugate the heathen world to God.

No other will be found mighty to pull down the strong holds of the god of this world. The weapons of our warfare must be spiritual. The enemy will laugh at the shaking of a spear, at diplomatic skill, at commerce, learning, philanthropy, and every scheme of social order and refinement. He stands in fear of nothing but the cross of Christ, and therefore we must rely on nothing else. With that we may boldly pass all his outworks and entrenchments, and assail his very citadel. So did Philip, when he preached Jesus as the way of reconciliation to the eunuch; so did Peter, when preaching to the centurion; so did Apollos, when preaching to the Greeks; so did Paul, through his whole missionary career. It is wonderful what faith those ancient worthies had in the power of a simple statement of the doctrine of salvation through the blood of Christ. But they had felt its power in their own hearts, they saw it on the hearts of others, and they found reason to rely on nothing else. And the experience of modern missions has done much to teach the inefficacy of all things else, separate from this. Who does not know, that the only cure for the deep-seated disorders of mankind must be wrought in the heart, and that nothing operates there like the doctrine of salvation by the cross of Christ? This is true in the most highly civilized communities; but perhaps it is specially true among benighted heathens. In their deplorable moral degradation, they need just such an argument, striking even the very senses, and convincing of sin, of their own lost state, and of the love of God. Nothing else will be found like that to bridge the mighty gulf which separates their thoughts from God and the spiritual world. Nothing else will concentrate, like that, the rays of divine truth and grace upon their frozen affections. With the truth, that God so loved the world as to give his only begotten Son that whosoever believeth on him should not perish but have everlasting life, we go forth through the heathen world; and, with any thing like the faith in its efficacy through the Holy Spirit which the apostles had, we shall be blessed with much of their success. Yes, my Brethren, this is the only effectual way of prosecuting missions among the heathen — *holding up Christ as the only Savior of lost sinners.* It requires the fewest men, the least expense, the shortest time. It makes the least demand for learning in the great body of the laborers. It involves the least complication in means and measures. It is the only course that may certainly look for the aid of the Holy Spirit. It keeps Christ constantly before the missionary's own soul, as an object of intensest interest and desire, with a vast sanctifying, sustaining, animating influence on his own mind and preaching. It furnishes him with a power transcending all that human wisdom ever contrived, for rousing and elevating the soul of man and drawing it heavenward — the idea of love, infinite and infinitely disinterested, personified in the Lord Jesus, and suffering to the death to save rebellious and ruined man! And if the doctrine comes glowing from our own experience, we shall not fail to get the attention of the heathen, and our success among them will far exceed what we might expect among gospel-hardened sinners here at home. I might dwell long on the history of missions, ancient and modern, in the most satisfactory illustration of this point, did the time permit; but it is not necessary.

Let me add, that there is no way so direct and effectual as this, to remove the social disorders and evils that afflict the heathen world; indeed, there is no other way. Every specific evil and sin does not need and cannot have a separate remedy, for they are all streams from one fountain, having a common origin in a depraved and rebellious heart.

Urge home, then, the divinely appointed remedy for a wicked heart; purify the fountain; let love to God and man fill the soul; and soon its influence will appear in every department and relation of life. If reforms in religion and morals are not laid deep in the heart, they will be deceptive, and at all events transient. The evil spirit will return in some form, and with seven-fold power. New England owes her strong repugnance to slavery, and her universal rejection of that monstrous evil, to the highly evangelical nature of her preaching. And were the whole southern section of our own land, or even a considerable portion of it, favored with such highly evangelical preaching, slavery could not there long exist. But in heathen lands especially, an effective public sentiment against sin, in any of its outward forms, can be created no where, except in the church; and it can be there created only by preaching Christ in his offices and works of love and mercy, with the aid of the ordinances he has given for the benefit of his disciples, especially the sacrament of his supper. Thus at length, even in barbarous heathen lands, the force of piety in the hearts of the individual members of the church will be raised above that of ignorance, prejudice, the power of custom and usage, the blinding influence of self-interest falsely apprehended, and the ridicule and frowns of an ungodly and perverse world. Indeed, if we would make any thing of converts in pagan lands, we must bring them to the ordinances of the gospel, and into the church, as soon as they give satisfactory evidence of regeneration; for they are too child-like, too weak, too ignorant to be left exposed to the dangers that exist out of the fold, even until they shall have learned all fundamental truths. And besides, the school of Christ for young converts from heathenism, *stands within the fold,* and *there,* certainly, the compassionate Savior would have them all gathered, and carried in the arms, and cherished "even as a nurse cherisheth her children."

Finally; This method of conducting missions is the only one, that will unite the energies of the churches — so far as Christians can be induced to prosecute missions for the purpose of reconciling men to God. Making this grand aim of missions, and pressing the love of Christ home upon the hearts and consciences of men, as the grand means of effecting this, will certainly commend itself to the understandings and feelings of all intelligent Christians. Not only will a large number of good and faithful missionaries be obtained, but they will be supported, and prayed for, and made the objects of daily interest and concern. And how delightful it is to think, that the Head of the church has been pleased to make the object and work of missions so entirely simple, so spiritual, and so beyond the possibility of exception, that evangelical Christians of every nation and name can unite in its promotion. But if we change the form of the work, and extend the range of its objects of direct pursuit, and of course multiply the measures and influences by which it is to be advanced, we then open the door for honest and invincible diversities of opinion among the best of men, and render it impossible that there should be united effort, on a scale at all commensurate with the work, and for a long period. The church militant becomes divided and weak, and is easily paralized and thwarted in its movements by the combined and united legions of the Prince of darkness.

It would seem, therefore, that missions to the heathen must have a highly spiritual nature and development, or prove utterly impracticable and abortive. Such, it is believed, are the convictions of all who have had much experience in such enterprises. Unless missions have this nature and development in a very high degree, they will not commend themselves strongly to the consciences and respect of mankind; they will neither command the requisite number of laborers, nor keep them cheerfully in the field; they will prove inadequate to the subjugation of the heathen world to God; nor will they unite in this great enterprize the energies and prayers of the churches. In a word, they will not continue long to exist, unless Christ the Lamb of God himself be in them, reconciling the world unto himself, and causing his servants to make the salvation of the souls of men their all-commanding end and aim. Men may *resolve* that it shall be otherwise; but their purposes, however decided, will be in vain against the unalterable laws, which God has given the work of missions to the heathen.

Beloved Brother, — In the system of missions, with which you are soon to be connected, the aim has been, and is more and more, as experience is acquired, to prosecute the work on the principles advocated in this discourse. So far as your own influence is concerned, see that the system be rendered still more spiritual in its temper, objects, and measures. See, too, that your own renunciation of the world is entire before you enter upon your self-denying work, and that it be your determination to know nothing among the heathen but Christ and him crucified. Only by looking constantly unto Jesus, will you be able to run with patience the race set before you. As an ambassador of Christ, sent to plead with men in his stead to be reconciled to God, see that you are true to your vocation, and faithful to your trust, and that you never descend from the elevated ground you occupy. Whatever oscillations in public sentiment there may be from time to time in the Christian mind at home, you need not fear, if your character, preaching and influence are formed on the New Testament, that you will be forgotten in the contributions and prayers of God's people. At all events, be faithful unto death, and whatever be your lot here below, the result in eternity will be more blessed to you, than it is possible for your mind now to conceive, or your heart to desire.

Fathers and Brethren, — Let it be our prayer, that God will be pleased to strengthen our own faith in the realities of the unseen world. Then shall we be better able to pray as we ought for our missionary brethren, that they may be intent on their single but great object of winning souls to Christ, and be so imbued with the spirit of Christ, that his image shall be fully stamped on all their converts. Let us urge upon our brethren among the heathen the imperative duty of making full proof of their ministry as *missionaries,* rather than as *pastors;* and let us lay upon them "no greater burden," than the "necessary things" appertaining to their high and peculiar vocation. We must indeed hold them to the principle, that they shall treat those only as loyal subjects of our infinite Sovereign, who give evidence of hearty submission and reconciliation; but we will leave it to their better-informed judgments to determine, — in the remote, vast and varied, and to us almost unknown fields of their labors, — what is and what ought to be satisfactory evidence of actual reconciliation. Then will our brethren rejoice in having a simple, well-sustained, and glorious enterprise before them, and also "for the consolation" of the liberty conceded to them by the "elders" and the "whole church." In this good old way, marked with the footsteps of the apostles, there is hope for the world, for the whole world, that it may be reconciled to God. And when the principles of love and obedience are once restored to men, and men are at peace with God, and united to Him, then will they be at peace with one another. Then wars will cease, and all oppression. Then the crooked in human affairs shall be made straight and the rough places plain, the valleys shall be exalted and the mountains and hills made low, and the glory of the Lord shall be revealed, and all flesh see it together.

> "In one sweet symphony of praise,
> Gentile and Jew shall then unite;
> And Infidelity, ashamed,
> Sink in the abyss of endless night.
>
> "Soon Afric's long-enslaved sons
> Shall join with Europe's polished race,
> To celebrate, in different tongues,
> The glories of redeeming grace.
>
> "From east to west, from north to south,
> Emmanuel's kingdom shall extend;
> And every man, in every face,
> Shall meet a brother and a friend."

Selection 4

DEVELOPMENT OF THE MISSIONS[1]

Experience has shown, that the great object of missions — the introduction of the gospel among the unevangelized — can be effectually accomplished only by a course of measures fitted to secure the establishment of the gospel institutions. These the apostles introduced wherever they went, but with far less difficulty than we experience. Were the heathen countries of our times like Asia Minor, Macedonia, and Achaia, we should need to provide only for the personal and family expenses of missionaries, and for printing the Scriptures and religious books and tracts; and even a part of this expense, and soon the whole, would be defrayed by the converts. Moreover, owing to the present state of the heathen nations, we have found stronger reasons than the apostle Paul had at Corinth and Thessalonica, for not looking to converts for the personal support of missionaries. The most we can expect from them is, that they shall support their own native teachers and preachers, and gradually assume the support of their schools, and of the press.

Among the developments common to the missions, the most important has been in the matter of preaching. While this has by no means been restricted to the Sabbath, there has been a tendency to give more and more significance to the day, by regular preaching in some one place. It has generally required long time and patience to collect and sustain even a small adult congregation, but not otherwise has it been possible to keep up the tone of the enterprise. The missionary has needed the preparation for such a duty, as well as its reacting influence upon his own mind and heart. He has needed a service where he could speak authoritatively as an ambassador, without the humiliation of

[1] *Memorial Volume of the First Fifty Years of the A.B.C.F.M.*; Boston: The Board, 1861, THE MISSIONS, Chapter III, pp. 242-252.

rude objections and foul abuse. The native Christians have also needed regular, well-studied exhibitions of the plan of salvation, and of their duty as Christians. They could not be adequately informed and elevated to the self-governing, self-sustaining basis by means of mere conversational preaching. They required the benefit, indeed, of every one of the auxiliary means of grace, but could never reach their full stature as Christians without the regular, stated, formal preaching of the word. The heathen then saw the missionary in his true place and dignity. If they did not often go to hear him, they knew there was a day which he regarded as specially set apart by the God of heaven for declaring and for hearing the truths of the Christian religion; and also a time when the missionary assumed authority to speak, and when it was the sole business of all others to hear.

Not only has he preached the gospel orally, statedly, formally on the Sabbath, and more familiarly during the week, but as a good Protestant Christian he has sought to give the Bible to the people. And as that could benefit them only as they were able to read, he found it needful to open schools; not with the expectation of teaching the whole population to read, nor even a considerable portion of it, — that being impossible, — but to form such a public sentiment as in the end would insure this result. A demand was thus created for school books and for the press. The schools served as an introduction and a tie to the people at the outset of the work, and as a means of infusing Christian ideas into the language. As converts multiplied, it became an interesting question how to provide native pastors for them, and how to convert the more promising of the pious youth into evangelists and teachers. Without such, the mission could never finish its work; hence institutions arose for training both males and females. When natives had thus been prepared to be helpers in the different departments, it became needful to aid in their support until the native churches should be able and willing to sustain them; otherwise some of the most valuable and costly results of missionary labor would be wholly sacrificed and lost.

Laws of Growth

The more important indications of progress in the missions have been these — collecting hearers, reducing languages to writing, translating the Scriptures, forming Christian schools, creating a desire for education, awakening anxiety to learn the way of life, multiplying converts, gathering churches, training up a native ministry, and leading the people to support it; and whatever else goes to improve and elevate the domestic, social, civil, and religious life of the people. And this leads to the remark, that continued progress has been found essential to the prosperity of the missions. Regarded in their spiritual nature, missions seem to be under the same laws with individual Christians, in whose spiritual life there is no such thing as standing still, but advancement is the condition of health. A living mission must needs grow and spread its branches, like a tree. It increases in its demands for labor, oversight, nutriment, and expenditure. We learn this from experience. The greater the disposition to hear, the greater is the need of preaching and of preaching houses. The more diffused and earnest the desire for schools, the greater is the demand for teachers, school houses, and school books. In proportion to the progress of mind and feeling upward from barbarism, has been the cost of printing, (if the means were at hand,) and the demand for the lights and advantages of general knowledge. But the most urgent among the growing expenses in a prosperous mission have been those for the training and support of helpers in the higher classes of native agency; and the measures for rearing this agency having been commenced, they have been found essentially progressive, but with this redeeming feature, that at length they begin to diminish the demand for foreign laborers.

A reference to the varying expenditure of the Board would not invalidate this statement; because the expenditure has been more or less subject to arbitrary limitations, — determined by the amount of receipts, rather than by the actual necessities of the missions. Who can tell what an amount of good in missions has been thus annually sacrificed? Who has not sympathized with the disappointments and griefs of the missionaries? It is melancholy to think of the waste of influence thus occasioned in the missions, since they reached the stages of manifest success. The churches have not seemed prepared for rapid progress. Instead of glad praises to God for thus answering prayer for the extension of his kingdom in foreign lands, the officers of the Board have often been put upon the painful task of showing that they have labored to the utmost to check the speed of their missionary trains.

There has been a growth of experience and skill in the conduct of missions during the past half century. It is indeed true that our fathers, at the outset, gave the preëminence to the preaching of the gospel, in their theory of missions, as really as do their successors. Thus they wrote as far back as the year 1813, and nothing stronger can be said now: "Important as the distribution of the Scriptures among the heathen in their own language, is held to be by us and by the Christian public generally, it should never be forgotten, that the *preaching of the gospel,* in every part of the earth, is indispensable to the general conversion of mankind. Though the Scriptures alone have, in many individual cases, been made the instrument of regeneration, yet we have no account of any very extensive diffusion of Christianity except where the truths of the Scriptures have been preached. Were the heathen generally anxious to receive the Scriptures and to learn divine truth, they would, like the Ethiopian eunuch, apply for instruction to those who had been previously acquainted with the same Scriptures, and, when asked if they understood what they had read, would reply, 'How can we, except some man should guide us?' The distribution of the Bible excites inquiry, and often leads those who receive that precious book to attend public worship in the sanctuary. But the preaching of the gospel is, after all, the grand means appointed by Infinite Wisdom for the conversion and salvation of men. Without this, the Scriptures, however liberally distributed, will have comparatively little effect among any people, whether Pagan or nominally Christian." And again, in 1817: "The translation and dispersion of the Scriptures, and schools for the instruction of the young, are parts, and necessary parts, of the great design. But it must never be forgotten, or overlooked, that the command is, to 'preach the gospel to every creature,' and that the preaching of the word, however foolish it may seem to men, is the grand means appointed by the wisdom of God for the saving conversion of the nations."

From this practical view of the work, taken by the Board at the opening of its career, there has been no intentional departure, either by the Prudential Committee or by the missions. Schools and the press have always been regarded as subordinate to preaching. When agriculture and the mechanic arts have also been taught, as in the Indian missions, and at first on the Sandwich Islands, it has been as a subordinate means. At the same time, there has been a tendency in the more important of the auxiliary influences to transcend their proper limits. Book-making has sometimes acquired an undue prominence, especially in the earlier periods, when some brethren may have found it easier even to translate the Scriptures, than to preach in a foreign tongue, and when preaching yielded little apparent fruit, and schools were easily multiplied, and tracts and books could be circulated to any extent. In the chapter on the difficulties in obtaining the Board's charter, it was seen how translating and circulating the Scriptures then preponderated, in the public mind, over preaching as a means of converting the heathen.

The subordinate agencies have been gradually falling into their places, and it is reasonable to expect, under the lead of the Great Captain, that the progress of the gospel will be more rapid in the second half-century than it has been in the first.

How the Work May Be Completed

It is an unsettled problem how the work of missions may be so finished, that the missionary force can safely withdraw, leaving the new Christian community to take care of itself. There are spiritual, intellectual, and social difficulties to be first overcome; and these are often much aggravated by adverse influences from abroad. Out of what depths of moral and social degradation is every heathen convert raised before he is fitted for membership in the church of Christ! "And such were some of you," — "fornicators, idolaters, adulterers, effeminate, abusers of themselves with mankind, thieves, covetous, drunkards, revilers, extortioners." (1 Cor. vi. 10, 11.) But though "justified in the name of the Lord Jesus," they are sanctified only in part, "babes in Christ," continually needing to be taught "which be the first principles of the oracles of God." Who can realize what it is, and what it must be, for an entire community of Christians to have had their home, for a long course of years before conversion, where truth had fallen in the street, and equity could not enter, without rule or protection of law, with no standard of morality, no domestic virtue, no culture of the affections, no correct public sentiment, and almost no conscience? And who, that has closely observed the weaknesses and imperfections of human nature in its most favored conditions, is not prepared for occasional and violent outbreaks of ingratitude, passion, waywardness, and wickedness, in churches gathered from the lower, and sometimes the lowest, depths of humanity? That such churches should live, thrive, and ever reach the self-sustaining point, is a miracle of grace.

Causes such as these had their influence in churches gathered by the apostle Paul, as we see in his Epistles. At Corinth he had occasion to lament the many who had been carried away by false teachers, their disorderly worship, their irregularities at the Lord's Supper, their negligent discipline, their party divisions, their litigations, debates, envyings, wraths, strifes, backbitings, whisperings, swellings, tumults. And how soon were the Galatians seduced from their loyalty to the truth, so that the apostle feared he had labored among them in vain! He exhorts the Ephesian church members to put away lying, to steal no more, to have nothing more to do with covetousness and fornication. Four years after this he speaks of his helpers in Lesser Asia as all turned away from him. That he had not full confidence in all the native pastors appears from his address at Miletus. At Rome, there were those who preached Christ of envy and strife, supposing to add affliction to his bonds; and at his first arraignment before Caesar, not a member of the Roman church had the courage to stand by him. To the Philippians he declares his belief that many professed Christians were enemies of the cause of Christ, and gloried in their shame, minding earthly things. In this same Epistle he speaks in desponding terms of his native helpers, who sought their own, and not the things of Jesus Christ. He thought it needful to exhort the Colossians not to lie one to another, and the Thessalonians to withdraw from such as walked disorderly. He cautions Timothy against fables, endless genealogies, and profane babblings, as if such were prevalent in some of the churches; and speaks of preachers destitute of the truth, with corrupt minds, ignorant, proud, addicted to controversies that engendered envy, strifes, disputations, and railings; and of some who had even made shipwreck of the faith, and added blasphemy to their heresies. The apostle John, somewhat later, declares that many "antichrists" had gone out from the church, denying the Father and the Son.

Yet it is generally supposed that the Apostolical Churches possessed as much piety as the best portions of the visible church of our times. Indeed, the great apostle speaks of Roman Christians, only a few years before the date of his Epistles to Timothy, as being noted for their faith throughout the world. At the very time of his censures on the Corinthians, he declares that church to be "enriched by Jesus Christ in all utterance and in all knowledge," so that it came behind in no gift. While he so seriously cautions the Ephesians, he ceases not to give thanks for their "faith in the Lord Jesus, and their love unto all the saints." He thanked God upon every remembrance of the Philippians; and when he wrote to the Colossians, he gave thanks for their faith in Christ Jesus, and their love in the Spirit, and to all the saints. And how remarkable his testimony in behalf of the Thessalonians! He remembered, without ceasing and with constant gratitude, their work of faith, and labor of love, and patience of hope in the Lord Jesus Christ, wherein they had become followers of him and of the Lord, having received the word in much affliction, with joy of the Holy Ghost, so that they were examples to all that believed, in Macedonia and Achaia.

The fact undoubtedly is, that visible irregularities and disorders, and even certain immoralities, are more to be expected in churches gathered from among the heathen, than in the churches of Christendom; and they are, at the same time, more consistent with grace in the church, than in countries that have long enjoyed the light and influence of the gospel. While the primitive converts from paganism were remarkable for the high tone of their religious feelings, and the simplicity and strength of their faith, they were wanting in respect to a clear, practical apprehension of the ethical code of the gospel. It is obvious, that Paul found the burden of his "care of the churches" much enhanced by the thoroughly wicked character of the age. His manner of treating the native pastors and churches is a model for missionaries and their supporters in our day, who ought to expect greater manifestations of ignorance, weakness, and sin in churches that are gathered in Africa, India, and the Sandwich Islands, than at Ephesus, Colossé, and Corinth, in the palmy days of Roman civilization.

This imperfect state of the native churches, and the circumstances in which they exist, have made it difficult for the missions to reach a point where these churches might be safely left, even after the native community had become Christianized. There is a limit beyond which it has not been found practicable to go, in procuring and supporting a foreign missionary force in any one field; as there has been in the support of an English army in India: nor are nations conquered by one simultaneous, universal onset, but by successive victories. It has been found, too, that a less number of foreign missionaries is needful for the work in a heathen country, than was once supposed. There must be room for the free growth and action of a numerous native ministry, and for devolving upon that ministry the heaviest responsibility it will bear.

The popular sentiment at home is believed to have required too much of the missions. A standard has been prescribed for their ultimate success, which renders their satisfactory termination quite impossible, or at best throws it into the far, uncertain future. The Christian religion has been identified, in the popular conception of it, with a general diffusion of education, industry, civil liberty, family government, and social order, and with the means of a respectable livelihood and a well-ordered community. Hence our idea of piety in native converts has generally involved the acquisition and possession, to a great extent, of these blessings; and our idea of the propagation of the gospel by means of missions is, to an equal extent, the creation among heathen tribes and nations of a state of society such as we enjoy. And for this vast intellectual, moral, social transformation we allow but a short time. We have expected the first generation of converts, even among savages, to come pretty fully into our fundamental ideas of morals, manners, political economy, social organization, justice, equity, — although many of these are ideas which old Christian communities have been ages in acquiring. If we have discovered that converts under the torrid zone go half clothed, are idle on a soil where a small amount of labor supplies their wants, sometimes forget the apostle's cautions to his converts, "not to lie one to another," and "to steal no more," in communities where the grossest vice scarcely affects the reputation, and are slow to adopt our ideas of the rights of man, we at once doubt the genuineness of their conversion, and the faithfulness of their missionary instructors.

It is an important and encouraging consideration, in the effort to bring missions to a successful issue, that an increasing outlay is not always necessary to meet the demands of a growing and prosperous mission. This results from an increase of intelligence, experience, and piety in missionaries, thus augmenting their superintending and executive power; from a similar growth in the native ministry; from substituting the less expensive native agency for the missionary, thus multiplying stations without increasing the foreign force; from developing the native churches; from new discoveries in the relations and powers of the missionary enterprise, increasing the simplicity and economy of its spiritual machinery; and from new arrangements and combinations, to meet the constantly increasing expenditure in some parts of the system, by a constantly diminishing outlay in others.

The work of the missionary has been performed mainly at central points; and when this work shall have been completed at all these points, and there is no more need of new stations, — when it is possible for gospel institutions to exist, through divine grace, without the longer presence of the missionary, — then the work of the mission in that community is obviously completed. The missionary, having "no more place in those parts," should go and preach the gospel elsewhere. It is a great point to know when to do this. After a native church is formed, it should have, as soon as possible, a native pastor and the needed church officers; and the native pastor should have ample scope for preaching, and for all his ministerial and pastoral abilities and duties. The local church is the divinely appointed illuminating power for its district. It is the great power in missions. It is a leaven, which may be expected in time to leaven the whole lump. With a somewhat reserved and discreet superintendence on the part of the nearest missionary, it will thrive best, after a proper organization, by being left to itself. Thus station after station may be finished, and new conquests be continually made, with almost no enlargement in the number of the foreign force, and also without any material increase of expenditure; provided the native pastors have not been rendered too expensive by an injudicious education, doing less to fit them for their work than to make them dissatisfied in it, and provided the duty of self-support has been properly urged upon the native churches.

Selection 5

PRINCIPLES AND METHODS OF MODERN MISSIONS[1]

I am now prepared to state, in a concise but positive form, what I believe to be the true and proper nature of a mission among the heathen. The mission of the Apostle Paul, as set forth in the fourth chapter, embraced the following things: —

1. The aim of the apostle was to save the souls of men.

2. The means he employed for this purpose were spiritual; namely, the gospel of Christ.

3. The power on which he relied to give efficacy to these means, was divine; namely, the promised aid of the Holy Spirit.

4. His success was chiefly in the middle and poorer classes, — the Christian influence ascending from thence.

5. When he had formed local churches, he did not hesitate to ordain presbyters over them, the best he could find; and then to throw upon the churches, thus officered, the responsibilities of self-government, self-support, and self-propagation. His "presbyters in every church," whatever their number and other duties, had doubtless the pastoral care of the churches.

Prominent, then, among the visible agencies in foreign missions, if we follow the great apostle, are LOCAL CHURCHES. I call them by no denominational name. They may be churches governed by popular vote, or by elders they have themselves chosen for the purpose. They are local bodies of associated Christians. The first duty of a missionary is to gather such a church. That will serve as a nucleus — and it is

[1] Chapter VII of *Foreign Missions: Their Relations and Claims;* N.Y.: Charles Scribner, 1869.

the only possible nucleus, a school not being one — of a permanent congregation. A missionary, by means of properly located, well organized,
well trained churches, may extend his influence over a large territory. In
such a country as India, or China, his direct influence may reach even
scores of thousands.

I find nothing in the history of the mission of the Apostle Paul,
which seems to me decisive, as to the manner in which these multiplied mission churches should be brought into social relations to each
other, and would cheerfully leave that to the good sense and piety of
missionaries on the ground.

I now inquire, What should be the nature of the mission church?
It should be composed only of hopeful converts; and should have, as
soon as possible, a native pastor, and of the same race, who has been
trained cheerfully to take the oversight of what will generally be a small,
poor, ignorant people, and mingle with them familiarly and sympathetic-
ally. And by a native pastor, I mean one recognized as having the pastoral care of a local church, with the right to administer the ordinances
of baptism and the Lord's Supper.

This necessity of a native pastor to the healthful and complete development of a self-reliant, effective native church, is a discovery of recent date. I cannot say, nor is it important to know, by whom this fundamental truth or law in missions was first declared. Like many discoveries in science, it very probably was reached by a number of persons, at nearly the same time, and as the result of a common experience.[2]

As soon as the mission church has a native pastor, the responsibilities of self-government should be devolved upon it. Mistakes, per-
plexities, and sometimes scandals, there will be; but it is often thus that
useful experience is gained, even in churches here at home. The salary
of the native pastor should be based on the Christianized ideas of living
acquired by his people; and the church should become self-supporting
at the earliest possible day. It should also be self-propagating from the

---

[2] "It may be said to have been only lately discovered in the science of missions, that when the missionary is of another and superior race than his converts,
he must not attempt to be their *pastor;* though they will be bound to him by
personal attachment, and by a sense of the benefits received from him; yet if he
continues to act as their pastor, they will not form a vigorous native church,
but, as a general rule, they will remain in a dependent condition, and make but
little progress in spiritual attainments. The same congregation, under competent
native pastors would become more self-reliant, and their religion would be of a
more manly, home character." —Rev. Henry Venn's *Letter to the Bishop of
Jamaica,* dated January, 1867. Mr. Venn is Honorary Secretary of the Church
Missionary Society, and no one is better informed on missionary subjects. (See
pp. 36-37 in Introduction on Venn and Anderson.—Ed.)

very first. Such churches, and only such, are the life, strength, and glory of missions.

A foreign missionary should not be the pastor of a native church. His business is to plant churches, in well-chosen parts of his field, committing them as soon as possible to the care of native pastors; himself sustaining a common relation to all, as their ecclesiastical father and adviser; having, in some sense, like the apostle, the daily care of the churches. He might stand thus related to a score of churches, and even more, however they were related to each other; and when he is old, might be able to say, through the abounding grace of God, "Though ye have ten thousand instructors in Christ, yet have ye not many fathers; for in Christ Jesus I have begotten you all through the gospel."[3]

Self-evident as this idea of a mission church may seem on its announcement, it is not yet adopted in all Protestant missions, and until of late, has seemed to gain ground very slowly. Its universal adoption, however, cannot be far distant, and will add immensely both to the economy and the power of missions.

It is upon this view of the nature and relations of native churches, that we build our missionary system.

Education, schools, the press, and whatever else goes to make up the working system, are held in strict subordination to the planting and building up of effective working churches. But though held strictly in such subordination, we see in it the utmost latitude for the exercise of a wise discretion in the conduct of missions. The governing object to be always aimed at, is self-reliant, effective churches, — churches that are purely native. Whatever missionaries believe to be most directly conducive to this end, comes within the scope of their privilege and duty; of course, under reasonable restrictions growing out of their fundamental relations. The use of schools and the press comes under the question, how far they are subsurvient to the great end, namely, the rapid and perfect development of churches.

We thus perceive the place which education must hold in missions. Without education, it is not possible for mission churches to be in any proper sense self-governed; nor, without it, will they be self-supported, and much less self-propagating. For the church-members there must be common schools. This results from the degraded mental condition of the heathen world, as compared with the field of the apostolic missions. Scarcely a ray of light reaches it from sun, moon, or stars in the intellectual and moral firmament. Mind is vacant, crushed, unthinking, enslaved to animal instincts and passions; earthly, sensual, terribly debased. The common school, therefore, is a necessity among the de-

[3] I Cor. iv. 15.

graded heathen, to· help elevate the converts, and make the village church an effective agency. And the church-members, as far as may be, should be educated within the bounds of their own villages; and in such manner that a large number of them will abide with their people, and help to support their native pastor and schools, and make their Christian village a power in the land. At first, these schools must be sustained by the mission; but it is better for them, not long afterwards, to be sustained by the parents.

The native preachers and pastors come, almost of course, from the same depths of mental degradation; and since they must be enabled to stand alone and firmly in the gospel ministry, and be competent spiritual guides to others, they should of course have a higher training. What this shall be, what it shall include and exclude, must depend on circumstances too various for general rules. But one thing is clear. Our army, liberated from the thralldom of pagan slavery, must be well officered in order to fight bravely.

The printing-press in missions is mainly for the schools and for the church-members, to whom, indeed, books are indispensable. Experience tends to the result of having missions cease to own printing establishments as soon as the needful printing can be secured from presses owned by others.

Wherein, then, do our modern missions differ from those of the apostolic age? They differ in several particulars.

1. Modern missionaries are sent forth and supported by churches in their native lands; by churches, too, of long standing and experience; and, so far at least as this country and Great Britain are concerned, by churches existing and operating in the midst of freedom and high religious intelligence. In this modern missions have certainly a great advantage over the primitive missions.

2. They have not the personal presence and active agency of apostles; but they have the four Gospels, the Acts of the Apostles, and their Letters of Instruction, all written under the guidance of inspiration; and the press, to multiply copies of these documents by thousands. A portion of the modern Evangelical Church, indeed, is coming into the practice of putting their missionaries under the control of missionary bishops, and regards these as successors of the apostles. But they evidently are not apostles, since they lack the "signs, and wonders, and mighty deeds," which St. Paul, in his Second Epistle to the Corinthians, declares to be the needful "signs of an apostle."[4]

3. The pastorate in modern missions differs from that of the apostolic age, in that it ordinarily has but one pastor for each church;

---

[4] 2 Cor. xii. 12; Rom. xv. 18, 19.

2.8517

whereas the New Testament always uses the plural in speaking of the pastorate in the churches planted by the Apostle Paul. "They ordained presbyters in every church"; being influenced in this, perhaps (as has already said), by the usage of the Jewish synagogue. This practice seems to have been lost, with the very idea of the apostolic church, in the great decline of the Early and Middle Ages; and when that idea was recovered, as it was at the Reformation, and put in practice, the usage of having but one pastor in each church was adopted by all evangelical denominations, as being more conformed to the demands of the age. And this is now the general usage in all the evangelical churches; and it has thence been transferred to the mission churches among the heathen. The apostolic principle is retained, but the form is changed. I speak only of the pastorate, in which the evangelical denominations agree; leaving entirely untouched the points concerning which the evangelical denominations differ.

Such is the simple structure of our foreign missions, as the combined result of experience, and of the apostolic example; in all which the grand object is to plant and multiply self-reliant, efficient churches, composed wholly of native converts, each church complete in itself, with pastors of the same race with the people. And when the unevangelized world shall be dotted over with such churches, so that all men have it within their power to learn what they must do to be saved, then may we expect the promised advent of the Spirit, and the conversion of the world.

It might be deemed an omission in my description of the missionary work, should I not advert to a series of efforts made in the cities of India, and more especially in Calcutta, to gain access for the gospel to the higher classes by means of English schools. In these schools a large number of high-caste Hindus have received a liberal Christian education, through the medium of the English language and literature. The result of the experiment is regarded as very hopeful by those who are making it. And there is certainly a development among the higher class of Hindus in Calcutta, and in some other of the India cities, that is worthy of attentive consideration. But the results of the experiments are not yet sufficiently developed to occupy a prominent place in a description of the fundamental nature of the missionary work.[5]

I close with a few general remarks.

1. The foreign missionary, the home missionary, and the pastor have each substantially the same object. It is to plant churches, and make

[5] The author here directs the reader to Appendices III and IV of the book on "English Mission Schools" and "The Brahmo Samaj," which need not be reproduced here. —Ed.

them shine as lights in the world. Our leading sentiment is as really applicable to home missionaries, as it is to foreign missionaries. The labors of the home missionary have a direct reference to the forming of self-governed, self-supported churches, and such churches are proofs of his success. The home missionary becomes then a pastor, or gives place to one sustaining that relation.

2. The great simplification in the use of means, and relying more on those which are spiritual, is a principal reason why a given amount of funds now sustains a more extended working mission than it formerly did. The grand object and means are the same; but the working process, becoming more spiritual, bears more effectively on the heart and conscience.

3. The proper test of success in missions, is not the progress of civilization, but the evidence of a religious life.

4. The gospel is applicable equally to all false religions. Generically considered, there can be but two religions: the one looking for salvation by *grace;* the other, by *works.* The principle of evil in all unbelieving men, is the same. The refuges of lies in Popery, in Judaism, in Mohammedanism, in Brahminism, Buddhism, and every form of paganism, are wonderfully alike. There is one disease, and one remedy. Before the gospel, the unbelieving world stands an undistinguished mass of rebellious sinners; unwilling that God should reign over them, unwilling to be saved except by their own works, and averse to all real holiness of heart and life. There is power in the doctrine of the cross, through grace, to overcome this. The doctrine of the cross — as will more clearly appear when we come to the evidences of success in missions — is the grand instrument of conquest. Not one of the great superstitions of the world could hold a governing place in the human soul, after the conviction has once been thoroughly produced, that there is salvation only in Christ. Be it what it may, the man, thus convinced, would flee from it, as he would from a falling building in the rockings of an earthquake.

Selection 6

ON RAISING UP A NATIVE MINISTRY[1]

The fact is important to be noted, that the elders, or pastors, whom the apostles ordained over the churches they gathered among the heathen, were generally, if not always, *natives of the country*. In this way the gospel soon became indigenous to the soil, and the gospel institutions acquired, through the grace of God, a self-supporting, self-propagating energy. While the apostles had not the facilities that we have for training men for this office by education, they had not the necessity. Among their converts at Ephesus, Berea, Corinth, Rome, and elsewhere, they had no difficulty in finding men, who required only some instruction in theology, and scarcely that, when endowed with miraculous gifts, to be prepared for the pastoral office. How they did, or would have done, beyond the Roman empire and the bounds of civilization, we are not informed; but in the use they made of a native ministry, we recognize one of the grand principles of their missions, and also the true theory of missions — simple, economical, practical, scriptural, mighty through God.

Our first remarks will be upon the manner of raising up a native ministry.

1. This must be by means of seminaries, schools of the prophets, such as, in some form or other, the church has always found necessary. There should be one such seminary in each considerable mission. It is an essential feature of the plan, that the pupils be taken young, board in the mission, be kept separate from heathenism, under christian superintendence night and day. In general the course of study should embrace a period of from eight to ten or twelve years, and even a longer time in

---

[1] American Board of Commissioners for Foreign Missions, *Annual Report, 1841*, pp. 44-47; and separately published as a tract at that time.

special cases. Pupils can be obtained for such a course of education in most of the missions; but, as a nursery for them, it is expedient to have a certain number of free-schools, which also greatly aid in getting audiences for the preachers.

2. There will be but partial success in rearing a native ministry, unless the seminary be in the midst of a select and strong body of missionaries, whose holy lives, conversation, and preaching shall cause the light of the gospel to blaze intensely and constantly upon and around the institution. Experience shows that in such circumstances we are warranted to expect a considerable proportion of the students to become pious.

3. The student, while in the seminary, should be trained practically to habits of usefulness. But this requires caution, and must not be attempted too soon. Those set apart for the sacred ministry, might remain as a class in theology at the seminary, after completing the regular course of study; or, according to the old fashion in this country, which has some special advantages, they might pursue their theological studies with individual missionaries, and under such superintendence exercise their gifts before much responsibility is thrown upon them.

4. The contemporaneous establishment of female boarding schools, where the native ministers and other educated helpers in the mission may obtain pious and intelligent partners for life, is an essential feature in this system. A native pastor, with an ignorant, heathen wife, would be greatly embarrassed and hindered in his work. In this manner christian families are formed, and at length christian communities, and there is a race of children with christian ideas and associations, from among whom we may select our future pupils and candidates for the ministry.

Our second topic is the employment of this native ministry.

The pupils in the seminaries will have different gifts, and the same gifts in very different degrees. All the pious students will not do for preachers. Some may be retained as tutors in the seminary, others may be employed as school teachers, others as printers, bookbinders, etc. Those set apart for the ministry, while they are taught the way of the Lord more perfectly, can be employed as catechists, tract distributors, readers, or superintendents of schools, and thus gain experience and try their characters. In due time they may be licensed to preach, and after proper trial, receive ordination as evangelists or pastors.

While care should be taken to lay hands suddenly on no man, there is believed to be danger of requiring too much of native converts before we are willing to intrust them with the ministry of the word. Generations must pass, before a community, emerging from the depths of heathenism, can be expected to furnish a body of ministers equal to that in our country.

Could the present native church members at the Sandwich Islands be divided into companies of one hundred and eighty each, a hundred churches would be constituted. Native pastors should be in training for these churches, and evangelists for the numerous districts where churches are not yet formed, and where the people are consequently exposed to the inroads of the enemy. In the other missions the chief employment, at present, must be that of evangelists. In the Tamul missions, hundreds might find ample employment; and in the Oriental churches, our leading object should be to bring forward an able evangelical native ministry with the least possible delay.

The power and economy there is in the plan, is our third topic.

In most of our missions we are opposed by three formidable obstacles, namely, *distance, expense,* and *climate.* England was opposed by the same obstacles in her conquest of India. And how did she overcome them? By employing native troops; and it is chiefly by means of them she now holds that great populous country in subjection. We too must have native troops in our spiritual warfare. Why not have an army of them? Why not have as numerous a body of native evangelists, as can be directed and employed?

Such a measure would effect a great saving of *time.* Indeed we can never leave our fields of labor till this is done. Our mission-churches must have native pastors, and pastors of some experience, who can stand alone, before we can leave them. Besides, we should make far greater progress than we do, had we more of such helpers.

And what economy of money there would be in the operation of this plan! The cost of a ten-year course of education for five natives of India, would not be more than the outfit and passage of one married missionary to that country. And when a company of missionaries is upon the ground, it costs at least five times as much to support them, as it would to support the same number of native preachers. The former could not live, like the latter, upon rice alone, with a piece of cotton cloth wrapped about their bodies for clothing; and a mud-walled, grass covered cottage, without furniture, for a dwelling; nor could they travel on foot under a tropical sun. They could not do this, and at the same time preserve health and life.

The cost of educating a thousand youth in India, from whom preachers might be obtained, and afterwards of supporting two hundred native preachers and their families, would be only about $25,000; which is but little more than the average expense in that country of twenty-five missionaries and families. Now if the preaching of two well educated native preachers, laboring under judicious superintendence, may be

expected to do as much good as that of one missionary, we have in
these two hundred native preachers the equivalent, in instrumental
preaching power, for one hundred missionaries, and at an expenditure
less by nearly $75,000 a year. And then, too, the native preacher is at
home in the country and climate, not subject to a premature breaking
down of his constitution, not compelled to resort for health to the United
States, or to send his children thither for education. Besides, the native
churches and converts might gradually be brought to assume a part or the
whole of the support of the native ministry; while it is very doubtful
whether it will ever be expedient for the missionary to receive his support from that quarter.

One hundred thousand dollars a year would board and educate
four thousand native youth. That sum would support five hundred or
six hundred native ministers with their families; and if the value of this
amount of native preaching talent equalled that of only two hundred
missionaries, the annual saving of expense would be at least $125,000.
But it would in the end be worth much more; so that we see, in this
view, how our effective force among the heathen may, in a few years,
be rendered manifold greater than it is at present, without even doubling
our annual expediture. Some progress has even now been made towards
this result. We already have five hundred male youth in our seven
seminaries; and a still greater number, male and female, in our other
twenty-seven boarding schools. But the scheme, however promising and
indispensable, cannot be carried into effect, without a large addition
of first rate men to the company of our missionaries.

Selection 7

THE VALUE OF NATIVE CHURCHES[1]

It was stated in the last chapter, that the grand object of foreign missions is to plant and multiply churches, composed of native converts; each church complete in itself, with presbyters of the same race, left to determine their ecclesiastical relations for themselves, with the aid of judicious advice from their missionary fathers.

The value of native churches must be learned by an estimate of the value of native converts, and of the native ministry. And should it be thought that I produce the richest specimens from our golden mines, it should be remembered that such specimens best illustrate the work of the Holy Spirit in extending Messiah's kingdom. They will best show what can and must be done before the glorious reign of our Lord and Saviour extends over all nations.

In estimating the *value of native converts,* I begin with Western Africa. The oldest mission on the West African coast is that of the English Church Missionary Society at Sierra Leone. Here, in the early stage of that mission, we shall find a native church of marvelous interest and power, gathered out of the most unpromising materials, in circumstances the most unpropitious.

It is fifty years since a plain German laborer in London, named William A. B. Johnson, offered himself to the Church Missionary Society to be sent as a school-master to Sierra Leone. He had only a common school education, but was rich in Christian experience. It soon appeared that he was called of God to the gospel ministry, and he accordingly received ordination in Africa. His was a wonderful ministry. When Mr. Johnson first took up his abode at what was after-

[1] Chapter VIII of *Foreign Missions: Their Relations and Claims;* N.Y.: Charles Scribner, 1869.

wards called Regent's Town, in Sierra Leone, the people numbered about a thousand. They had been taken at different times from the holds of slave-ships; were wild and naked; and being from twenty-two different nations, were hostile to each other. They had no common medium of intercourse, except a little broken English, had no ideas of marriage, and lived crowded together in the rudest huts. They were devil-worshipers, and most of them lazy, thieving, plundering, brutal savages.

Mr. Johnson was at first exceedingly discouraged. But he resolved to preach Christ to them as the Saviour of sinners, in the simple manner of the gospel, and to open to them the miserable state of a sinner rejecting such a Saviour. His resolution was the same with that of the Apostle Paul, when he surveyed the desperate pollutions of the Corinthians, — "to know nothing among *them,* save Jesus Christ and him crucified." There is no other adequate power of deliverance. After pursuing this course the greater part of a year, preaching salvation through the Lord Jesus, a remarkable change began to come over the people. Old and young became concerned for their souls. There was, in short, an outpouring of the Spirit. Many sought retirement in the woods for prayer; and soon the neighboring mountains echoed, in moonlight evenings, with the hymns of worshippers. Mr. Johnson has left a record of the experience of many of the converts, in their own simple and broken, but expressive language, when examined, as they all were, for admission to the Lord's Supper. I am impressed by his record of their convictions of sin; their acknowledgments of the divine forbearance; their distrust of their own hearts; their inward conflicts; their tender consciences; their faith and patience; their benevolence; and their love for souls. The outward changes were most striking. The people learned trades, became farmers, attached well-kept gardens to their dwellings. They built a stone church large enough, with the help of galleries, to seat closely nearly two thousand persons; which was regularly filled with decently dressed, orderly, and serious worshippers. They built a parsonage, school-houses, store-houses, a bridge of several arches — all of stone. Most of the adult population were married. Their night-dances and heathenish drumming ceased, and so did their oaths, drunkenness, and stealing; and the schools contained a thousand children.[2]

---

[2] See *Memoir of Rev. W. A. B. Johnson,* London, 1852, Preface, and pp. 168, 169, 245, 275, 279, 283, 299, 305, 419, 423, 424, 426. Also, *London Missionary Register* for 1819, pp. 5, 378-381, 486-492; and for 1829, pp. 18, 107-113, 197, 252-256, 371. Also, and especially, *Twentieth Report of the Church Missionary Society;* extracts from which are embodied in *Missionary Register* for 1820, pp. 473-476.

All this Mr. Johnson lived to see; but he died in 1823, only seven years from the commencement of his mission! Was there ever a more wonderful religious change? It shows the power of the simple gospel, both to convert the savage, and to civilize him. It shows the power of the cross of Christ. It shows, also, the illuminating, reforming influence of such a church, regarded as a missionary agency. Would that the same influences could have been continued in all their power. But this was more than forty years ago, and it was then too early for native pastors; their necessity to the full development of a native church not having then been discovered. A worthy missionary successor to Mr. Johnson was not soon found, and Regent's Town suffered a decline after his death. But the foundations he had laid were sure, and there was progress on the whole. In the year 1842, twenty-four years after Mr. Johnson began his mission, one fifth of the population of Sierra Leone was at school, and the attendance at public worship was estimated at twelve thousand. In 1862, native pastorates were established, and ten parishes undertook the support of their own pastors; and no less than six different missions were sent by the people to the unevangelized tribes beyond the colony. The present number of nominal Christians in the colony, is said, on high authority, to be eighty thousand, of whom twenty thousand are communicants; and the missionary work at Sierra Leone is regarded as having been accomplished.[3]

I venture to say, to the glory of God in the gospel, that not one of the "seven churches of Asia" shone with a brighter light, than did this one, at that time, gathered from the slave-ships of Western Africa. And were such churches now along the whole extent of that coast, and in the vast interior, the darkness, crime, and misery of that benighted region would give place to the blessedness of a Christian civilization.

Look, next, at the great island of Madagascar, situated on the eastern coast of Africa. Here we shall see, as of old, infant churches struggling successfully against the utmost efforts of the civil power to destroy them. The London Missionary Society commenced a mission on that island in 1820, under the protection of the King Radama. The missionaries gave the people a written language, a grammar and dictionary, school books, a hymn-book, and the Bible, and taught some thousands to read the Scriptures.[4] The converts were virtually, if not formally, embodied in churches. A pagan queen, the widow of Radama, succeeded her husband in 1828, and, being hostile to the Christian religion, forbade the observance of its ordinances, and the reading of the Bible; and persistence in either was punishable with death. Per-

---

[3] *Church Missionary Intelligencer,* 1868, pp. 203, 250.
[4] Ellis's *Madagascar Revisited* (London: John Murray, 1867), p. 2.

ceiving that the gospel continued to gain ground, notwithstanding her decree, she, in 1835, banished all the missionaries. The Christians, still increasing, were then subjected to fierce persecution, which continued through twenty-five years, until her death in 1861. They were poisoned; they were hanged; they were speared; they were stoned, and the stoning was a most barbarous mode of execution. They were thrown down a fatal precipice. Loaded with heavy iron collars, and chained together, they were driven into banishment. They were burned at the stake, and some were crucified. Many were sold into slavery. It is believed that more than two thousand persons suffered as Christians, during this persecution, in some cruel form or other.

So far as was possible, they associated together as Christian communities; and there were those of their number intelligent and courageous enough to act as pastors and teachers, though always at the peril, and sometimes at the sacrifice, of life. The result was a continual growth in numbers through all the persecutions.

The queen was succeeded by her son; who favored the Christians, and invited the return of the missionaries. This was seven years ago; and now, as we have the account from the well-known Dr. William Ellis, in his work recently published, entitled "Madagascar Revisited," dedicated by permission to the Queen of England, and from other sources, there are, within and around the capital of Madagascar, ninety churches, with more than five thousand members; one hundred and one native pastors; and twenty thousand claiming the Christian name. In the space of four years, the number of nominal Christians was more than doubled, and the number of the communicants was increased tenfold.[5] And we hear that a queen, lately come to the throne, has virtually embraced the Christian religion, and that, if she should live, we may expect Christianity to be soon adopted as the national religion.

We may read the history of Roman persecutions from Nero down, and we shall find none more cruel than the one in Madagascar, and none more distinguished for the inflexible firmness of its martyrs; upon whom, it should be remembered, the fiery tempest burst in the very infancy of their religious life. Nor should we forget that these heroic martyrs belonged to the negro race.

Another case illustrating the same thing, but bearing on a more numerous people, is the remarkable steadfastness of native Christians in the great India rebellion of 1857. This was wholly unexpected. The native Christians at the twenty missionary stations which were swept away in that terrible mutiny of the native army, exceeded two thousand in number. A very large portion of these were compelled, as Christians,

---

[5] Ellis's *Madagascar Revisited,* pp. 469, 501.

to flee for their lives. They were beaten, their houses were plundered, and eleven of them suffered death. Everywhere Moslems or Hindus urged them to apostatize, and threatened and persecuted them; but they were firm to their Christian profession. Of the whole number only six yielded, and these returned as soon as the rebellion ceased.[6] Dr. Mullens, long time a leading missionary at Calcutta, and now the able Foreign Secretary of the London Missionary Society, wrote thus, while in India, concerning these native Christians: —

"Drawn, to a very large extent," he says, "from the artificial hot-house system of orphan and boarding schools; helped from first to last by missionaries; not only fed and taught, but in a measure having employments created for them; the community, as a whole, had grown up in the possession of sound principles, but weak in character, with little self-reliance, and a great deal of the petulance of spoiled children. The mutiny has driven all this away; and they who were thrown headlong into the troubled waters, and had to swim for their lives, without the aid of the corks and bladders on which they had relied, gained health and vigor in the process, and landed, not only alive, but *men*. The old system has been flung away forever."[7]

We see in these converts the nature of the materials for Hindu churches. Indeed the examples thus far adduced go to show, that the mission churches of our times are formed of the same material with the churches of the apostolic and martyr ages, and have, through the grace of God, the same power of endurance.

Let us next see what manner of converts, through divine grace, are produced in Eastern Turkey. It is true, that the churches in that empire are not composed of converts from heathenism; but then the knowledge of the way of salvation through faith in Christ had perished from among them, and they stood, in that respect, very much on a level with Mohammedans and Pagans.

At Harpoot, on the upper waters of the Euphrates, the mission of the American Board formed a station in 1856; and eleven or twelve years ago, a church was gathered there, which, after two years, received a native pastor, and at once guaranteed a portion of his salary, and doubled the amount in the next year. A training-school for the native ministry was opened; and of the eighteen young men in the first class sent forth from that school in the year 1864, eight were licensed to preach the gospel, and most of the others occupied out-stations as catechists and teachers. Churches were soon formed in the villages, to

[6] Mullens' *Ten Years in India* (Joseph Mullens, *A Brief Review of Ten Years' Missionary Labour in India;* London: Nisbet, 1863), p. 24.
[7] Mullens' *Ten Years in India,* p. 25.

which these native preachers were sent, which showed great readiness to support their pastors and preachers. As soon as a village became interested in the truth, it earnestly desired a native pastor of its own, and was easily pleased with him, and opposed to a change.

You will bear in mind, that Harpoot is only one of the five stations composing what is called the Eastern Turkey mission; and I have selected it to show how, in the use of appropriate means, with the divine blessing, a mission church may become as leaven thrown into the lump, and how its offshoots, developing into other churches, and they becoming the nuclei of congregations, grow and multiply until they fill the land. At the end of eleven years from the commencement of that church, the work had so extended, that there were connected with it thirteen churches; four hundred and eighteen church-members; eleven native pastors, more than half of them supported by their own people; twelve licensed native preachers; twenty-one native teachers, and forty-one other helpers. The people were very poor; but, as in the Macedonian church of old, "their deep poverty abounded unto the riches of their liberality." Of pupils there were two thousand and forty-one; and scores of unpaid laborers went spontaneously forth every Sabbath-day, as missionaries into the harvest fields around. This was the growth of a single missionary station, and of a single church, in less than twelve years.[8]

The missionary stations in Aintab and Marash, in the Central Turkey mission, are illustrations of the speedy gathering of large mission churches and congregations. It lately became necessary to divide the churches at each of those stations, and the number of members in each of the four churches, thus constituted, was about one hundred and fifty, with congregations of from six to eight hundred. It is not twenty years since the first missionary sent to Aintab was stoned and driven away by the people. Eight years after that time, visiting Aintab, I was myself met by a cavalcade of Christian men, several miles from Aintab, who escorted me into the very heart of the city, and I saw nowhere among the people so much as a look of disapprobation. It is only twelve years since a missionary station was begun at Marash; but it was not effected until the messengers of the gospel had been driven repeatedly away by violence. Yet, in 1861, the late Dr. Dwight from Constantinople, being in Marash at a communion season, had the joy of addressing an orderly assembly of twelve hundred people.[9]

8 *Ten Years on the Euphrates,* and *Letters from Eden,* by Rev. C. H. Wheeler (*Ten Years,* Boston: American Tract Society, 1868).

9 Harrison Gray Otis Dwight. For an account of this experience at Marash, see: Anderson, *History of the Missions of the A.B.C.F.M. to the Oriental Churches,* vol. II, pp. 70-72. —Ed.

Time would fail me to speak of the growth and value of churches elsewhere. Enough has been adduced to show, that the chief work of evangelical Christendom for the conversion of the heathen world, is to plant churches, instinct with gospel life, in all the central and influential districts of the unevangelized land.

I next illustrate the value of the *native ministry*. This also I do by adducing some of the more remarkable cases.

The first is that of a Karen preacher, pastor, and missionary, named Quala (or Sau Quala), a convert of the Baptist mission in Burmah.[10] Quala signifies "Hope," and the name was given him by his parents because of hoped-for relief from Burmese oppression, awakened by the entrance of British ships into Burman ports at the time of his birth; but it was not till the boy was fifteen or sixteen years old, that the British took actual possession of Tavoy. Three years after this, the first Karen convert was baptized by Dr. Judson, and began immediately to preach, and the first sermon of this convert was in the house of Quala's father. That sermon was blessed to the inquiring youth, who was received into the church in the year 1830, thirty-eight years ago.

As with so many of his countrymen, so with him; the first impulse of his spiritual life was "to declare what God had done for his soul, and to invite all whom he could reach to believe and live." His father was an unbeliever almost to the day of his death; but his mother is said to have been a "lovely picture," when sitting under the sound of the gospel, with large beaming eyes, full of intelligence, fixed on the speaker.[11] Quala resembled his mother. He was employed some years by the missionaries in assisting to translate the New Testament into the Karen language. For fifteen years he accompanied the missionary in his jungle-tours in Tavoy and Mergui, tours sometimes extended three or four hundred miles; and they together laid the foundations in those regions of many Karen churches. Thus was this young servant of the Lord prepared for more responsible service.

It is a striking illustration of the excessive caution of early missionaries in putting native converts into the ministry, that Quala did not receive ordination until fourteen years after his reception into the church.[12] Some time after this, he felt strongly moved to enter on what proved to be the great work of his life, a mission to the Karens in the province of Toungoo. This was a great trial to the churches in Tavoy

[10] Some references to Quala in Torbet, Robert G., *Venture of Faith;* Phila.: Judson Press, 1955, pp. 212-213, 215. —Ed.

[11] *Gospel in Burmah,* p. 215. (by Mrs. Macleod Wylie; London: W. H. Dalton, 1859. —Ed.)

[12] *Gospel in Burmah,* pp. 231, 236.

and Mergui, all of which joined in a written remonstrance to the missionaries against his leaving them. It was like our sending to the heathen our most useful, learned, and valued pastors and ministers. But it was decided to be his duty to go, as may yet perhaps be true of some such men among ourselves. Quala reached Toungoo in December, 1853, the year after that province, by the annexation of Pegu, came under the protection of English law. The first baptism he performed was in the following January. Before the close of that year, the number of converts connected with his labors was seven hundred and forty-one, who were associated in nine churches. In less than three years, the number of churches was increased under his ministry to thirty, with an aggregate of two thousand one hundred and twenty-seven members, more than two thousand of whom were baptized by Quala himself.[13] Nor do those converts appear to have been admitted to the church without due consideration. His labors and fatigue were truly apostolical, and such was his success. His singleness of purpose was like that of the Apostle Paul. He received no salary in Toungoo, and, being constantly on the move, he found it necessary, for two years, to leave his lovely wife in Tavoy, who is represented as "the flower of the jungle." One and another of the native disciples gave him a garment when he needed it, and, having no house, he got his food where he labored.

The wild mountain Karens, in "regions beyond," sent a petition, that he would come and tell them of the "Eternal God." The English Commissioner, hearing of this, offered Quala a salary from the English government, if he would become the head and overseer of that wild tribe. Quala gives this very touching account of his conference with the Commissioner. His reply was: "Sir, I cannot do it. I will not have the money. I will not mix up God's work with government work. There are others to do this thing. Employ them. As for me, I will continue the work in which I have been engaged." The Commissioner asked, "Where do you obtain money to live on? Why do you not like money? We will give you money, and you may continue your work as teacher as heretofore. Will it not make it easier for you?" He answered, "No, sir; when I eat with the children of poverty, my heart sleeps. I did not leave my dear wife, and come up hither in search of silver, or agreeable food. I came to this land that its poor people might be saved. Be patient with me, sir. Were I to take your money, the wild Karens would turn against me." Admirable man! Where shall we find his equal in devotion to the cause of Christ?

[13] *Gospel in Burmah,* p. 241; also *Reports of the American Baptist Union* for 1856, pp. 72, 76; and for 1855, p. 86.

This servant of God is still living, and his character shines, in a venerable old age.[14] Though he stands out preëminently above his brethren in the native Karen ministry, we still recognize him as a Karen, and as owing all that he was and is to the grace of God, who can easily raise up many such apostolic men from among heathen converts.

Many of the older missions in other heathen countries have also had native ministers of distinguished ability and usefulness, but I shall specify only two more.

The Rev. John Thomas, a distinguished missionary of the English Church Missionary Society in Southern India, having the care of ten thousand native Christians, speaks thus of a native preacher among the Shanars: "Without any exception, he is the most able and eloquent native preacher of the gospel now in India." "I have no hesitation," Mr. Thomas adds, "in saying, that if such sermons as are generally preached by him, were delivered in any pulpit in London, the church would be crowded to overflowing. Nor am I singular in this opinion, for several of my brother missionaries, after hearing him, have expressed themselves in terms of the highest admiration of his pulpit abilities. The people, also, everywhere, listen to him with great attention and delight."

In 1860, death deprived Mr. Thomas of this beloved native co-laborer, and the missionary thus testifies to his worth: "His affection, his simplicity, honesty, and straightforwardness, his amazing pulpit talents, and profound humility, endeared him to me more than I can describe. The last sermon I heard from him was, without exception, the greatest sermon I ever heard. The text was, 'Enduring the cross, despising the shame.' Never did I hear Christ so exalted by human tongue. The effect was perfectly overwhelming."[15]

My third specimen is Bartimeus, an eloquent blind native preacher at the Sandwich Islands.[16] From the lowest physical, intellectual, moral, and social degradation and wretchedness, in his state of heathenism, Bartimeus (so named at his baptism) gradually rose, under the new-creating power of the gospel, to be a devoted, active, eloquent, and successful minister of the Word. The late Dr. Armstrong, a judicious and able missionary, who was with him five years, speaks thus of him: "He is a short man, and rather corpulent, very inferior in appearance when sitting, but when he rises to speak he looks well, stands erect,

[14] In the *Annual Report of the Baptist Missionary Union* for 1864, he is called "the Prince of Preachers."

[15] Quotations not identified. See Stock, Eugene, *History of the Church Missionary Society*, vol. 2, pp. 179-180. —Ed.

[16] Anderson, *History of the Sandwich Islands Mission*, Ch. XXV, "Bartimeus, the Blind Preacher," pp. 209ff. —Ed.

gesticulates with freedom, and pours forth, as he becomes animated, words in torrents. He is perfectly familiar with the former as well as the present modes of thinking of the islanders, which gives him a power in comparisons, allusions and direct appeals, which no foreigner will ever possess. Often, while listening with exquisite delight to his eloquent strains, have I thought of Wirt's description of the celebrated blind preacher of Virginia."

Bartimeus died in the autumn of 1843. "His funeral," says the Rev. E. W. Clark, one of the older members of the mission, "was attended by a large congregation of sincere mourners. The voice which had so often been heard among us in devout supplication, and in earnest entreaty, calling the sinner to repentance, was silent in death. His purified spirit, raised from the darkest heathenism, by the blessing of God on missionary labor, was at peace with the Saviour."

His calling to be a preacher was evidently of God. He had original endowments for that service. He had great strength of memory, and there has already been a reference to his eloquence. An illustration of both is given by Mr. Clark, writing from Wailuku soon after his decease.

"In January last, I met him at a protracted meeting, and was then more than ever impressed with the extent and accuracy of his knowledge of the Scriptures. He was called upon to preach at an evening meeting. His heart was glowing with love for souls. The overwhelming destruction of the impenitent seemed to be pressing with great weight upon his mind; and this he took for the subject of his discourse at the evening meeting. He chose for the foundation of his remarks, Jer. iv. 13: 'Behold, he shall come up as clouds, and his chariots shall be as a whirlwind.' The anger of the Lord against the wicked, and the terrible overthrow of all his enemies, were portrayed in vivid colors. He seized upon the terrific image of a whirlwind or tornado as an emblem of the ruin which God would bring upon his enemies. This image he presented in all its majestic and awful aspects, enforcing his remarks with such passages as Ps. lviii. 9: 'He shall take them away as with a whirlwind, both living, and in his wrath;' Prov. i. 27: 'And your destruction cometh as a whirlwind;' Isa. xl. 24: 'And the whirlwind shall take them away as stubble;' Jer. xxx. 23: 'Behold, the whirlwind of the Lord goeth forth with fury, a continuing whirlwind; it shall fall with pain upon the head of the wicked;' Hosea viii. 7: 'For they have sown the wind, and they shall reap the whirlwind;' Nahum i. 3, Zech. vii. 14, and other passages in which the same image is presented — always quoting chapter and verse. I was surprised to find that this image is so often used by the sacred writers. And how this blind man, never having used a concordance or a reference Bible in his life, could, on the spur of the moment, refer to all these texts, was quite a mystery. But his mind was stored with the precious treasure, and in such order that he always had it at command. Never have I been so forcibly impressed, as while listening to this address, with the remark of the apostle, 'Knowing, therefore, the terror of the Lord, we persuade men;' and seldom have I witnessed a specimen of more genuine eloquence. Near the close he said, 'Who can withstand the fury of the Lord, when he comes in his chariots of whirlwind? You have heard of the cars in America, propelled by fire and steam, with what mighty speed they go, and how they crush all in their way; so will the swift chariots of Jehovah overwhelm all his enemies. Flee, then, to the ark of safety.' "

These three remarkable men were from the lowest grades of heathen life. What they became was the result of the grace of God, through the gospel. And I bring them forward that our hopes may be raised as to what God may be expected to do through a native ministry. We must not, however, expect such eloquent native preachers to bear a larger proportion among the ministers of their own respective countries, than such men do in our own. As in old Christian countries, so among preachers of heathen lands, such men give a character to their profession. We thereby obtain a more exalted and just view of the capabilities of the profession; and they help to overcome the natural backwardness in missionaries to throw responsibilities on a ministry so recently rescued from the pollutions of idolatry.

My own estimate of the value of a native ministry has been rising for more than a score of years. A large number of the Christian islands in Central and Western Polynesia are properly reckoned among their trophies. They have been the fearless pioneers of the white missionary, facing dangers which to him would have been fatal, and which were sometimes fatal to themselves; and many a beautiful Christianized group in the broad Pacific is now manned solely by native missionaries and pastors.

The question naturally arises, and needs a brief reply, Whether mission churches may be expected to hold fast to their profession, in case the missionaries should withdraw, and leave them to themselves? There are some very interesting facts bearing on this question.

The churches of Tahiti, one of the Society Islands, were thus situated, for twenty years after the English missionaries had been excluded by the French. They were living under French rule, and fully exposed to French vices and to Roman Catholic influences; and were left by the missionaries, moreover, without native pastors. Yet, as is related elsewhere, they at once instituted pastors from among themselves, and more than held their ground. Tahiti and its dependencies are still under French rule; but it was stated last year by a London journal, that there are now thirty-seven native Protestant parishes and churches with only native pastors, containing three thousand communicants; and that Pomare, the queen, and nearly all her people, still adhere to the Protestant faith.[17]

And we have seen how it was in Madagascar, after the banishment of the English missionaries, and during five and twenty years of persecution. I know of no more remarkable firmness in the primitive churches. The blood of the martyrs in Madagascar, as in ancient times, was the seed of the church. We have seen, too, how it was with the native Christians in India, during the great rebellion; which had for its object not only the overthrow of the English power, but the utter destruction of Christianity, and when the native Christians were without the presence and support of their missionary fathers and brethren. Nowhere — never, was greater firmness shown by persecuted Christians than by those.

As the rebellion did not extend to Southern India, the native Christians there had not to pass through the fiery ordeal of their brethren at the north. Yet the Rev. Mr. Thomas, the venerable missionary already quoted, bears the most pleasing testimony concerning the native Christians under his missionary care. "I do not for a moment doubt," he says, "but that this people would retain their religion, if the English government in India, and all the missionaries, were providentially withdrawn from the country. Their stability arises very much, I think, from their knowledge of God's holy word, and the very great extent to which the power of reading that word has been afforded by means of our village vernacular schools."[18] Thus showing wherein lies the strength and glory of Protestant missions, as distinguished from those of the Romish Church.

It is natural also to inquire, Whether what are called revivals of religion are common in churches among the heathen? They appear to me to be not unfrequent, and to be evidently the work of the Holy Spirit. Indeed, revivals of religion do not seem peculiar to any age, or country, where there is vital religion. The reformation in the days of Hezekiah is declared to have occurred "suddenly."[19] It was both sudden and rapid. So was that in the time of Ezra. So was that in the time of John, the forerunner. So was that of the Pentecost. Such must have been the character of much of the success of the Apostle Paul; else why was he represented, by his opposers, as creating so great a disturbance? Such was the reformation in the time of Luther, whose

[17] *London Patriot,* Aug. 16, 1866, p. 542.
[18] *Church Missionary Report,* 1864-5, p. 134.
[19] 2 Chron. xxix. 36.

grand victory was achieved within ten years after he first raised the standard of reform. The "Great Awakening" in New England was also sudden and rapid. So was that at the Sandwich Islands. In a very few years, subsequent to 1836, more than thirty thousand hopeful converts were added to the church. Nor was the progress of the gospel less rapid in the Islands of the South Pacific. We have seen how it was in Sierra Leone, in Madagascar, and among the Karens of Burmah. In the missions of Western Asia there have been frequent revivals, though no one was very extensive. And we have reason to believe that this general law of progress in the kingdom of Christ will be more and more exemplified as the time for the world's conversion draws near.

In the Christian Church, which is yet but partially sanctified, the stream of gospel grace has not a continuous, even flow. It meets with obstructions; and when it rises above them and overflows them, we call the overflow a revival, a reformation.

The influences that modify revivals of religion are clearly seen in the heathen world. The really great awakenings hitherto, have all been among what may be called the aboriginal races, where the gospel encounters less of organized antagonism than in the conquering and dominant races. And by pressing the work among these more pliant races, the Evangelical Church has not only gained important positions and advantages, but has had the encouragement it so much needed at the outset of its great work, to labor hopefully and patiently in the fields of greater difficulty, where the harvest must needs be delayed, but will be more abundant when it comes.[20]

[20] The reader should remember that Dr. Anderson was still fighting a battle for the breaking up of great central mission stations under missionary pastors, for the organization of village churches, and for the ordination of native pastors over them. The presentation of such concrete evidence for the soundness of his theory was necessary to gain acceptance. —Ed.

Selection 8

THE CONTROL TO BE EXERCISED OVER MISSIONARIES AND MISSION CHURCHES[1]

The Board adopted the following Resolution at its last Annual Meeting, viz.: — "That the Prudential Committee be requested to present a written report, at the next annual meeting, on the nature and extent of the control which is to be exercised over the missionaries under the care of the Board; and the moral responsibility of the Board for the nature of the teaching of the missionaries, and for the character of the churches." The Prudential Committee have attended to this duty, and present the following Report.

It will be seen, that this call upon the Prudential Committee involves a discussion of the whole working of the system of Foreign Missions. We must determine the ecclesiastical standing and liberty of missionaries, and of the churches they gather among the heathen; inquire whether ecclesiastical liberty be not as safe for missionaries abroad, as for pastors at home, and whether missionaries and pastors are not in fact controlled by similar means and influences; show in what manner missionaries are obtained, what are the powers and responsibilities of the Board, and what is the actual extent of the claims of missionaries upon the Board and upon the churches. This will exhibit the working

---

[1] This document appears to be principally the composition of Rufus Anderson, but it is signed and was presented by three secretaries: Rufus Anderson, David Green, and Selah B. Treat. ABCFM, *Annual Report, 1848,* pp. 62-80; separately published as pamphlet, Boston: 1848. It reveals how Anderson was contending against the growing denominational spirit in America which wanted the exportation of confessional and denominational forms. It also shows how, despite general acceptance of Anderson's principles, his colleagues were refraining from acceptance of their full implications and reveals the force of missionary paternalism. The tension with regard to slavery is also evident.

of the principle of voluntary association in missions, involving, as the main reliance, influences that bear directly on the reason, judgment and heart, and a brief mention must be made of the more important of these influences. The Prudential Committee will also be expected to show the adaptation of the constitution of the Board to its various trusts and duties. In respect to the native mission churches, the inquiry will arise, how far they ought to be independent of the jurisdiction of all bodies of men in this country; how they are to be trained to self-support and self-government; what expectations it is reasonable to cherish concerning them; and what are the responsibilities of the Board for the teaching of the missionaries, and for the character of the mission churches.

I

The Missionaries

1. The Ecclesiastical Liberty Belonging to Missionaries

The Board affirmed at Brooklyn, in the year 1845, that "the missionaries acting under the commission of Christ, and with the instructions of the New Testament before them, are themselves at first, and subsequently in connection with the churches they have gathered, the rightful and exclusive judges of what constitutes adequate evidence of piety and fitness for church-fellowship in professed converts."

It was doubtless intended, by this declaration, to recognize the missionaries under the care of the Board as entitled to equal liberty, in all ecclesiastical matters, with ministers at home. They certainly are equally the ministers, messengers and ambassadors of Christ; they equally receive from him their call, commission, office and work. *As a body, they sustain to the churches at home a relation equally as close as do the body* of the pastors. The several Christian denominations acting through the Board have, in all practicable ways, given to the missionaries it has sent forth their countenance, sanction, and adoption. "These missionaries," says a standard work on the Constitution of the Congregational Churches, "may justly be considered as sent abroad by the churches, inasmuch as they are supported by their contributions, attended by their prayers, and protected by their constant solicitude. It is true that the immediate agents, in designing and arranging their departure, are Missionary Societies; but these Societies, when the subject is rightly considered, are only the agents and representatives of the churches."* It should be added, that the missionaries are ordained to their office, as really as pastors, and by the direct representatives of the churches, and with the same formalities, and almost always with the knowledge that they are to be sent forth and directed by the Board. In this manner, the Board itself has been recognized by the churches and accredited as an Agent in the work of foreign missions; as it has been, also, by resolutions and other formal acts of General Associations, Synods, and General Assemblies, and by thousands of collections in aid of its funds made in the house of God on the Sabbath, and at other times and places, with the concurrence of pastors and churches.

The denial that a missionary is an office-bearer until a Christian church has invited him to take the oversight of it in the Lord, is made in utter forgetfulness, as it would seem, of the commission by which a preaching ministry was originally instituted. The primary and pre-eminent design of that commission was to create the *missionary* office, and to perpetuate it till the gospel should have been preached to every creature.

It is not claimed for missionaries that they are Apostles, since they have not the "signs of an Apostle," and since the apostolical office was not successive and communicable to others. That office was extraordinary, in the range both of its objects and its powers, and the Apostles can have no proper successors. Missionaries are Evangelists. They do the work of Evangelists; and such they are, as Timothy and Titus were in the primitive missions, and as Eusebius says many were in the second century. "These," says that historian, "having merely laid the foundations of the faith, and ordained other pastors, committed to them the cultivation of the churches newly planted; while they themselves, supported by the grace and co-operation of God, proceeded to other countries and nations." The method of conducting missions has, indeed, been considerably modified by the altered condition of the world; rendering it possible to send forth a far greater number of missionaries than in ancient times, and to augment their value as instruments and to accelerate what may be called national conversions, by sending missionaries forth in the family state, and making their labor less itinerant and transitory than in early times; but the true relation of missionaries to the churches at home, and to the heathen world, appears to be that of Evangelists.

Considering the weakness and waywardness so generally found in men just emerging from heathenism, native pastors must, for a time, and in certain respects, be practically subordinate to the missionaries, by whom their churches were formed and through whom, it may be, they

* Upham's Ratio Disciplinae, p. 128.

are themselves partially supported. This is true, also, of the mission churches; as will be explained in another part of this report. Should a practical parity, in all respects, be insisted on between the missionaries and the native pastors, in the early periods when every thing is in a forming state, it is not seen how the native ministry can be trained to system and order, and enabled to stand alone, or even to stand at all. As with ungoverned children, self-sufficiency, impatience of restraint, jealousy, and other hurtful passions will be developed. The native pastors themselves are, for a season, but 'babes in Christ,' children in experience, knowledge and character. And hence missionaries, who entertain the idea that ordination must have the effect to place the native pastors at once on a perfect equality with themselves, are often backward in intrusting the responsibilities of the pastoral office to natives. They fear, and justly, the effects of this sudden comparative exaltation; especially when aggravated by ordination formalities multiplied and magnified beyond the scriptural precedents; involving a convocation of ministers and people, an ordination sermon, a formal charge, perhaps a right-hand of fellowship, and possibly an address setting forth the importance of the occasion, in place of the simple laying on of hands and prayer, as in the apostolical ordinations. All this may be well in old Christian communities; but whatever advantages it is supposed to have among the heathen, these are thought to be overbalanced by its tendency to inflame the self-conceit and ambition remaining in the heart of the heathen convert, however carefully he may have been educated in the doctrines and duties of Christianity. We scarcely need any great amount of experience, indeed, when our thoughts are once turned to the subject, to see that there is wisdom in the apostolical view of the pastoral office in mission churches, and in their mode of bringing forward a native ministry and training it for independent action.

It must be obvious, that the view just taken of this subject involves no danger to the future parity of the native ministry, considered in their relations to each other; for, in the nature of things, the missionary office is scarcely more successive and communicable to the native pastors, than was the apostolical office to evangelists.

The point specially insisted on is this, — that ministers of the gospel lose none of their ecclesiastical standing and liberty by engaging in the work of foreign missions. No plea for abridging their ecclesiastical liberties can be founded on the fact of their support coming from the churches at home; because the obligation of the churches to support missionaries rests on precisely the same basis with the obligation of missionaries to become such. Both the service and the support are to be rendered as a duty owed to Christ. The one is no more voluntary, no more optional, no more a work of supererogation, than the other.

Missionaries are no more objects of charity, or beneficiaries, than are pastors at home. Their labors as truly entitle them to a support from some quarter. When the reality of the missionary's call from the Head of the Church to go on a mission has been settled by competent and acknowledged testimony, an obligation arises and exists *somewhere* to send him forth and support him. And after he has gone into the field, he can no more properly be *starved* out of his appropriate liberty by those to whom he looks for support, than he can be legislated out of it by those who direct his labors. Nor do missionaries become, in any servile sense, the servants of those who support them; they are not their hired-servants, but their fellow-servants. Christ is their common spiritual Head, and he sends his missionaries forth a free ministry. And the Board seeks to accommodate itself to this principle in Christ's kingdom. "With great care, it seeks out competent men as missionaries and worthy of confidence; and then sends them out under the broad commission of the great Head of the Church, to preach the gospel to every creature, themselves free, to propagate a free Christianity in the field of their labors. With a scrupulous regard for the rights of the missionaries in this particular, it places them among the perishing heathen, to gather as many as possible into the fold of Christ, and there leaves them, in the free and untrammeled exercise of their own judgment, under a due sense of accountability to Christ, to decide on the spot, in each particular case as it occurs, what is sufficient evidence of genuine conversion, and what is the proper and sufficient ground for the admission of the heathen convert to the privileges of the Christian Church."*

When the Committee came to treat of the checks and influences under which missionaries operate, it will be seen that this degree of liberty is compatible with as perfect a responsibility, as is attainable in the present state of human nature and of the world. But it is important to remark here, that this responsibility can never be perfectly enforced, except by guarding the religious liberties of missionaries with the most scrupulous care. Men must be free, and must feel that they are free, in order to rise to the full capacity and dignity of moral agents, and be subjected to the full control of law, reason, and the moral sense. And, of all gospel ministers, the missionary among the heathen most needs to have his mind and spirit erect, and to feel that all good men are his brethren. This is necessary to the unity, peace, order and efficiency of every mission. The law of liberty is an all-pervading law in Christ's kingdom.

* Prof. William Smyth, of Bowdoin College.

2. HOW THE RESPONSIBILITY OF MISSIONARIES IS SECURED

So far as the Committee can rely on the experience of more than thirty years, they regard it as not less safe to concede ecclesiastical liberty to missionaries, than to pastors. And how eminently safe it has been at home, the last two centuries can testify. In each of the denominations of Christians represented in this Board, the understanding, conscience, and heart of ministers is supposed to operate with equal freedom in the performance of their spiritual duties; and it is the prevalent belief, in each of these denominations, that this liberty could not be advantageously diminished.

What the Prudential Committee are to show is this: — *That foreign missionaries are subjected to similar controlling influences with pastors at home.* These influences are exerted in the selection of missionaries; in their voluntary engagements; in the terms of their pecuniary support; in their mutual watchfulness over each other; and in the direct influence of truth upon their minds and hearts.

1. Missionaries are, in an important sense, selected for the work, and it thus comes to pass that they have, as a body, a trust-worthy character.

The Board does not, indeed, extend a "call" to them, as churches do to those whom they would have for their pastors. This has sometimes been recommended, as preferable to the course now pursued. But few missionaries would be obtained in this way. The missionary spirit has not yet strong hold enough upon the churches, or upon the colleges and theological seminaries, for the adoption of such a plan. Were the responsibility to be thus taken from students and candidates for the ministry, and assumed by missionary institutions, the young men in our theological schools would seldom be found in a state of mind or in circumstances to give an affirmative answer to a "call," by the time their characters and qualifications should have been sufficiently developed to warrant one. It is found to be better to lay the case before all, and leave the result to the providence and grace of God. Consecration to the foreign missionary work for life involves a somewhat peculiar experience of its own; and the earlier and more thoroughly that experience is wrought in the soul, the better is the prospect of continuance and usefulness in the work of missions.

The Committee have been accustomed, generally, to wait for written *offers* from the candidates to go as missionaries under the direction of the Board. These are usually made some time before the theological course of studies is completed, and are commonly preceded by personal conferences or an informal correspondence with the Secretaries. The offer is accompanied by testimonials from pastors, instructors in colleges and seminaries, and others. If the testimony be decisive and satisfactory, the individual is invited to visit the Missionary House in Boston. This arrangement is found useful and satisfactory to all parties. There is now, if there has not been before, a free conference with him as to his religious principles and experience, his social relations, his motives in choosing the missionary work, his adaptations and preferences with respect to a field of labor, and whatever else is important in determining the question of his appointment and designation. Should it now appear to be the candidate's duty not to engage in a foreign mission, it is generally easy to convince him of the fact, and his case does not proceed to any formal action on the part of the Committee. Where the duty to go is clear, an appointment follows. The candidate next seeks ordination, at his discretion, from some ecclesiastical body; which body subjects him to as thorough an examination, as if he were to settle as a pastor. He is not taken on trust from the Board, but his call to the missionary work is brought under a renewed investigation.

It is believed that the missionaries laboring in connection with this Board are equal, as to ministerial qualifications and character, to the body of pastors in either denomination represented in the Board, in any one of the States of the Union; and this fact is evidently one of great importance, in an inquiry as to the possibility of exerting a reasonable control over their proceedings.

2. Missionaries come voluntarily under similar engagements with pastors at home.

The pastor's engagements are made to his church and people, to the body that ordains him, and, through that body, to the churches; in addition to his solemn and well-understood vows to his Lord and Master. The missionary's engagements are to the Board, acting in the way of a general superintendence over his proceedings as a missionary, and to the ordaining body, and, through those bodies, to the community from which he is to derive his support; and he also makes explicit vows to his divine Master.

The missionary engages, on accepting his appointment, to conform to the rules and regulations of the Board, the nature of which he is supposed distinctly to understand. He thus pledges himself, among other things, to be governed by the majority of votes in his mission, in regard to all questions that arise in their proceedings; the proceedings being subject to the revision of the Prudential Committee. He comes, moreover, under certain other distinct and well-understood pledges:— (1.) As to his *manner of life;* which is to be one of exemplary piety and devotion to his work. (2.) As to his *teaching;* which must be conformed to the evangelical doctrines generally received by the churches, and set forth in their well-known Confessions of Faith. And (3.) as to *ecclesiastical usages;* to which he must conform substantially as they prevail among the churches operating through the Board. He must hold to a parity among the clerical brethren of his mission. He must hold to the validity of infant baptism. He must admit only such to the Lord's Supper as give credible evidence of faith in Christ. So far as his relation to the Board and his standing in the mission are concerned, he is of course not pledged to conform his proceedings to any other book of discipline than the New Testament.

3. The missionary's claim for continued support, like that of the pastor, depends upon his fulfilling his engagements.

Unless faithful to these engagements, the missionary cannot claim a continuance of his support. And the Board not only may, but it must insist on his performance of them. It is bound to know, that the missionary preaches the gospel and administers the ordinances according to his expressed and implied pledges; which of course he must do, or retire from his connection.

The responsibilities and powers of the Board, in this aspect of the case, are easily defined. While it cannot depose a missionary from the ministry, nor silence him as a preacher, nor cut him off from the church, it can dissolve what it formed, namely, his connection with itself and with the mission. While the Board may not establish new principles in matters purely ecclesiastical, it may enforce the observance of such as are generally acknowledged by the churches, and were understood to be acknowledged by the missionaries when sent to their fields. While the Board may not require that baptism shall always be performed by sprinkling, nor forbid that the Lord's Supper shall be administered to converts after they have given what the missionaries believe to be credible and satisfactory evidence of piety; it may require, (for such are the established and acknowledged usages,) that he receive none into the church, except such as are believed to be truly pious persons; that he baptize in the name of the Father, the Son, and the Holy Ghost; and that he do not refuse baptism to the infant children of the church.

Where the opinions of the great body of its patrons are divided in regard to the *facts* of Scripture, the Board may not undertake to decide, positively, as to the nature of those facts, with a view to binding the conduct of its missionaries. Such a fact, at present, is the admission of slave-holders into the apostolical churches. The Board may not undertake to decide, that this class of persons was certainly admitted to church-membership by the Apostles, nor that they were excluded, in such a way as to have the effect on the missionaries of a statute, injunction, or Scripture doctrine, in respect to the admission of such persons into churches now to be gathered in heathen nations where

CONTROL OVER MISSIONARIES AND MISSION CHURCHES

slavery is found.[2] The Board, the Prudential Committee, and the Secretaries may have their opinions on this subject, as well as on all others, and (as will be stated more fully hereafter) may freely express those opinions in their correspondence with the missionaries, and ought to do so, if they see occasion, with such reasonings, persuasions and remonstrances, as they may think proper. But they cannot properly go farther. Nor can the Board assume, as the basis of any of its proceedings, or imply in any manner, that the apostolical usages are not the wisest and best for all modern missionaries to follow, who are similarly situated with the Apostles. Nor can it do any thing in direct and manifest contrariety to the great Protestant maxim, on which our own religious liberties depend, that *the Scriptures are the* ONLY *and the* SUFFICIENT *rule of faith and practice.*

On the other hand, if it was an usage of the Apostles to give definite and positive instructions to the holders of slaves as to their treatment of them — instructions which had a tendency to do away the institution — and if such instructions are found in their Epistles, then modern missionaries may be expected to conform to that usage, and to give the same instructions in like circumstances; though the time and manner of doing thus must be referred, in great measure, to their own discretion, as with ministers at home, in respect to the direct inculcation of specific duties. The successful inculcation of such duties presupposes a certain amount of doctrinal knowledge in those who are to be operated upon, as well as of moral susceptibility, and also a due adaptation in the instructions to time, place, and circumstances.

But while the Board may require that the missionaries under its care instruct all classes of men after the manner of the Apostles, it is not at liberty to restrict the missionaries to the identical instructions given by the Apostles; because there is no good reason to suppose, that all the instructions are recorded in the New Testament, which the Apostles were accustomed to give. Missionaries may go farther, if their convictions of duty require it, and may apply what they regard as the obvious and generally conceded principles of the gospel to the case. They have the same liberty, in their preaching, with ministers of the gospel elsewhere. They may instruct their converts, among other things, on the Christian duty of fully conceding the right of marriage to the slaves; of not holding them as property; of sacredly respecting the relation between husbands and wives, and between parents and children; and of securing to all the right of worshiping God, and of

---

[2] A growing number of the constituency of the American Board in New England were seeking to force the Board to sever relations with the Cherokee churches, in which slaveholders were members. They eventually withdrew and formed the American Missionary Association. —Ed.

reading his holy .word. And the Committee have no hesitation in urging the duty of such instruction upon their brethren among the heathen; with the plain inculcation, in the prosecution of their ministry, of whatever obligation grows out of the fundamental law of love, as given by the Lord Jesus Christ, "Whatsoever ye would that men should do to you, do ye even so to them;" — it being understood that the missionaries are to have the liberty of exercising their discretion as to time and manner.

Nor have the Committee any hesitancy in saying that, since the gospel was so preached by the Apostles as ultimately to root out the most extensive and terrible system of slavery the world has ever seen, so ought missionaries now, in times and ways within the range of their own discretion, so to hold up the doctrines, duties and spirit of the gospel, that it shall have the same beneficent tendency on the social condition of the heathen.

A writer of unquestioned opposition to slavery, to whose discriminating pen the Board is indebted, has justly remarked, that it would seem to be within the discretion of a missionary in a slave-holding community, whether he will attack slavery directly, and by name, or "whether he will strike at some one or more of the things which enter essentially into it, and the wrong of which can, in the actual circumstances of that community, be set home with convincing power upon the conscience of the slaveholder."*

Slavery is, indeed, at variance with the principles of the Christian religion, and must disappear in any community, in proportion as the gospel gains upon the understandings and the hearts of men. But the Board and its missionaries are restricted to moral means, and these must have time and opportunity to exert their appropriate influence. Missionaries should be employed who *deserve* confidence, and then confidence should be reposed in them; nor should results be required, which are beyond the power of their labors to produce. Many things which, at first, it might seem desirable for the Board to do, are found, on a nearer view, to lie entirely beyond its jurisdiction; so that to attempt them would be useless, nay, a ruinous usurpation. Nor is the Board at liberty to withdraw its confidence from missionaries, because of such differences of opinion among them, as are generally found and freely tolerated in presbyteries, councils, associations, and other bodies here at home.

Polygamy stands on a somewhat different footing from that of Slavery. Little difficulty is apprehended from it in gathering native churches. The evidence that polygamists were admitted into the church by the

* Prof. Smyth.

Apostles, is extensively and increasingly regarded as inconclusive, by the patrons of the Board. We no where find instructions given in the New Testament to persons holding this relation. Nor is there evidence of the practice having existed in any of the churches subsequent to the apostolical age. The Committee believe, that no positive action by the Board in relation to this subject is needed, or expedient. Unsustained as the practice is by any certain precedents in the apostolical churches, and unauthorized by a single inspired injunction, the native convert will rarely be able to prove the reality of his piety, should he persist in clinging to it, or refuse to provide for the education of his children, or for the support of their mothers, (when they need such provision,) if he may not be permitted to regard the mothers as his wives.

Should the missionary violate his compact in respect to the character or amount of his preaching and teaching; or in respect to the administration of the ordinances of the gospel; or by refusing to conform to the resolutions of his mission, or of the Prudential Committee, or of the Board, or in any other manner; the Prudential Committee, on being certified of the fact, is in duty bound to consider and act on the bearing this ought to have on his relations to the Board, and his claim for a continued support.

This claim for support, so far as it applies to the Board, is understood to be only for an equitable proportion of the sum-total of funds actually placed at the disposal of the Board, for the expenses of the year. The Board can divide only what it receives. The missionary goes forth trusting in God that there will always be enough for his wants.[3] He cheerfully incurs the risk, whatever it may be, and which past experience of God's goodness shows to be small. And he does this the more cheerfully, because his work is so eminently a work of faith. Mere pledges for his support from churches and ecclesiastical bodies, are too delusive to be depended on. It is only to a small extent that pledges can be obtained from individual Christians, and even the precise import and obligation of these are apt to be forgotten by those who give them. Nor are the formal pledges of support given to the Board worth any thing, except so far as they represent the deep-seated missionary principles and sentiments of the Christian community. There is, indeed, no firm footing for the missionary, except in the promises of his Lord and Master. Faith in Christ is the basis of his enterprise. It is so in respect to himself, his children, his work, and the desired results of all his sacrifices and labors, — pre-eminently so, compared with that

---

[3] The "faith principle" was as universal and as strong in the early church missions as in the later nondenominational, or interdenominational, missions, popularly called "faith missions," which follow the pattern of J. Hudson Taylor and the China Inland Mission.

of the pastor at home. And herein lies the special dignity of his calling.
He goes on his mission in the discharge of his own personal duty, because he believes his Lord and Savior requires him to go as his servant
and ambassador. If he have a proper view of his mission, he would
regard it as lowering the work immeasurably, to bring in the churches,
or the Board, as *principals;* as any thing else, indeed, than mere *voluntary helpers,* selected and chosen by himself to carry out the benevolent
purpose of his own independent self-consecration. The idea that a mission is a contract between the churches and the missionary in any such
sense, that he may cease to perform missionary labor, and claim a
pension, (as the servants of the East India Company do,) after a certain number of years, and while he is yet able to labor — should it
ever become an effective element in the reasoning of missionaries —
would prove destructive to the faith and vitality of the enterprise. If this
idea has sometimes been advanced by missionaries, it has been when
reasoning under the pressure of parental solicitude, and in great part on
the assumption that the work of publishing the gospel was committed by
Christ to the church as a society, or corporate body, to act as a principal in the matter; and as such, in the discharge of its own pre-eminent
duty, to send forth and support preachers in all the world; whereas the
command was given to individual disciples, before an organized Christian church existed, and whatever use was made of social organizations
during the apostolical age, the work was always regarded as the discharge of an individual and personal obligation. It is not less an individual and personal duty now, than it was then. The enlisting in the
missionary enterprise is wholly voluntary, as well on the part of the
missionary who goes abroad, as on the part of his fellow-christian who
remains at home. They are co-workers and mutual helpers; and the co-
operation of the donor may be as essential to the prosecution of the
work, as the labors of the missionary. On the part of all concerned,
the consecration, whether of person or property, must be a voluntary
offering by individual subjects of Christ's kingdom. Churches, in their
organized capacity, have no authority to prescribe to any one of their
members what he must do; but each must decide for himself, as the
result of his own consciousness of duty and privilege, what he ought to
do, and to what part of the work he should devote himself. It is a question of individual responsibility. "As we have many members in one
body, and all members have not the same office, so we, being many,
are one body in Christ, and every one members one of another;" and
whatever any one does, he is to feel that it is in the discharge of his
own prescribed duty. Christians at home will no more feel that they
are really indebted to the missionary, than that the missionary is indebted to them. They will no more feel, that the missionary is doing

their work, by going on a mission, than that they are doing his, by giving to support him. Each will regard himself as a fellow-servant of a common Master, engaged in a common service, and performing just that part of the work, which the Master has assigned to him. This view of the subject is doubtless the correct one, and the only one that will comport with the successful prosecution of missions, for a prolonged period of time, and on an extended scale. It is necessary for all parties to feel, *that they are discharging only their own personal obligations, that they are performing only their own appropriate work.*

The system, as it has been described, is found to work easily and well. The missionary is as free, in every sense, as the pastor. One is no more really held accountable for the manner of expending his salary, than is the other. One can no more absent himself from his field of labor and his work, without the concurrence of the body that furnishes the means of his support, than the other. The pastor can no more travel at the expense of his people, whether for health or business, without their consent, than the missionary can do so at the expense of the Board, without the consent of the Committee, or, in certain specified cases, of his mission. The greatest embarrassments experienced in the working of the system, are when the Committee are constrained to interpose their action in order to relieve a mission from the influence of one of its own members, and where the questions at issue relate to points in missionary practice and expediency, with which the community at home have not yet had opportunity to become fully conversant; or to mere matters of fact dependent on testimony, and requiring to be heard on both sides; — giving advantage to a disaffected missionary, should he choose to address himself to the popular mind. In a case of immorality, if it be flagrant, the compact may be annulled; and every one is ready to appreciate the reason. So if the missionary, however conscientiously, break fellowship with his brethren, and deny their baptism, or their ordination, his right to continue in the mission would cease; — it being a well-ascertained fact, that such opinions, in addition to violating the understood engagements, usually prove destructive to the harmony of a mission, when embraced by any of its members. The same is true if there be error in respect to important doctrines of the gospel. It is not the mere doctrinal errors that are to be considered, but their distracting, disastrous effect on the happiness and efficiency of the mission. There is no need of making out formal charges to prove a case of heresy by a formal trial, as an ecclesiastical body would do. The question assumes a plain business form, — whether there is an actual departure from the basis, on which the missionary appointment was made, and what effect it has exerted on the peace and usefulness of the mission, and on the operations of the Board.

That the action of the Prudential Committee, dissolving the connection of a missionary with his mission and the Board, is not of the nature of an *ecclesiastical* proceeding, technically speaking, is evident from the fact that it leaves his ecclesiastical relations undisturbed. His regular standing, both as a minister of the gospel and a member of the church, is not directly affected. As his appointment to the mission did not destroy his relations to his association or presbytery, so neither does his dismission. The Committee of course leave the ecclesiastical relations of the case for the ecclesiastical body (if it choose to consider them) with which the missionary may happen, at the time, to be connected.

It will often be found, where difficulties between a returned missionary and the Committee come out to the view of the community, that the original difficulty was not between the missionary and the Committee, but between the missionary and his brethren of the mission; and that the Committee interfered and assumed responsibility in the matter only when it became necessary, in order to relieve the mission from distracting and paralyzing divisions. The Board has had as few unpleasant relations to its missionaries, it is believed, in proportion to the number of persons, as any other missionary society in the new or old world.

It should be stated, that the missionary has his safe-guards, as well as the pastor. The latter is not dismissed from his people without the intervention of a council or presbytery. Such a direct ecclesiastical intervention is manifestly impossible, as the case stands between the missionary and his directors. But the Committee do not see that the case would be otherwise, were the Board elected by an ecclesiastical body, a General Assembly, for instance. As it is, the missionary has the right of appeal from the Prudential Committee to the large body of ministers and laymen composing the Board. If the question between him and the Board relate merely to Christian doctrine, or to alleged immoralities, and has sufficient importance to awaken the interest of an ecclesiastical body, he can obtain an opinion on his proper Christian or ministerial standing from his presbytery or classis, or from a council, and have the benefit of such a result. With this right the Committee have never attempted to interfere.

Enough has been said to show, that whatever of salutary influence there is in the connection between a pastor's faithful performance of his engagements and the continuance of his support from his people, there is no less with the missionary.

But the grand reliance for the proper conduct of missionaries, is

4. On their mutual watchfulness over each other, and the direct influence of truth on their minds and hearts.

As soon as a mission contains three or more missionaries, it is expected to organize itself as a self-governing community, under the laws, regulations, and general superintendence of the Board. Mutual watchfulness thus becomes the official duty of each member. It is also in a high sense the interest of each one to exercise a fraternal watchfulness over his brethren, in order to the safety and success of the enterprise in which the common welfare and happiness are embarked. And as brethren in Christ, as members of his church, and as jointly and severally his ambassadors to the heathen, — by the force of each of these relations they are impelled to the same duty. Nor have the several missions under the care of the Board been a whit behind the ecclesiastical organizations of their native land in mutual and faithful watchfulness.

The influence of truth on the reason, judgment, and heart of missionaries, is mainly through the intercourse kept up with the Christian world, and especially with their native land, and through their reading and studies, and the reacting effect of the faithful discharge of their missionary duties.

The interest which missionaries feel in their native land is not diminished by distance. Their home for Christ's sake, the home of their duty, is among the heathen, and grace makes them more than willing to live and die there. But nature has another home, dear to memory and ever interesting to thought and feeling, and with this they keep up an active correspondence during life. It is striking to observe the number of letters passing between missionaries and their friends. The effect of this correspondence must be great in cherishing the social feelings, and especially in preserving the desire for a good name in their native land. This effect is increased by the reading of religious and other newspapers, and of magazines and books, that are continually going to the missions, and causing the public opinion at home, on all subjects, to bear directly on missionaries, as it does on pastors. The Committee have long deemed it wise to pursue a liberal policy with repect to these matters, since well-informed, active and growing minds, yield most readily to wholesome rules and decisions, and to reason and common sense.

The correspondence of the executive officers of the Board with particular missions is more or less extended, at different times, according to circumstances. The free use of reasoning has always been awarded to them on all subjects, upon which they believe it would be useful to correspond with their brethren in the missions. No points are so much in dispute, but the Secretaries feel themselves at liberty to advert freely to them, — always being subject of course to have their correspondence revised at pleasure by the Committee, or by the Board. They may write upon caste, polygamy, slavery, creeds, preaching, education, the use of the press, modes of worship, evidence of piety, the Christian life, and numberless other kindred subjects. And they may give all the weight they can to their arguments, by bringing the experience of other missions, and what they know of the state of the public mind at home, to bear on the questions at issue. The religious newspapers and other periodicals furnish the means of performing this latter service in respect to all subjects that interest and excite the community. It is believed to be the duty of the Secretaries, acting under the direction of the Committee, to see that the missions are well furnished with the lights of truth. The Committee have had ample evidence of the value of this method of control. No class of ministers being more select than that which is engaged in the foreign missions, on none does correct reasoning, and especially that which is founded on the word of God, have more influence. In general, nothing more is needed, in the actual relations and responsibilities of missionaries, to control the opinions and operations of a mission, than good scriptural arguments. And in all cases affecting the conscience, the less there is of an appearance of authority, the better the result.

Libraries are connected with the several missions, some of which are large and valuable; the *material* for labor, in all the departments, is abundantly supplied; and the missionary, in common with the pastor, has his peculiar inducements to study, and to cultivate his mind and heart, growing out of the exigencies of his position. And the more devoted, laborious, and faithful he is in his work, the less need does he commonly stand in of influence and direction from without. Truth, conscience, a sense of duty, regard for unity and peace, deference to public opinion, and concern for God's glory and the good of mankind, — things such as these (not without some thought, it may be, of engagements to the Board and its patrons, and of the inconveniences resulting from their violation,) have rarely failed to be sufficient, with the divine blessing, to secure order and efficiency in the working of Christian missions in foreign lands. In other words, it is the blessing of God on the free and vigorous working of the voluntary principle in missions, based on Christian piety and intelligence.

The Committee believe it would be found, on a careful examination of the history of missions, that no method of controlling missionaries differing substantially from the one described in this report, has ever been effectual. Protestant missions, especially, and most of all from this country, can in no other way be long kept in existence.

Should it be supposed, that the great distance of the missions from the community which supports them, must weaken the controlling influence, two things are to be considered: — (1.) The public attention is more generally and intently fixed on the conduct of the missionaries, than it is upon that of ministers any where at home. (2.) There is no greater probability that all the members of one of the larger missions will go wrong together, or will countenance one of their own number in so doing, than that there will be similar wrong doing in almost any body of ministers, of equal numbers, which can be named in our own country. For they are as intelligent, as pious, have as much principle and sense of character, and as much desire to please God and do good; and they know that they are watched by Christians over the world.

It is due to the patrons of the Board, who may entertain doubts whether its constitution is well adapted to secure the safest and most efficient prosecution of missions among the heathen, to advert briefly to the subject; indeed, the discussion would not otherwise be complete.

The Prudential Committee have not been able to see that the Board would increase its working power, by any considerable changes in its constitution. So far, indeed, as the greater part of New England is concerned, there does not seem to be a possibility of forming what is called an Ecclesiastical Board, unless the relations of the Congregational churches to each other are first essentially modified. And were such a Board to be created, it would no more possess authority to perform purely ecclesiastical acts, than has the present Board. The Committee presume that it would not be wise to attempt a change in the present organization, until the details of the change are clearly proposed and understood, and well considered; nor until there is good reason to believe the new or modified organization would work better than the present; that it will command more confidence at home among the churches, and more abroad with the missionaries; and that it will secure the confidence which the present Board has gained in the mercantile world. Our fathers were providentially led to adopt the existing form of organization for conducting foreign missions, as best adapted to their day; and when the existing form is found not to answer the purpose, their children will doubtless change it. It was instituted solely for the spread of the gospel among the heathen, and in times favorable for taking an unbiased view of the subject; and hitherto it has actually worked better than any of its founders ventured to expect. It has, indeed, signally enjoyed the blessing of God. . . .

The Board is to be viewed as an AGENCY, acting for such as choose to employ it. It does not profess to be, and it is not, a distinct power with separate interests from the churches; nor are its agents sent into parishes as a substitute for the pastor, or as a co-ordinate power, to advocate a distinct and independent interest, in which the pastor and people have no concern; but, for the time being, they are mere auxiliaries to the pastors — the *agents of the pastors* — the pastors being the responsible persons. When the present organization is no longer deserving of confidence, it will soon die as a thing of course. So far as the Board is an active and influential body, it is a mere creature of the public mind. It must go along with the permanent majority. It has no authority. It cannot, except by an abuse of terms, be said to levy taxes. It taxes no one. It can only state the command of Christ, the necessities of the heathen, the facilities for doing the work of missions, its own plans and operations, and God's blessing upon them; and argue, exhort and plead. Men give or not, just as they please; and it is best that it should be so.

The corrective power, in respect to the undue multiplication and irregular working of voluntary associations, lies with the pastors and churches. It is for them, individually, to decide what objects shall and what shall not have access to their pulpits by means of agents. Here lies the only corrective power — where it ought to lie — in the primary associations and assemblies of the Christian Church; and here there is such a power, easily applied, and, if applied, adequate to the emergency.

II

THE MISSION CHURCHES

1. THE LIBERTY BELONGING TO MISSION CHURCHES

The Mission Churches in foreign lands, connected with the missions under the care of the Board, do not come properly under the jurisdiction of any body of men in this country. This is true of course so far as the Board is concerned, since that is not a body having ecclesiastical authority; and it is believed to be equally true in respect to all ecclesiastical bodies. The influence exerted upon the mission churches by the ecclesiastical bodies of this country, must be through the missionaries. We can claim no jurisdiction over them because we planted them.

The great object of foreign missions is to persuade men to be reconciled to God, as their rightful and only Sovereign; and the organization of churches is as really a means to this great end, as the preaching of the gospel, or the printing of the Holy Scriptures. When the time comes for organizing native converts into churches, the missionaries, acting in behalf of these children in knowledge and in the power of self-organization and government, cannot properly be restrained, by foreign interference, from conforming the organization to what *they* regard as the apostolical usage in similar cases; — having respect, of course, to those necessary limitations already mentioned, to which they have voluntarily subjected themselves for the maintenence of their social existence as missions, and for securing a regular and competent support from the Christian community at home. (See pp. 126-129.) The result may be a much simpler organization for the mission churches, than is found in lands that have long sat under the light and influences of the gospel. Indeed, experience has clearly shown, that it is not well to attempt the transfer of the religious denominations of Christendom, full-grown and with all their peculiarities, into heathen lands; at least, until the new-born churches shall have had time to acquire a good degree of discriminative and self-governing power. The experience acquired in lands long Christian partially fails us when we go into heathen countries. We need to gain a new experience, and to revise many of our principles and usages; and for this purpose to go prayerfully to the New Testament.

The religious liberty which we ourselves enjoy, is equally the birthright of Christian converts in every part of the heathen world, on coming into the spiritual kingdom of Jesus Christ, which they may claim as soon as they are prepared for it; just as American freedom is the birthright of our own children. The right of our children is not infringed by that dependence and control which they need during their infancy and childhood. It is even their right to claim, that the parent *shall* thus act for them in the early stages of their existence. But the wise parent will always form the principles and habits of his child with reference to the time when the right of self-control must be fully exercised and yielded. In like manner the missionary must needs give form, at the outset, to the constitution and habits of the mission churches; and for a time he must virtually govern them. But he will do this with a constant regard to the coming period, when those churches must and will act independently. He will train them, as the Apostles evidently trained the churches under their care, so that they may be early freed from the necessity of missionary supervision. In the infancy of the Christian community that is placed under his care, he will act on such scriptural principles and usages as he deems best fitted to make the most of every individual member of the church. And this he will do at any amount of personal inconvenience to himself; remembering that the power of carrying burdens is acquired by practice, and that native converts can be inured to responsibilities only by having responsibilities placed upon them, and by a conviction that they are trusted. At the risk of multiplying his most painful cares and disappointments, he will also aim to provide a native pastor for each church, just as early as he can in the period of his own missionary supervision, that the spiritual machinery may be homogeneous and complete in all its parts, and may the sooner be made to work without foreign aid. In no other way, indeed, can he secure the grand result for which he labors — the development of the self-sustaining, self-governing power in the native Christian community.

Nor may we expect to require of the mission churches, as the condition of giving them the gospel and its institutions, that they shall always think, judge, and act just as we do. We ought cheerfully to abide the consequences of the full assertion of our principles; and have patience, and bear long, and not give over, till it is evident that our moral means are exhausted, and that our enterprise has failed.

The necessity for long-suffering forbearance with churches gathered from among the heathen, will be the more obvious, if we consider three things.

One is thus stated in the Cambridge Platform.* "The weakest measure of faith is to be accepted in those that desire to be admitted into the church; because weak Christians, if sincere, have the substance of that faith, repentance and holiness, which is required in church members, and such have the most need of ordinances for their confirmation and growth in grace. The Lord Jesus would not quench the smoking flax, nor break the bruised reed, but gathers the lambs in his arms and carries them in his bosom." None will question, that the liberty of mission churches, with respect to the admission of members, goes to this extent. Of all churches, those gathered among the heathen have most reason for asserting this freedom, since nowhere are the lambs of the flock so much exposed while out of the fold, and nowhere, comparatively speaking, are they so many.

Another thing is this. There are not several churches existing in one place, as in most of our towns, formed to a great extent on the principle of elective affinity. All who give credible evidence of Christian character, must come into one and the same church, or be excluded altogether from church-membership, and the ordinances of the gospel.

Again, we should consider the extreme moral and social degradation of all heathen communities, in which mission churches are gathered. Read the first chapter of the Epistle to the Romans. Read the journals of modern missionaries. Consider the decline of mind among the masses of the people, under the long reign of paganism; the paralysis of the moral sense and conscience; the grossness of habits, physical and mental, in speech and action, in domestic life and all social intercourse. Consider the absence of almost all those ideas which lie at the foundation of moral elevation in character; the absence of words, even, to

* Ch. XII., §3. (The Massachusetts Puritans defined church order in the Cambridge Platform of 1648. —Ed.)

serve as pure vehicles of holy thought and sentiment; the absence of a correct public opinion on all things appertaining to manners and morals; and the constant and all-pervading presence of polluting, degrading, soul-destroying temptations.

Causes such as these had their effects in the churches gathered by the Apostle Paul, as we see in his Epistles.[1] When the Apostle directed his attention, for instance, to the church at Corinth, on which he had bestowed so great an amount of labor, he found occasion to lament the many who were carried away by false teachers, the disorder of their worship, their irregularities at the Lord's Supper, their neglect to discipline immoral members, their division into parties, their spirit of litigation, their debates, envyings, wraths, strifes, backbitings, whisperings, swellings, tumults. And how soon were a portion of the Galatians seduced from the gospel, and from their loyalty to the truth, and turned again to their old bondage unto weak and beggarly elements, observing days, and months, and times, and years; so that the Apostle confesses his fears that he had labored in vain among them. He thinks it needful to exhort the Ephesian church to put away lying, and to exhort those who had been dishonest before their conversion to steal no more, and those who had been avaricious and impure to have nothing more to do with fornication and covetousness. Four years after he had addressed his Epistle to the Ephesians, he informs Timothy that all his helpers in Lesser Asia were turned away from him, and even two who had attained to some distinction. Before the date of his Epistle, he evidently had not full confidence in some of the native pastors in that province, as appears from his address to them at Miletus. While at Rome, he writes that some in that city preached Christ of envy and strife, supposing to add affliction to his bonds; and at his first arraignment before Caesar, not a member of that church had the moral courage to stand by him. Writing to the Philippians, he declares his belief that many church members were enemies of the cross of Christ, whose god was their belly, who gloried in their shame, and minded earthly things. In this same Epistle, he speaks in desponding terms of his native helpers, among whom were none like-minded with Timothy, but all sought their own, and not the things which were Jesus Christ's. He thought it needful to exhort the Colossians not to lie one to another; and the Thessalonians to withdraw from such of their number as walked disorderly. He cautions Timothy against fables, endless genealogies, and profane and vain babblings, as if such were prevalent in some of the churches; and speaks of preachers destitute of the truth, possessing corrupt minds, ignorant, proud, addicted to controversies which engendered envy,

[1] The following paragraphs are much the same as the passage on pp. 94ff.

strifes, and perverse disputations and railings; and of some who had even made shipwreck of the faith, and added blasphemy to their heresies.

And it should be added, that the Apostle John, somewhat later, declares that many "antichrists" had gone out from the church, because they did not really belong to it in spirit and character, and of course had been in it, denying, as he says, the Father and the Son.

Yet it is generally supposed, whether correctly or not, that the apostolical churches possessed as much piety as exists in any portions of the visible church of our country and times, if not more. Indeed the Apostle Paul speaks of the Roman Christians, only a few years before the date of his Epistles to Timothy, as being noted for their faith throughout the world. At the very time of his censures on the Corinthians, he declares that church to be "enriched by Jesus Christ in all utterance and in all knowledge," so that it came behind in no gift. And while he so seriously cautions the Ephesians, he ceases not to give thanks for their "faith in the Lord Jesus, and their love unto all the saints." He thanked God upon every remembrance of the Philippians; and when he wrote to the Colossians, he gave thanks for their faith in Christ Jesus, and their love in the Spirit and to all the saints. And how remarkable his testimony in behalf of the Thessalonians. He remembered without ceasing and with constant gratitude their work of faith, and labor of love, and patience of hope in the Lord Jesus Christ, wherein they had become followers of him and of the Lord, having received the word in much affliction, with joy of the Holy Ghost; so that they were ensamples to all that believed, in Macedonia and Achaia.

The fact undoubtedly is, that visible irregularities and disorders, and even scandalous immoralities, are more to be expected in churches gathered from among the heathen; and are, at the same time, to a certain extent, more consistent with grace in the church, than in countries that have long enjoyed the light and influence of the gospel. While the primitive converts from paganism were remarkable for the high tone of their religious feelings, and the simplicity and strength of their faith, they were wanting in respect to a clear, practical apprehension of the ethical code of the gospel. It is obvious, indeed, that Paul found the burden of his "care of all the churches" much increased by the deceptive, impure, and thoroughly wicked character of the age and countries, in which he labored as a missionary and apostle. His manner of treating the native pastors and churches, notwithstanding their imperfections, is a model for missionaries and their supporters in our day; who ought to expect greater external manifestations of ignorance on moral subjects, and of weakness and sin, in churches that are gathered in Africa, India, the Sandwich Islands, and among the Indian tribes, than in churches that existed at Ephesus, Colosse, Corinth, and the cities of Galatia, in the palmy days of Roman civilization.

In reasoning, however, about mission churches among the heathen, whether ancient or modern, we should take into view the moral imperfections found in all human associations, in every land and every age. How many such imperfections do actually exist now in the churches of which we are members, and how difficult it has been found to apply a remedy. How much time and labor has it cost, in our most favored States, so to affect the public sentiment of professed Christians, as to induce them universally to abandon and avoid the trade in ardent spirits; how hard to restrain multitudes of professors of religion from divers conformities to the world, having no countenance in the gospel; and how impossible hitherto, to create a public sentiment in any church, that shall give the sin of *covetousness,* for instance, the place expressly assigned to it in the word of God.

2. How Far the Board Is Responsible for the Teaching of the Missionaries, and for the Character of the Mission Churches

The Board is responsible *directly,* in the manner which has been described, for the *teaching of the missionaries.* It cannot guaranty, however, an entire uniformity in their teaching. That diversity in mental habits, opinions, preaching, and social intercourse, which exists without rebuke among ministers of the same denomination at home, must be expected and tolerated among missionaries.

The Board can require of missionaries a compliance with their express and implied engagements, and the performance of all duties that are manifestly essential to the success of the enterprise. But in respect even to those fundamental obligations, when the mind of the missionary has swung so far off from the line of his duty as to refuse a compliance, *enforcement* is commonly found to be out of the question; generally, no other course is left but to dissolve his connection. The Board cannot, therefore, be held responsible for the invariable continuance of its missionaries in the path of their duty, even in respect to matters of vital importance. Its responsibility is limited to the proper selection of fields to be cultivated; to the judicious appointment and designation of missionaries; to the constitution and laws by which the several missions are formed into self-governing communities; to the equitable distribution of the funds placed at its disposal; to the just and proper instruction of the missionaries in matters within the province of the Board; to timely and needful suggestions, admonitions, exhortations and àppeals, fraternally addressed; and, finally, to a faithful superintendence of the missions, and a decisive intervention when there are manifest departures from duty in the missionaries.

But while the Board is directly responsible for the *teaching* of the missionaries, it cannot be held to a full responsibility for the *results* of their labors. Paul may plant, and Apollos water, but God giveth the increase. The Apostle to the Gentiles, as we have seen, had to sorrow much over the imperfect results of his labors. As *he* was not fully responsible for the character of the churches he planted, so *missionaries* cannot now be held to a full responsibility for the character of their mission churches. But the *Board,* as a missionary institution, (and the same would be true, were it an ecclesiastical body,) is even less responsible, than are its missionaries, for the character of the mission churches. It is not even directly responsible for the character of those churches, but only through the missionaries; and only so far through them, as it is properly held accountable for their character and teaching. If there be stupidity, ignorance, weakness, waywardness, perverseness, and even more scandalous wickedness in the mission churches — as the history of the apostolical churches would lead us to expect, even when the churches are gathered by the most able and faithful missionaries — they can be operated upon only through the missionaries. The Board cannot wisely address those churches directly on the subject, nor can any other body of men in this country, however constituted.

But when evil exists in the mission churches, the Prudential Committee may and must inquire, whether the *missionaries* are perfoming their duty. In one instance, some years ago, having reason to apprehend that admissions were made to a church in one of the missions, without a proper attention to the evidences of piety, the Board, at its annual meeting, instructed the Prudential Committee to inquire into the facts, with a view to a correction of the evil; and such inquiries were made by the Committee, and with a satisfactory issue. Inquiries have also been made by the Committee, as to the teaching of missionaries in some of the missions, with respect to alleged irregularities and evils in mission churches, and in the social and domestic state of native Christian communities. So far as a judicious and proper correspondence with the missionaries may properly affect their incipient measures, in the formation of churches, and their subsequent teachings, and so far as those measures determine the character of the churches, the Board is responsible for the character of the native churches.

Its responsibility in respect to the *existence of slavery* in several of the Indian churches, has some peculiar modifications in the circumstances of the case. The *incipient* measures for the formation of churches among the Cherokees and Choctaws, were taken thirty years ago —

long before the subject of slavery came up for discussion among the churches at home. God was soon pleased hopefully to renew the hearts of a number of slaveholding Indians, and, upon giving credible evidence of piety, they were received into the church. What the missionaries *could then* have done, had they perceived all the bearings of that subject, cannot be known. The Indians are *now* partially civilized, and have organized governments. There are slaveholding whites without, who are supposed to take an interest in continuing slavery among them, and slaveholding whites within, married to Indian wives, and thus become a part of the nation; and their churches are organized Congregationally in one tribe, and Presbyterially in another. So that the missionaries, like pastors among ourselves, are obliged now to depend wholly on instruction and persuasion for their influence on the churches under their care. The religious liberty of those churches is to be respected. We should stand firm in support of our principles as to the rights of churches. Unless the missionaries are able to produce conviction — however desirable it may be that they should do it — the *churches* in the one case, and the *sessions* in the other, will vote in opposition to their views. It is admitted, however, that the missionaries should do all in their power, in the exercise of their best discretion, to lead those churches and sessions to a right appreciation of their duty in this matter; and that they should use a direct influence, at their discretion, to eradicate the evil of slavery, as well as all other evils, from the churches under their care. But it is obvious, that the Board, and the missionaries under its direction, have not precisely *the same degree* of responsibility for the existence of slavery in the churches just referred to, that they would have in respect to churches yet to be formed among the tribes of the African continent, or were churches now to be formed, for the first time, among the Indian tribes.

How long we should bear with mission churches, that do not come up to our standard of duty, and may even greatly try our spirits, is what the Committee are not able to decide. But they cannot doubt, that we should imitate the example of Him, who "maketh his sun to rise on the evil and on the good, and sendeth rain on the just and on the unjust;" and who "so loved the world that he gave his only begotten Son, that whosoever believeth in him, should not perish, but have everlasting life;" and who "is long suffering to us-ward, not willing that any should perish, but that all should come to repentance." We need an abounding charity, a most Christ-like feeling, when we come to the question of withdrawing our support from churches we have gathered among the heathen, because they are slow in rising to our standard of Christian excellence. Should their deficiency be in any measure owing to our lack of knowledge on the subject, when we commenced our labors among them, it will strengthen our motives for forbearance. Before deciding a question so momentous to the interests of souls, and to our own future peace of conscience, it would be well to see whether we do not find in those churches the same spiritual results, the same living Christianity, and the same moral defects, that existed in the churches planted and nurtured by the Apostles; and whether the Lord Jesus does not bless them with outpourings of his Holy Spirit, though they cannot yet be persuaded, in all important respects, to follow us.

We should remember, that none of us are principals in this work of missions. The work is Christ's, not ours; and we are all his servants, to do his will. And if we look into our own churches, and consider their manifold imperfections, we shall find abundant cause for charity and forbearance in respect to all churches gathered among the heathen; and if we study the intellectual and moral condition of the pagan world, we shall only wonder that the first generation of converts from heathenism can be so far raised in the scale of Christian morals and general excellence of character.

By order and in behalf of the Prudential Committee.

Rufus Anderson,
David Greene,   *Secretaries.*
Selah B. Treat,

Missionary House, Boston, Sept., 1848.

Selection 9

MISSIONARY SCHOOLS[1]

It is thought by some, that modern missionaries among the heathen give too much attention to schools, and that they do this at the expense of time which ought to be devoted to the preaching of the gospel. There may have been something to justify this opinion in a few of the missions, especially in their earlier stages. In general, however, the impression is probably a mistaken one; at least in respect to the missions with which I am acquainted. The misapprehension may be owing to two causes. First, in the annual reports of missionary societies, the statistics of education are usually given more in detail and with greater precision and prominence, than those of preaching — a result not easily avoided. Secondly, the precise object of education, as a part of the system of modern missionary operations, appears not to have been generally understood hitherto by the community. Perhaps I ought to add, that its proper object has not always been well understood by the directors of missions. What this object is, will be explained in the sequel.

The proportionate attention given by missionaries to schools, is by no means as great as many seem to suppose. Those who attended the last annual meeting of the American Board of Commissioners for Foreign Missions, will remember the result of inquiries on this subject there proposed to the Rev. William Richards, of the Sandwich Islands mission. It appeared that not only was the average attendance of natives on preaching, at the fifteen stations of that mission, greater than it is in any one considerable district of our own country, but that the

[1] Reprinted from *The Biblical Repository*, vol. XI, no. XXXI, July, 1838, pp. 87-113. A second pamphlet of the same title was published in 1861, quite different in content. See also Dr. Anderson's chapter on schools in the *Memorial Volume*, Ch. VII, pp. 304-332.

missionaries preached oftener than is here customary among the settled pastors. And in general, the missionaries of that board among the heathen will bear comparison, in respect to the frequency of their preaching, with their more zealous brethren in the pastoral office at home. And the same is no doubt true of the missionaries of other societies.

Still it is admitted, that schools constitute a prominent part of the system of modern missions, and that there is no evidence of their having formed any part of the missions prosecuted by the apostles. The inquiry therefore is very natural and proper. *Why this departure from apostolic usage?* To this inquiry the present article is designed to furnish a reply.

Our first object will be to ascertain *the extent of territory embraced by the apostolic missions.*

The inspired history gives no information that the apostles and their companions extended their personal labors beyond the Roman empire. Fabricius has collected from the New Testament the names of all the places there mentioned, at which they planted churches, some forty or fifty in number; and also the names of the different countries which they are said to have visited.* These countries were Judea, Syria, Asia Minor, Macedonia, Illyricum, Greece, Italy, and the islands of Cyprus and Crete, with several others of less note. Mesopotamia should probably be added, on the strength of 1 Pet. 5:13. All the principal districts or provinces of Asia Minor are named in the Acts of the Apostles. The parts of Arabia in which Paul spent several years, are supposed to have been adjacent to Damascus, and within the modern Syria; and there is no evidence in Scripture that this apostle actually made his contemplated journey into Spain. The whole territory, therefore, traversed by the apostolical missionaries, so far as the Scriptures inform us, was within the Roman empire, and formed but a part of it; and, so far as territory is concerned, but little more than was afterwards governed by the eastern or Byzantine emperors.†

If we inquire what further light ecclesiastical history throws on this subject, we shall not be able greatly to extend the travels and labors of the apostles. Mosheim[2] gives it as the result of his researches, that "the

---

* Fabricii Lux Evan. exoriens, etc. p. 83. (Johann Albert Fabricius, 1668-1736, *Salutaris lux Evangelii toti orbi per divinam gratiam exoriens,* etc.; Hamburg, 1731. —Ed.)

† The countries mentioned Acts 2:9-11; add Media and Parthia to the above named.

[2] Two translations of J. L. von Mosheim's work were popular in America: *An Ecclesiastical History, Ancient and Modern,* tr. by A. Maclaine, 6 vols., Phila.: S. C. Ustick, 1797-8; and *Institutes of Ecclesiastical History,* tr. by J. Murdock, 3 vols., N.Y.: Stanford & Swords, 1832. —Ed.

stories often told respecting their travels among the Gauls, the Britons, the Spaniards, the Germans, the Americans, the Chinese, the Indians, and the Russians, are too recent and fantastic to be received by an inquisitive lover of the truth." "A great part of these fabulous stories," he continues, "were got up after the days of Charlemagne; when most of the christian churches contended as vehemently about the antiquity of their origin, as ever the Arcadians, Egyptians and Greeks did." Dr. Murdock, the American translator of Mosheim, believes — chiefly in view of the authorities quoted by Fabricius — that Peter, after preaching long in Judea and other parts of Syria, probably visited Babylon, Asia Minor, and finally Rome; that Paul, after his captivity, visited Judea, Asia Minor and Greece, and returned to Rome, but did not proceed further westward than Italy; that John, after remaining many years in Judea, removed to Ephesus, where, excepting the time of his banishment to Patmos, he remained till his death; that James the younger (the elder James was put to death by Herod) spent his life in Judea; and that Andrew probably labored on the shores of the Black Sea near the modern Constantinople, and perhaps in Greece. "Philip," he adds, "either the apostle or the evangelist, is reported to have ended his days at Hierapolis, in Phrygia. Thomas seems to have travelled eastward, to Parthia, Media, Persia and India. Bartholomew took perhaps a more southern course, and preached in Arabia. Matthew is also reported to have travelled east, in the Modern Persia. Of Simon the Canaanite, nothing to be relied on can be said. Thaddeus, Lebbeus, or Jude the brother of James, the author of an epistle, is reputed to have preached at Edessa, in the north of Syria. Of the companions of the apostles — Timothy, after accompanying Paul many years, is said to have been stationed at Ephesus, where he suffered martyrdom under Domitian or Nerva. Titus, another companion of Paul, is reported to have been stationed in Crete, where he died. Mark, or John surnamed Mark, attended Paul and afterwards Peter, and probably preached the gospel in Egypt. Of Luke, little can be said, except that he accompanied Paul, and wrote the book of Acts and a Gospel. Of Barnabas, nothing can be said worth relating, except what is learned from the New Testament. — From this account, imperfect as it is, we may conclude that the apostles and their companions scarcely extended their labors beyond the boundaries of the present Turkish empire."*

To the countries, then, which are mentioned in the New Testament as favored with the missionary labors of the apostles and their companions, ecclesiastical history adds Egypt, Southern Arabia, Persia, Media, Parthia, and India. But we have nothing that throws light on

* Mosheim's Eccl. Hist. vol. I. p. 55, 56 —*Note.*

their manner of proceeding in these countries. For information of this kind, we must look solely to the missions described in the New Testament. These were in Syria, Asia Minor, Macedonia, Greece, Italy, and the islands of Cyprus and Crete. I say Crete, for although we have no account of the labors of the apostle Paul in that island, we have his epistle to Titus, instructing him how to proceed in his mission to the Cretans. — I omit Judea, as being the source of the missions, and not a heathen country.

Our next inquiry relates to *the state of education in these countries.*

The mere mention of Syria, Asia Minor, Macedonia, Greece and Italy, is enough for the reader of history. What were they in those times but the very foci of civilization? Where were other countries in the wide world, to be compared with them in this respect? And the time, too, in which the apostolical missions were performed, was it not in the palmy age of Roman literature? But though the evidence of the high state of general civilization and individual intelligence in those countries at that period, is unquestionable, it is not easy to show precisely what means of education were possessed by the people at large, nor to what extent the multitude was actually educated.

Two events must have exerted a powerful influence on the minds of men and the tone of education throughout the field traversed by the apostles; — viz. the general dispersion of the Greeks, with their language and philosophy; and the general dispersion of the Jews, with their inspired books and their religion.

The Macedonians, upon the conquests of Alexander the Great, planted their colonies everywhere. They built Grecian cities even in Media. "On the Tigris, Seleucia was principally inhabited by Greeks: to the southeast was the magnificent Ctesiphon; and to the northwest was Sitace. Babylon imitated Macedonia; in its neighborhood lived Greeks and Macedonians. From thence along the Euphrates upwards lay Nicephorium, a Grecian city, surrounded also by other Greek towns; and further on in Mesopotamia was Charrae, a settlement of the Macedonians. But not to enter into details, we refer (in Appian) to a large catalogue of cities in Further and Hither Syria, which were reckoned to the Greeks. Tigranes, the Armenian, in his march to Phenicia by way of Syria, destroyed no less than twelve Greek cities. Between Syria and Babylonia we meet with the ruins of Palmyra, on which are found more Greek than Palmyrene inscriptions. Even some written in the Palmyrene character, are nevertheless in their language Greek. In Hither Syria, on the boundaries of Palestine, and in Palestine itself, the Greeks, as was natural from the situation and neighborhood, made still greater intrusions." Antioch, the capital of Syria, was peopled by its founder with Greeks and Macedonians, and acquired a reputation for

Greek refinement and science. Tyre and Sidon adopted the Greek language. Caesarea was peopled chiefly by Greeks. Gadara and Hippos, on the east of the Jordan, became Greek cities, and the former possessed men learned in Greek science. So also did Gaza, a city on the southwest border of Judea. Philadelphia, east of the Jordan, is still majestic in its Grecian ruins. Indeed the country east of the Jordan, was towards the north Greek, and towards the south mostly in possession of the Greeks.*

In this manner were the Greek language, manners and institutions generally diffused. As early as the time of Cato, that language was understood and spoken throughout the civilized world. Homer was read in Persia, and it is supposed even in India. In Carthage navigators described their voyages of discovery, and Hannibal wrote a history of his wars, in the language of the Greeks.† "Graeca leguntur," says Cicero, "in omnibus fere gentibus." During the reign of Augustus, the study of the Grecian philosophy was so generally prevalent, that almost every statesman, lawyer and man of letters was conversant with the writings of the philosophers. This philosophy originally embraced all inquiries about the nature of God, the origin and destiny of man, and the phenomena and powers of the material world. Afterwards the consideration of physical topics was to be a great extent excluded. Socrates, as is well known, exerted his influence to direct the investigations of philosophy to subjects in morals and religion, and in social and political economy. It is no doubt true, that comparatively few of the people knew anything of the different sects of Grecian philosophy, yet the fact that their disciples were so generally dispersed, must have had no small influence on the minds of men.‡

A consideration of the schools and the public libraries which are known to history, will assist our impressions as to the state of education in those large cities, in which were the *recorded* labors of the apostles and their associates. Athens for many ages had been renowned for her schools; and though at one time these were removed to Alexandria, and at another suffered much in the conquest of Greece by the Romans, yet they revived, and were resorted to from all quarters by those who

* Hug on the prevalence of the Greek language in Palestine, etc. Bib. Repos. vol. I. pp. 536-550. Prof. Pfannkuche, in his dissertation on the prevalence of the Aramean language in the same country in the time of the apostles, restricts the use of the Greek to the narrower limits. Bib. Repos. vol. I. pp. 317-363. The reader will incline to the views taken by Prof. Hug.

† Schlegel's Hist. of Literature, vol. I. p. 111.

‡ Eschenburg's Manual of Class. Lit. translated and edited by Prof. Fiske; and Enfield's Hist. of Philosophy. (Johann Joachim Eschenburg, 1743-1820; William Enfield, 1741-1797, *History of Philosophy,* London: 1791. —Ed.)

were eager for learning. They even survived the incursion of the Gauls in the fourth century, and continued to flourish till after the time of Justinian. In the period under consideration they had rivals at Apollonia on the western shore of Macedonia, where Augustus finished his education, not far south of Illyricum and Dalmatia; at Rhodes; at Pergamus, where was one of the seven churches; at Tarsus, the birthplace of Paul; and especially at Alexandria in Egypt. The law school at Berytus, in Syria, was of a subsequent date; and the schools of Antioch, Smyrna, Caesarea, Edessa and Seleucia, were of christian origin, and arose after the death of the apostles. The christian school at Alexandria was opened in the latter part of the second century. But the school of pagan philosophy in that city, at the era of our Saviour's advent, was thronged from all quarters, and is said to have sent forth eminent philosophers of every sect to distant countries. The celebrated library at Alexandria needs no description. About one hundred and fifty years before Christ, Pergamus contained a library of 200,000 volumes, rivalling the collection of the Ptolemies. Before the era of our missions, Mark Antony had presented it to Cleopatra, to replace the one in the Museum, which had been destroyed by Julius Caesar during the siege of Alexandria.

As to the influence of the Jews in their dispersion, it may be remarked, that as long ago as the reign of Ahasuerus, or Artaxerxes Longimanus, they were found in considerable numbers in all the provinces of Persia. The evidence of this is in the book of Esther. At the commencement of the christian missions, this people were dispersed over the Roman empire. The geographer Strabo, quoted by Josephus, says, "The Jews have already passed into every city; nor were it easy to find any place in the world, which has not received this nation and been occupied by it." Strabo flourished in the Augustan age. At that time, the antiquities and sacred books of the Jews began to attract the attention of pagan scholars, and conversions from paganism to Judaism were not uncommon. Synagogues, composed in great measure of proselytes, existed in many of the Grecian cities. Schools are said to have been common among the Jews; and no one can doubt that this dispersion of the Jews must have had a great effect on the gentile mind.*

From all this it would seem, that education and knowledge must have been considerably prevalent in the countries where were the missions described in the New Testament. Especially is it almost certain that men of education would be found in those cities generally, in which they gathered churches. Some of them would already be among the proselytes to Judaism, and it is highly probable that these would occa-

* Eschenburg's Manual, etc. p. 282.

sionally embrace the christian faith. The apostle Paul does indeed say, that "not many wise men after the flesh" were called. By these he may perhaps have meant the philosophers. It was, however, then no doubt much as it is now. In every city where converts were multiplied, there were a few from the less proud and ambitious classes of educated men. These would be superior to most of the apostles in respect to mere learning, and sometimes, it may be, quite equal to Paul himself, the best educated among the apostolic missionaries. In point of fact, the standard of education among the Gentiles, in Syria, Asia Minor, Greece and Rome, was at that time higher, than it was among the Jews, and the amount of education was greater.

I am now prepared *to state some facts, illustrative of the apostolical missions,* which are important to the main object of this discussion. One of the most prominent of these is, the small number of missionaries sent by the Holy Ghost into the several heathen countries. The New Testament gives no evidence that more than three apostles visited Asia Minor. If we call in the aid of ecclesiastical history, we have but four. To these add Barnabas, Luke, Mark, Silas and Apollos, and there are but nine missionaries in all. Timothy was a native of the country. So was Titus; at least he was a Greek. The list of the seventy disciples now extant, which would make nearly all the Christians named in the Epistles to be missionaries sent from Judea, is rejected by ecclesiastical writers as fictitious. But even if this list were authentic, it would then appear that not more than a dozen missionaries were sent to the countries of Asia Minor; and, excepting Syria, no other country appears to have been so much favored in this respect.

Now we are told that Paul and Barnabas, in their missionary tour through Asia Minor, "ordained elders in every church." Whom did they ordain? Sixteen cities are named where there were churches, and passages might be quoted from the Acts and Epistles, implying that a far greater number of churches were planted. Paul also informs Titus, that he had left him in Crete, among other reasons, that he might "ordain elders in every city." Whom? Not men sent for the purpose from the churches of Judea. Not missionaries. The elders thus ordained were chosen from among the native converts themselves.

Such was the usage of the apostles. They preached the gospel. Converts were multiplied. These were embodied in a society, and one or more of their number best qualified by talent, education, or miraculous gifts, or it may be in all these ways, were ordained over them in the Lord.

Now, in what manner did the apostles obtain, in every city, men qualified for such a trust?

It appears that their missionary labors, so far as they are recorded in the New Testament, were in the best educated, and in some respects highly educated, portions of the world; that they were chiefly in cities, and, excepting Rome and a few others, in Grecian cities, including most of those which were distinguished for learning and general civilization in those times; that in most places they must have preached more or less to educated men, rendering it not improbable that some of these were among their converts; and that these men, with some special instructions in the knowledge of the gospel, would be fitted to preach the gospel and take the pastoral charge of churches. During the three years Paul spent at Ephesus, and the year and a half he labored at Corinth, he might have trained numerous candidates for the ministry. Wherever the apostles went preaching the gospel, they found mind in that erect, intelligent, reasoning posture, which is the result of civilization — a more learned and refined civilization even, than existed in the communities from which the missionaries themselves proceeded.

It would seem, however, that whatever was the amount of education in the communities favored with the labors of the apostles, it was impossible to supply the gentile churches properly with teachers, without a miraculous agency; for, in these churches, the Holy Ghost saw fit to put forth a supernatural influence to raise up prophets, teachers and governors, that they might the more speedily and effectually be built up in the faith and order of the gospel.

Thus were the apostolical churches among the heathen furnished with religious teachers and guides. The apostles (excepting Paul) after spending three years in the most intimate connection with one who spake as never man spake — in a school for which any candidate for the ministry would gladly exchange the most favored of the halls of science — were wondrously endowed by the Holy Ghost with miraculous gifts and graces. Paul, pre-eminently the apostle to the Gentiles, spent his youth, probably, in the schools of Tarsus, but completed his education at the feet of Gamaliel in Jerusalem. He received his knowledge of the gospel by immediate revelation; "for I neither received it," says he, "of man, neither was I taught it but by the revelation of Jesus Christ." Next were the evangelists, often companions of the apostles in travels and labors, also endowed supernaturally for the work of missions. Next came prophets, teachers, etc., in the several churches. And these supernatural gifts appear not to have been restricted to one or two

[The editor has deleted the following few pages given to a discussion of offices and the gift of tongues in the early church, based on the works of eighteenth-century scholars, long since superseded.]

members of each church, but, sometimes at least, were bestowed, for mutual edification, upon numerous members, if not upon all.*

Now we must believe that the Holy Ghost would not have exerted this supernatural agency upon the minds of the first Christians, had it been unnecessary. And whence the necessity? Why were their minds strengthened, made the subjects of a spiritual illumination, and endowed with a facility and force of utterance beyond the reach of their natural powers in their circumstances? And why was this supernatural agency gradually withdrawn, as the churches became more enlightened by education, and able to train up her own teachers in her schools at Alexandria, Caesarea, Antioch, Edessa, and elsewhere? It has been said that the church grieved away the Spirit by her corruptions and follies. But it is far more reasonable to suppose, that the agency was withdrawn because the exigency which called for it had ceased.

We now turn our attention to modern missions, and *contrast their circumstances with those of the missions described in the New Testament.*

Modern missions have been sent to the Oriental churches, to the Mohammedans, and to — omitting some small districts — the pagan nations in western and southern Africa, India, the Archipelago, Polynesia, and the territories occupied by the native tribes of North America. The Oriental churches and the Mohammedans occupy most of the countries that were the scene of the apostolical missions. These I pass by at present, to contrast the circumstances of the modern and ancient missions to pagan nations.

One obvious and most important fact in modern missions to the heathen is, that they are prosecuted in the less civilized, and to a great extent in uncivilized, portions of the world. What heathen nation of these times will compare with the nations visited by the apostles? India is partially civilized; the rest are in a state of barbarism, and most of them, except as they have been affected by the gospel, are absolutely savage. On the score of education and intelligence, they stand immeasurably below the Greeks and Romans. The aboriginal-American, the Polynesian, and the African nations were without an alphabet until they received it from the missionaries. The larger nations of the Indian Archipelago have long had the use of letters, but scarcely one in forty of the inhabitants can read, and books of every kind are rare. Concerning India, the Abbé Dubois is good authority,

---

* I Cor. 14:23, "If therefore the whole church be come together into one place, and *all* speak with tongues." v. 24, "If *all* prophesy." v. 26, "When ye be come together, *every one of you* hath a psalm, hath a doctrine, hath a tongue, hath a revelation." v. 29-31, "Let the prophets speak *two* or *three,* and let the others judge. If any thing be revealed to another that sitteth by, let the first hold his peace. For ye may *all* prophesy one by one."

except where he speaks of Protestant missions. He says the brahmins regard the sciences as their own exclusive property, that they make a mystery of them to the vulgar, and have always taken the greatest pains to prevent their spread among other classes of men. At the same time they have themselves made no progress in learning beyond their ancestors of the era of Pythagoras, and stand, with the whole body of the Hindoos, where they did two thousand years ago. It is worth while to add, that the sciences above referred to, which are the ones that in ancient times gave so much celebrity to the Indian philosophers, are astronomy, astrology and magic. The native schools now existing in India are so unlike those of Europe or America, and so inferior to them, as not to bear a comparison. The Abbé says they are in the larger towns, or within the precincts of some large temple, and are without method, or plan for study, or discipline, without excitement for the student, or encouragement for the teacher.*

I hesitate not to advance the proposition, that mind, in all the pagan nations, now open to missionaries, is in such a case that the converts, without either the supernatural gifts of early times, or the substitute for those gifts (imperfect as it may be) which is found in education, will not be fitted for the offices and duties of the christian church, nor to stand alone without the help of missionaries.

They need such extraneous influences far more than did the early converts. This is true of the nations of India; and it is pre-eminently true of the more barbarous pagan nations in which the experiment of Protestant missions has been made. How it would be in China, I do not know. A more thorough and practical discipline appears there to be given to the mind in the class of students called "literati," than is known to any class of minds in India. But in the large portions of the heathen world just named, it is impossible, without either miraculous gifts, or education, fairly and fully to introduce the christian church, in any one of its existing forms; or if introduced, there is no reason to believe that such churches could be sustained and flourish without the constant presence of missionaries. They could not on the plan of *Congregationalism;* — for want of that intelligence and discretion among the members, which are so necessary where every man has a vote and a direct agency in the affairs of the church, and for want also of men qualified to act as deacons and committees. Even now, after all that has yet been done in the way of education, Congregational missionaries (and the same is equally true of all others) are obliged to ex-

---

* Description of the People of India; vol. I. p. 354. (Jean Antoine Dubois, *Description of the Character, Manners, and Customs of the People of India,* tr. from the French, 2 vols., Phila.: M. Carey, 1818. —Ed.)

ercise a governing influence in the churches they have gathered very analogous to that exercised by the apostles. — They could not on the plan of *Presbyterianism;*—for want of suitable men to be entrusted, as ruling elders, with the government of the church. — Neither could they on the plan of *Episcopacy;* for want of men qualified to perform the duties of priests and bishops. Indeed, the want of well qualified teachers and pastors would be equally felt, and equally fatal to success, whatever form should be given to the ecclesiastical organization. I repeat; without either miraculous gifts, or that intellectual and moral discipline which is not ordinarily attained without more education than is to be found in the heathen world, the native churches, if left to themselves, would soon run into confusion, and the institutions of the gospel would perish from among them. One has but to study the writings of the apostolical Fathers to see, that even in their times — in the centre of the civilized world, and almost in the brightest period of ancient learning — the churches founded by personal ministry of the apostles, as soon as miraculous gifts ceased, and earlier, were kept with the greatest difficulty in the doctrines of the apostles.* And we know that it took the church three long centuries to acquire even the ascendency in the Roman empire, and that the hour of her triumph may be regarded as the commencement of her decline. It would be an interesting inquiry, how far this slow progress, (it must be regarded as slow, if we take only the time into view,) and the early, rapid, and terrible decline of the church, followed by ages of darkness, were owing to the want of those very facilities for general education, with which God, chiefly through the medium of the press, has furnished his people in these latter days.

Not to pursue this subject, let us illustrate somewhat more the intellectual degradation, into which the great body of the present heathen world has fallen.

To how great an extent have all useful ideas perished from the minds of pagan nations! In those which make the greatest pretensions to learning, in India for instance, the researches of christian scholars have discovered that there is but little of truth on any subject. Their history, chronology, geography, astronomy, their philosophical notions of matter and mind, and their views of creation and providence, religion and morals, are exceedingly destitute of truth. It is not, however, so much vacuity of mind that we have here to contend with, as plenitude of error; the mind being filled with theories and systems of geography, astronomy, metaphysics and theology, all mingled together — the ac-

---

* See Osburn on the Doctrinal Errors of the Apostolical and Early Fathers, *passim*. (William Osburn, Jr.; published London, 1835. —Ed.)

cumulations and perversions of three thousand years — and all claiming the same divine origin, the same infallibility and authority. So that, happily, even the simplest course of elementary instruction in schools, could not be otherwise than a direct attack upon their false religions; and the overthrow of any one of their systems of learning would be a subversion, in their apprehension, of theological error, and the substitution of theological truth.

But when we go beyond the limits of civilization, among the wild children of paganism living on our western wilderness, in Africa, and the islands of the sea, then it is a vacuity of mind, and not a plenitude, we have to operate upon. The savage has few ideas, and those few relate to his physical experience and wants. The relations of things escape his attention. He sees only the objects just about him. He knows nothing of geography; nothing of astronomy; nothing of history; nothing of his own spiritual nature and destiny; nothing of God. His mind, if it were possible for it in these circumstances to be expanded, would still be empty. It could not stand erect. It would have nothing to support it.

The worst consequence of all this in connection with the natural depravity of the savage, is that paralysis of the thinking power, especially on spiritual subjects, so often mentioned and lamented by missionaries. This indisposition to thought is well illustrated by the Rev. Lorrin Andrews, principal of the missionary Seminary at the Sandwich Islands, in an essay on native schools at the islands written about six years since.* I will quote a few of his more striking facts.

"The worst thing in their *reading*," he says, speaking of the natives, "is, that they get no ideas. I have taken great pains to ascertain this fact, and I am convinced that ninety out of a hundred that are called readers, hardly know that any meaning ought to be attached to the words. Indeed a great many think there is a kind of mystery, or perhaps magic, in reading. Their notion is, that they must say over a word or two, or a sentence, and then from some quarter a thought will come to them — that is, when they have any thought at all. I have spent hours at a time, in the high school, trying to make the scholars believe that a word written on paper, or printed in a book, meant just the same thing as when spoken with the mouth." — "The mass of the people," he adds, "gain nothing from conversation with their countrymen who are better informed, as in enlightened countries, for they are all alike unthinking." — "It is remarkable that we are obliged to teach in a formal manner many things to this people, which are easily understood by the most illiterate in civilized countries, or which they would find

* See Appendix to the 25th Annual Report of the ABCFM, 1835, pp. 135ff.

out by inference. We are called upon frequently to answer questions which appear to us foolish. To mention only one; about three months ago, the wife of Kauwa, one of the Society Island teachers, died; a very respectable and, I believe, pious woman. She died on the Sabbath day. Some few days after her death, the question was agitated among our Lahaina church members, whether or no she could now be happy? And the conclusion pretty generally, if not universally, was that she must be miserable, since the last act of her life consisted in dying on the Sabbath; in other words, breaking the Sabbath; and as they had been taught that there was no repentance after death, it was not discoverable at all by them how she could be saved. This reasoning was among the best informed people of Lahaina, who have enjoyed almost ten years of faithful instruction. Kaio, my teacher (in the native language), who for thought, reflection, and knowledge of the Scriptures stands third, if not second, in the island, was completely puzzled with the question, and came to me for a solution."

"The study of Colburn's Intellectual Arithmetic," says the same missionary, two years later, "has done more than all other books in teaching the scholars *to think*. Geography has greatly enlarged their views of things, and added much to their stock of knowledge. But for much mental discipline in a little space, this little book has exceeded all others they have yet had. After going half way through the book, they were astonished at themselves. When I commenced with it, they laughed at the simplicity of the questions on the first page, and said it was like the Child's Arithmetic.* I turned over thirty or forty pages of the manuscript, (the translation had not then been printed), and read off several questions. They thought of them a while, and said, nobody knows these things, they are exceedingly entangled. I told them they could soon comprehend them, if they would go straight on from the beginning of the book. They said, perhaps so. Sometime after they had passed over the place they thought so difficult, they asked me when they should get to the hard questions I had formerly read to them? On being told they had passed over those questions without making a mistake, they exclaimed, what fools we were!"

How very unlike the field which God has given *us* to cultivate among the heathen, to that cultivated by the apostles and their associates. Moreover, we go forth to our work without their power of performing miracles, and our converts must be built up in the faith and order of the gospel, and qualified to stand alone and extend the triumphs of the Redeemer of men, without those gifts of teaching, prophe-

---

* Members of the high school, or seminary, were at that time adults.

cy and government, which were supernaturally conferred on the first
gentile converts.

Would any one, notwithstanding this vast difference of circumstances, still restrict us to the single method of oral preaching, because
only that was employed by the apostles? But why overlook the supernatural qualifications, the miraculous powers of the apostles! Why overlook the supernatural gifts conferred upon their converts? Why lose
sight of the fact that the apostles did actually press into the service *all*
the natural powers they possessed, *all* their intellectual acquisitions, *all*
their gifts and graces, and *all* the providential facilities within their
reach, and brought these all to bear to the utmost upon the people to
whom they were sent? And would they not have been grateful for more
power, and greater means and facilities? Would they not have used
them if they could? Would not the apostle Paul, for instance, in the
prosecution of his missions, have rejoiced in such providential facilities, as rail-roads by land; steam-boats by water; paper instead of papyrus, or parchment; printed books instead of manuscripts; bills of exchange, by means of which to remit the contributions of the Macedonian and Grecian churches to Jerusalem, rather than the necessity
of sending messengers all the way thither to carry the money; and the
log-line and compass, in that terrible tempest when for many days neither
sun nor stars appeared? Would he not gladly have favored the whole
body of his converts with the *reading,* as well as the *hearing*, of the word?
And when laboring with his own hands at Corinth and Ephesus, because
he deemed it inexpedient to be chargeable to the Christians of those
cities, would it not have been grateful to his feelings and facilitated
his missionary work, if some society in Judea could have relieved him
from this necessity?

Nothing can be more illogical, than the objection brought against
missionary schools, because the apostles established none. How many
things the apostles omitted to do, which they would have done if they
could. And how absurd to restrict the church of the nineteenth century
to the means that were at its command in the first. Must no use be
made of the numberless providential gifts to the church since then?
Must no notice be taken of the subsequent changes in her circumstances? Must no regard be had for the very different attitude and
relations of the pagan world towards her? The heathen to whom the
church then sent her missions, were as well instructed in human science,
as she was herself; now, the heathen are as much lower on the scale
of intelligence, as the church is higher; and does this fact create no additional obligation? Besides, where is the divine command to restrict
ourselves to *one mode* of propagating the christian religion? The apostles certainly had *two*. They preached; and then, by the laying on of

hands, they instrumentally conferred extraordinary gifts of teaching, prophecy, government, tongues and miracles on certain of the converts.* The first we do as they did; the second, in the only manner within our power, viz., by a course of instruction. And as the command to do a thing includes the means which are necessary for its performance, this, being essential to the accomplishment of the work enjoined, is also commanded. Moreover, by what authority do we limit the meaning of the Saviour's last command to the public, oral, formal proclamation of it to a congregation? When has it been shown, that the apostles delivered sermons in the manner of modern times? — And why make *adults* the only object contemplated by the injunction? Should the gospel not also be proclaimed to youth and children, and the manner of proclaiming it be suited to their years? Why tie up this blessed command, so full of good will for mankind, to one single method of conferring the benefit? Why limit its applicability to one single combination of circumstances? Is the consecrated church the only place where the gospel can be, where it ought to be preached? May the gospel not be preached in an upper, private room? May it not be preached, in conversational tones and manner, to a single family? May it not be preached by the way-side to a single traveller? May it not be preached in the Bible-class, and Sabbath school, and even in the weekday school; and then may not the *media* of truth, common in such circumstances, be employed to make it known to the youthful mind? I would ask, too, if *the writing of Paul's Epistles* was not an act of obedience to the command under consideration? No one doubts that it was; and if so, and if a copy of his Epistle to the Colossians was made out for the church of the Laodiceans,† was not the copying of the epistle in obedience both to the letter and spirit of the Saviour's command? And when we, availing ourselves of the manifold copying powers of the press, *print* this epistle and the other portions of the word of God, and distribute them by thousands, is not this obeying the command? And when we teach the unlettered to read the word of God for themselves, and thus enable them to confer the same ability on others, and to grow more in knowledge and grace than they otherwise would, is not this also obeying the command? Yes verily; it is intelligent obedience. For the printing of the word of God, and teaching men to read it, are not something different from the work enjoined. They are not designed to open and smooth the way for the gospel. They are not *preparatory* work. They are the very work itself — as much so as the conferring of miraculous gifts of prophecy and teaching, or the

---

* Rom. 1:11. Acts 8:17. 1 Tim. 4:14. Acts 19:6.
† Col. 4:16.

writing of the Gospels, or the inspired Epistles anciently were. The schools are — if they are what they ought to be — nurseries of piety, places and means for.the direct inculcation of gospel truth in youthful minds and hearts. They are folds where the lambs of the flock are to be fed.

Lest I should be misunderstood I will say here — what will more fully appear in the sequel — that a due proportion is to be observed in the different parts of the work. The different gifts, like the different members of the body, though all essential to the completeness of the whole, have their relative degrees of importance, and should each be kept in their several places, and each have no more than their respective proportions of time. Preaching has the first place. It has that place at home, and it has it and should have it abroad. It is the grand means of operating upon the conscience and heart. It is the grand means of conversion. In some form or other, adapted to the circumstances of the missionary, it should be the leading pursuit of his life. In every mission it should be the focal point, the ultimate, grand object, the final cause with the members in all their plans.

It is now time to state, more precisely, *what place education should hold in the system of modern missions.*

1. If we were to regard education simply as a convenient method of inculcating a knowledge of the gospel on minds of a certain class, still it may properly be used by the missionary. So far as heathen youth are concerned, it is found in practice to be the only method of getting early access to their minds, the only method of preaching the gospel to them. It is often the most direct and effectual means of bringing others, and especially parents, under the preached gospel.* The visitation and superintendence of schools also gives a fine field of usefulness to missionaries recently come upon the ground, and not enough acquainted with the native language to preach formally to the adults. It is almost the only thing they can do; and in the larger missions there will almost always be some missionaries in this condition.

2. In barbarous pagan countries, if we could make any use of the press and the printed word of God, elementary schools are indispensable. If we withhold the Bible from the pagan, no matter how, in what respect does our policy differ from that of the church of Rome? I need not say that books and the press are useless in a community which cannot read.

3. Ages of experience in protestant Christendom have shown, that connecting a small system of schools with the stated and frequent

* Acts 19:9.

preaching of the gospel, is wise as a means of increasing the effect of preaching and the durability of its influence. And if it be so within the bounds of Christendom, why not beyond? The ministry throughout the world, acts under one and the same commission, and is governed by one and the same code of laws. The gospel they preach is the same. Human nature, with which they have to deal, is the same. If the circumstances differ, as they do very greatly, the difference only shows the greater need of connecting schools with preaching among those who know not the gospel. The ordained missionary will indeed engage no more than is necessary in their elementary instruction. He will commit this as soon as may be to native teachers. But when occupying a fixed station, he will no more be without such schools than the pastor at home, and no more will he withhold from them his fostering care, and watchful guardianship. The missionary who has them not, will do well from year to year to compare their respective congregations, and the results of their preaching. Let their native churches also be compared, and their prospects among the rising generation.

4. After all, we cannot undertake to educate the youth of the whole heathen world, nor even any considerable proportion of them. The labor and the expense are both out of the question. Whatever it may be proper or desirable for us to do, in a general point of view, the scantiness of the means placed at the disposal of missionary societies renders it expedient, yea unavoidably necessary, that schools at the expense of such societies be established on a limited scale. We can educate only the few, and they must educate the many. Our pupils, as far as possible, should be select, and selected with some regard to the ulterior employment of the most promising of them as helpers in the mission. Our schools should be model schools. They should be nurseries of teachers. They should be introductory to the higher seminary, and preparatory to it. The preached gospel must at all events be sustained, and the number of schools should be regulated by the means placed at the disposal of the society, and the balance remaining of what is appropriated to the mission, after providing for the support of its preaching members. Still I must doubt, — if missionaries are not to be mere itinerants, if they are to have a fixed residence and operate within the bounds of some one district, — whether the church has any right to insist upon their laboring wholly without schools; or, in other words, without a system of means in operation around them for rearing up native helpers and successors in their work. Do the Scriptures confer any such right on the churches? Do they impose any such obligation on the missionary? Had missionaries the power of conferring supernatural gifts by the laying on of their hands, as the apostles and some of their associates had, the case would be very different.

5. While I assert the legitimate use of schools as one of the means of propagating the gospel in foreign missions, and while I maintain the right of missionaries to be furnished with them to a certain extent, I would suggest a general rule in relation to their establishment; having respect in this rule to the average amount of funds which experience has shown may be relied on by missionary societies, and the proportionate demand which will be made on these for sending forth and supporting preachers of the gospel. The rule is this — *That the system of education, in all its parts, so far as it is supported by the funds of the mission, should have a direct reference to the training up of native teachers and preachers.* To this, in the smaller missions, and also in the less concentrated missions, there must be exceptions. A liberal construction should always be given to it. In some missions, as among the Tamul people of Ceylon and South India, the rule itself may require a considerable number of schools; — to awaken attention, give tone to the public mind with respect to education, furnish a better selection, give importance to the subject in the view of the select pupils, open a field for the occasional trial of their powers while pursuing their studies, and strengthen their motives to arrive at high attainments. Still, whatever scope is allowed for the exercise of discretion in arranging and managing the details of the system, there will be a great practical advantage in having the one definite object proposed by this rule. And it is a question, whether missions themselves ought not to be established, organized, and prosecuted with more reference to the same end. Are not many of our missions modelled as they should be, if our object and expectation were to furnish a *full* supply of preachers from Christendom for all the nations of the heathen world, now and for ages to come; and as they should not be, if our object be to imitate the apostles by throwing the great amount of permanent labor upon converted natives, and introducing what the Holy Spirit may be expected to make a self-sustaining, self-propagating Christianity?

The plan suggested would involve a seminary of a higher order in each considerable mission, which would receive pupils from the preparatory schools, and conduct them through a course of liberal education more or less protracted. These seminaries should be commenced on a small scale, and enlarged no faster than shall be necessary. They should combine the college and the school of theology. The notion that instruction in the principles of human science must precede the study of theology, is derived from the schools of philosophy, and is not countenanced by the word of God. The plain, simple theology of the Scriptures can be taught to youth, and even to heathen youth, in every stage of their education. The institutions should be eminently missionary institutions. The whole course of education, from beginning to end, should be christian. It should be no part of the object of these seminaries to educate natives for the law, nor for medicine, nor for civil affairs, nor for trade, except so far as this will directly promote the legitimate objects of the missions with which they are connected. The course of instruction should be planned with a view to raising up, through the blessing of God, an efficient body of native helpers in the several departments of missionary labor — to be teachers of schools, catechists, tutors and professors in the seminaries, and, above all, preachers of the gospel, pastors of the native churches, and missionaries to the neighboring heathen districts and countries. For this purpose the seminaries should be furnished with competent teachers, and with all necessary books and apparatus, and a press should generally be in their neighborhood.*

These missionary seminaries will be as really subordinate to the preaching of the gospel, as are the theological seminaries of our own country. If we teach in them, and in so doing, turn aside in any degree from the formal ministry of the word, it will be that we may multiply teachers and ministers of the word. Our object will be the more effectually to plant those instrumentalities, which, with God's blessing, will secure for the gospel a permanent footing and constant increase in heathen countries.

Our protracted discussion now draws to its conclusion. We should not forget, however, to glance at the claims of education among the oriental churches. The oriental churches are the Coptic, Syriac, Greek, and Armenian, and they number about six millions of souls. The Copts are found in Egypt; the Syrians, in Syria, Mesopotamia, the mountains of Koordistan, and on the western shore of Hindoostan; the Greeks, in Greece, European Turkey and Asia Minor. Many of the Arabs in Syria are of the Greek church; and so is the Georgian nation, living at the northern base of Mount Caucasus, between the Black and Caspian Seas. The country of the Armenians lies between Asia Minor and Persia, but the Armenians are a commercial people widely scattered. About a hundred thousand Maronites on Mount Lebanon, and nine thousand for each of the sects above mentioned, are converts to papacy. These are relics of the churches planted by the apostles. To them were first given the oracles of God, and from them emanated the light of the glorious gospel which shines upon us. "But in treading over again the tracks of the apostles," says the Rev. Mr. Smith, "I

---

* See a Statement of Principles, on which missionary Seminaries should be reared, in the Appendix to the 28th (last) Annual Report of the A.B.C.F. Missions, pp. 151-155.

have sought in vain for an individual that now breathes the spirit of
Jesus, unless he had borrowed it from a foreign source."* I shall content myself with affirming, that the state of education and intelligence
is much lower now, in the countries where the oriental churches are
found, than it was in the apostolical times. Even if it were not, regarding education as taking the place of miraculous gifts, and as our
only means of raising up teachers and preachers, it is to be numbered
among the legitimate objects of modern missions to these churches.
The necessity for schools sustained by missionary societies, is, however, less urgent among the oriental Christians, than in heathen
nations; and recent indications encourage the belief, that we may pretty
easily and without great expense "provoke" those churches to do far
more than they are now doing in the way of self-instruction.

Thus the case stands. Apostolical usage has been urged upon us
to exclude the use of education from our missions, only because the
immense difference in our circumstances has been overlooked. It has
been forgotten that their missions were to the most civilized nations
of the world, and that ours (I speak not only of those to pagans) are
to the least civilized; that theirs were to a people comparatively educated and refined, and ours are to a people uneducated, and to a great
extent barbarian, and even savage; that miraculous gifts were conferred by the Holy Ghost upon their gentile converts, so that the
churches might be promptly and effectually supplied with pastors and
teachers, while notwithstanding the present intellectual degradation of
heathen nations, Infinite Wisdom no longer sees it best to bestow such
gifts. Thus far the comparison is against us; but now the tables turn.
We have a knowledge of the world such as they had not; facilities for
travelling far exceeding theirs; paper, printing-presses, printed books,
where they had only the papyrus, parchment, the written page and the
voluminous and costly manuscript. In these circumstances, so diverse
from those of the apostles, why demand of us that we use no means
for publishing the gospel except what they used? Are not means and
opportunities talents to be employed — providential gifts bestowed
upon us with special reference to the advancement of God's kingdom
of grace on earth? Why, when the Head of the church bids *us* go into
all the world, and has provided for us rail-roads, and steam-boats, and
the thousand improvements in modern navigation, should we go on foot,
or venture out to sea, without compass, or quadrant, in some "ship to
Alexandria"? Why, when he bids *us* make known the gospel to every
creature, should we depend only on the living voice and the manuscript?

* Missionary Sermons and Addresses, p. 223. (Eli Smith, Boston: Crocker &
Brewster, 1833. —Ed.)

Why should we not avail ourselves of the progress of mind, of art, of science? It is said, that means are nothing in themselves, that the power which must accomplish the work is of God, and that an extended array of instrumentalities has a tendency to make us rely on them and forget his power? This is all true. But did Paul do less because his planting was rather by itself, and God must give the increase? Did he not exert all his strength, and plant and water, and become all things to all men, and put into requisition every possible means to save them? Unquestionably he did; and so should we. Creation, education, grace, and providence go to make up the degree of our accountability. Still it is a precious truth, that we are no less dependent on the influences of the Holy Spirit, than the apostles were. None of our plans will succeed, none of our efforts prosper, without his influences. Go where we will, if the Holy Spirit go not with us, our missions, however vigorously prosecuted, will fail. Missionaries and their directors and patrons have not felt this dependence enough. There is no danger of feeling it too much. When weak in ourselves, we are strong in God. But faith is not the only grace we are to exercise. We must practise obedience. We must act, as well as believe. Looking unto Jesus, we must do with our might whatsoever our hand findeth to do, for the honor of his name and the advancement of his cause on earth.

Selection 10

VERNACULAR VERSUS ENGLISH SCHOOLS[1]

The authorities upon which you have relied have led to an erroneous statement of the opinions and proceedings of the American Board, and especially of that one of its Secretaries, who was sent to visit the missions in India, and has now the honor of addressing you; and this is equally true as regards the Rev. Dr. Thompson, my respected associate in the Deputation. Among other things, you say: "These brethren, especially the Secretary, evidently came to India with a foregone conclusion;" that, "it appears plainly, from the minutes of the Board itself and from the writings of the Secretary, that he had made up his mind that schools are not the proper mode of conducting missions; that mission schools were not a fair object of the expenditure of mission funds;" that in their visit to India "right and left they seem to have put down the schools;" that "the Board and the Deputation reported against the expenditure of their funds on the mission schools," "that *that* was a blow all but fatal to the missions;" and "that the Board are now in the course of retracing their steps."

*   *   *   *   *   *

I now proceed to the facts:

1. Excepting a single point, I can recollect no "foregone conclusion" in my own mind, when I went to India. Having then been for more than thirty years connected with the foreign correspondence of the

---

[1] Portion of a *Letter to the Rev. Robert S. Candlish, D.D.,* Boston: T. R. Marvin & Son, 1862, pp. 3-8. On the issue of the English Language Schools, one must refer to the *Reports and Letters connected with special meetings of the Mahratta and Tamil Missions of the A.B.C.F.M.,* Boston: printed for the use of the *Prudential Committee,* 1855, being collected reports first published in India. See references on pp. 25-27 to English Schools, Instruction in English Language, etc.

Board, and intimately conversant with all its missions beyond sea, I could not but have a variety of definite opinions as to the best method of conducting missions; but I recall only one such conclusion, and that was, if possible, to bring about the institution of a *native pastorate* in the missions. I rejoice to say, that this was effected in each of the three older India missions.

2. You refer to "the writings of the Secretary," as affording proof that mission funds ought not, in his estimation, to be expended on mission schools. All the writings of the Secretary and of the Deputation, that have as yet been committed to the press, are lying before me. Nothing is said in them against such schools, but only as to the manner of using the schools. In their Report to the Board, the Deputation declare the doctrine they inculcated in India, as well as the result to which the missions everywhere arrived in their proceedings, to have been this; — *"That the system of education in all its parts, so far as it is supported by the funds of the mission, should have a direct reference to the training up of native preachers."* In their letters to the missions, they used the following language concerning various classes of native teachers and helpers; — "We now have better use for our funds, than in the payment of heathen schoolmasters." "If we would have teachers worth employing, we must educate them. The same is emphatically true of catechists. This latter class will not need the same amount of education; and we concur most fully with you in the opinion, that they should not be taught the English language." — "Our experience strongly inclines us to believe, that we have repeatedly begun too early, and expended too much money and strength in training helpers; and that it is better to defer the systematic effort — the [high or training] school — till the converts adapted to our purpose justify the expense of the institution. How large a number of your present helpers are uneducated men, except in the ability to read the Scriptures, and to expound, mainly from their own experience, the leading truths of the gospel! And yet how useful they have been! With more education, they would almost of course have been more valuable; but, at the outset, who would have rejected their co-operation? Let us employ such helpers as we have, in the *beginning* of our efforts, and the better educated will come in due time. We only add, that you may rely on the disposition of the Prudential Committee to aid you, to the extent of their ability, in really promising efforts for bringing forward an efficient native ministry at the earliest possible day."

In one of their letters to a mission, the Deputation wrote thus concerning an English-language school of a secondary rank, at an interior station: "The school has been in operation twenty years. Not far from five hundred boys have enjoyed its advantages. A great amount of missionary time, thought and labor has been given to it. All has been done for it that the nature of the case permitted. No one can doubt it has been useful to society. But not a member of the school has ever been known to receive a saving impression from the truths of the gospel. God has withheld from it his seal. We believe that the experiment has been sufficiently tried."

In their reasoning concerning the kind of schools to be employed, and especially those in which the English language was to be taught, the Deputation made a distinction between rural districts and great cities, — a distinction, as will appear in the sequel, which has since been recognized and sanctioned by Dr. Duff. Not only did they forbear all criticism upon the great English-teaching schools of your own and other kindred bodies in Bombay, Madras and Calcutta, but they never expressed an opinion that such schools were not what the peculiar exigencies of those great cities required. On their return from India, they thus reported to the Board: "A distinction should be made between the *great cities* of India, and the *rural districts*. If we would gain access for the gospel to the inhabitants of such cities as Bombay, Madras and Calcutta, and especially to the higher classes, it *may be* that measures must be adopted there, which are neither necessary nor expedient in the rural districts, especially for the masses of the people. The best method of conducting missions in such cities is still subject to costly experiments, which have not as yet had time enough for testing their results. There are peculiar circumstances in them, which will more or less control our plans and movements. The question of chief difficulty in respect to Madras is, whether it will be expedient for the Board to retain its present mission there. In case it should do so, it is a fact of importance, resulting from the comparative isolation of this city, that the plans there pursued will not probably have the effect to interfere with the working of the Arcot and Madura missions. But it is thought to be otherwise with Bombay. The most difficult question is, how to prosecute the Bombay mission so as not to draw down the more enterprising converts from the interior villages to the metropolis, from whence few of them would ever return."

In the "Memorial Volume of the First Fifty Years of the American Board of Commissioners for Foreign Missions," — a copy of which I take the liberty of sending you, — the writer of this letter, in the chapter on Schools, thus describes the relation which the Board sustains, and has sustained, to education and missionary schools.

"(1.) In the present advanced state of most of its missions, it finds a more profitable use for its funds, than in the support of heathen schoolmasters. Nor does past experience encourage any great outlay for common schools composed of very young heathen children, even with Christian masters; nor for boarding-schools that are chiefly made up of such children. Christian children should of course receive a Christian education; but, even here, it is not wise to be forward to relieve parents of one of their most obvious and sacred duties. Into these schools as many heathen children should have admission as can find room; and there should be schools also expressly for such, if there be reliable teachers for their instruction, and funds for their support.

"(2.) The Board has been obliged, in the progress of its work, to decline connection with expensive educational institutions for general education to prepare young men for secular and worldly pursuits. Its higher schools, whether for males or females, have been more strictly training institutions, with express and direct reference to carrying out the great purposes of the missions. Moreover, it has been found necessary to exclude the English language, in great measure, from the training schools for educating village teachers, preachers, and pastors.

"(3.) The education in the missions under the care of the Board, regarded as a whole, was never so effective, in a missionary point of view, never so valuable, as at the present moment. Perhaps there are as many common schools as the missionaries can well superintend. What these schools most need is better teachers, and to derive more of their support from the parents of the pupils. The self-supporting principle among native Christians, in all its applications, needs an unsleeping guardianship and culture. It is here that the grand practical difficulty lies in the working of specific charities. Where a man can support himself, it would be cruel to support him."

Thus much as to our "writings;" and the "Minutes of the Board" will be found entirely consentaneous with these.

Decidedly Christian schools, adapted to the condition of the people, following in the train of the preached gospel, and purely auxiliary to its ministrations, we all regard, and have long regarded, as an essential element in a well-conducted mission.

PART III

THE MISSIONARY

Selection 11

OUGHT I TO BECOME A MISSIONARY TO THE HEATHEN?[1]

The principal means of deciding the important question, 'Ought I to become a missionary to the heathen?' are obvious; viz., the word of God — the providence of God — and the indications of the Spirit of God. The first is, of course, very general, and counsels all alike. The second is more particular, and if narrowly observed, the finger of Providence may often be very clearly discovered, pointing out the path of duty. Frequently, however, there are no data discoverable, from which to draw any conclusion on this ground, as when providential circumstances are very general in their character.

In case both these fail of being sufficiently definite, recourse may be had to the third means mentioned above — the counsel and guidance of the Spirit of God. This cannot fail, if sought aright. And it ought to be a source of unfeigned gratitude to God, that we have the sure promise of his unerring Spirit, to guide us in the way of truth and duty, provided we inquire for it with humble docility. Thanks to our Father in heaven, that he has said, "If any man lack wisdom, let him ask of God, who giveth to all men liberally, and upbraideth not, and it shall be given him."

But as the Holy Spirit, in this matter, makes use of the natural faculties and desires of the human mind, it will readily occur, that here again we fallible mortals are liable to err — liable to mistake the in-

[1] Missionary Tract No. 8; Boston: The Board, 1851.

On the subject "The Missionary" see also Selection 3 in Part II, THE THEORY OF MISSIONS TO THE HEATHEN, which was also published as Missionary Tract No. 1 with the title *The Office and Work of the Missionary to the Heathen.*

clinations of our own hearts for the suggestions of the Spirit of God:
or to neglect the real drawings of the Spirit, as the fanciful products of
an adventurous or romantic mind. It may not, therefore, be improper
to suggest a few thoughts for the purpose of guarding against mistakes
on this important topic.

And, first: We are not, generally, to expect *any extraordinary influence of the Holy Spirit,* taking occasion, suddenly, or from some circumstance apparently trivial, to infuse into us an ardent desire for the
work of missions. This, it is true, may happen in some rare cases, when
even the individual himself cannot give any satisfactory account of his
convictions: as in the case of the person irresistibly led to the determination to devote himself to the cause, by reading the passage: "Unto
me, who am less than the least of all saints, is this grace given, that I
should preach among the Gentiles the unsearchable riches of Christ."

And such rare and manifestly extraordinary cases should no more
teach *us,* to wait for a similar call, than the occasional awakening of a
careless sinner, by some trivial circumstance, amidst all his gaiety and
folly, should teach others to give themselves no trouble, but pursue
the same giddy course, until they are arrested by a similar interposition
of the Spirit of God.

This suggests a second remark: that, in guiding us by his influence
into the path of duty, the Holy Spirit operates on the heart, as in other
cases, *by means of the truth.* There is a constant tendency in the
human mind, when looking for divine direction, to expect it in some
remarkable manner. So it was in the case of Naaman the Syrian, so
it is with impenitent sinners in every age: and Christians themselves
are liable to fall into the same error: and the more so, in proportion
to the magnitude and responsibility of the case under consideration.
Now in relation to the question of duty to the heathen, are there not
many who deem it amply sufficient, simply to ask the Lord to guide
them by his Spirit, believing that if it be their duty to go, it will then be
made known to them somehow, without further trouble on their part?
Thus many think it unnecessary, or at least neglect entirely to make a
full investigation of the subject, because they do not feel a strong desire, or any premonition that duty leads that way: and others, who once
had some anxiety, and, it may be, prayed frequently over the subject,
are discouraged, because their desires for the work grow weaker, or at
least, are stationary; and their views do not grow clearer, as they expected. Now it is not enough occasionally to pray for divine direction,
and then fold our arms in half careless expectation. No; we must read
much upon the subject — we must investigate it deeply and thoroughly,
just as though we were at last dependent on our own resources; and
then, with humble prayer that God would aid us by his Spirit, would

bless the truth we have acquired, and through it influence our hearts to choose the way of duty, we may, almost infallibly, determine what that duty is.

A third remark is, that we should not take the absence of a *strong desire* for the work of missions, as conclusive evidence that it is not the mind of the Spirit that we should go to the heathen. This indeed flows necessarily from the preceding remarks; for a man cannot know what the will of God respecting him is, unless he is diligent in the use of all the means by which he may arrive at that knowledge. Interest is excited and desire awakened, only in view of the truth; and to look and pray for a missionary spirit, while we are not employing the appropriate and only means of exciting it, is both unphilosophical and sinful. It was when Nehemiah and his companions went out by night "and viewed the walls of Jerusalem which were broken down," that their hearts were moved, and their purpose was formed to repair the desolation. It was when Paul entered Athens, and *"saw* the city wholly given to idolatry," that "his spirit was stirred in him." And when we have carefully surveyed the foreign field, when we have made ourselves familiar with the miseries, prospects, and wants of the heathen, then, and not till then, can we expect to feel deeply in their behalf. Till we have done this, our want of interest in missions, so far from being the fruit of the Spirit, and an indication, therefore, that we should remain at home, is the fruit of our own willful blindness, and an indication of our infitness for acceptable service either at home or abroad.

Even a decided *aversion* to a self-denying service, when it is first contemplated, is no proof that we are not required to engage in it. Moses and Jonah were unwilling, at first, to discharge the commission with which they were intrusted by the Lord of Hosts. But they were not, for this reason, excused. The former, meek and submissive as he was, held back until "the anger of the Lord was kindled against him;" and the latter, by his presumptuous disobedience, drew upon himself the severe judgments of the Almighty.

Again: that the church has failed in the discharge of her high responsibilities must be evident to every one who inspects for a moment the broad command of the Saviour; and yet, doubtless, she has acted according to her inclinations. Surely, in her case, the want of a desire to do her duty to the heathen cannot be construed into an expression of the mind of the Spirit of God. In Scotland alone there were, a few years ago, not less than one thousand educated ministers without charges, — many of them employed as farmers, and many of them as common parish schoolmasters, — waiting for the removal of the present incumbents, that they might succeed to their livings. Can it be possible that not a single one of this vast number of useless ministers should have gone to point the heathen to the way which leads to ever-lasting life and glory? And though one stirring appeal after another was made by the Scottish Missionary Society for laborers in the Lord's vineyard, yet not one of this class volunteered. Let no one, therefore, conclude, simply because he has not an ardent desire for the work, that the question is settled that it cannot be his duty to go. It may, or it may not be so. There is very great danger in making our feelings and our desires a test of our duty, especially in a service which requires much self-denial. This must be perfectly obvious to every one who is experimentally acquainted with the deceitful workings of the human heart. It is demonstrated by the history of the church ever since the days of the Apostles.

By far the most obvious reason of this failure in duty, on the part of Christians, is that they have approached the examination of the subject, if they examined it at all, with a strong bias in favor of *home*. Indeed this is notoriously the fact. Now if there has been actual error in this point heretofore, is there not at least great danger of error at present?

It is admitted, indeed, that no man ought ever to enter the foreign field, without an ardent desire for the work. But it is a desire springing from supreme love to the Saviour — burning zeal for the salvation of sinners, and an earnest wish to labor where there is the widest prospect of usefulness. Now it is plain that this desire — the only one necessary — is consequent upon a decided conviction of the judgment, after a thorough, impartial, and prayerful examination, that the wants of the foreign are more urgent than those of the domestic field, and the call from abroad louder than at home. But what *Christian,* in these circumstances, would not have this desire? It is nothing mysterious or uncommon — nothing but the feelings common to every pious heart, directed by a judgment under the influence of truth, and the Spirit of God, strongly drawn out toward the heathen by their wretched, helpless, perishing condition. This is the true, much talked of, but much mistaken, *missionary spirit*.

We contend, moreover, that a similar desire springing from the same course, and the result of an equally firm conviction of the judgment, that the *domestic* field most needs our labors, is equally important, before we determine to remain at home. Let every one, therefore, who intends to remain, examine and see if his determination springs from supreme love to the Redeemer, and an ardent wish to do the greatest possible amount of good. If so, well: but if not, let him examine anew the whole question of duty.

In order to a correct decision, therefore, a thorough examination is absolutely necessary: and previous to this, no bias either way ought generally to be expected. And indeed, if it do exist, it ought to be narrowly examined, lest it may have originated from some unworthy source — either from adventurous or romantic feelings, on the one hand; or a love of ease, distinction, and influence, on the other. And this close scrutiny manifestly becomes the more necessary, if the desire or inclination be to a course of conduct requiring little or no self-denial. Do we thus jealously analyze our motives: or do we not often think it unnecessary rigidly to investigate the subject, taking it for granted, that as a matter of course, we are to labor at home, unless we have some *special call* to go to the heathen? But why should we require all the evidence on one side? Who does not see, that, with these views and feelings, it is impossible to investigate and decide the question with entire impartiality; because, when the mind has once adopted an opinion, it requires far more evidence to change it, if erroneous, than to direct it to the truth, had the judgment been suspended. But why, we ask again, is it necessary to have a special call to India, or Burmah, or the Sandwich Islands, or any foreign station, rather than to the West of our own country? "The field is the world." The foreign and domestic are but departments of the same grand field. Then why this distinction? If the paramount claims of either portion of the field are to be presumed, should not the presumption be in favor of the foreign department? For, to say nothing of its greater extent and destitution, the fact that so many who would gladly preach among the Gentiles the unsearchable riches of Christ, are prevented by providential circumstances beyond their control, gives the foreign field a peculiar claim upon all who are at liberty to enter it.

It is true, the missionary is exposed to peculiar trials, and needs patience, and perseverance, and a spirit of self-denial. But our blessed Master has told us, that if a man have not these, he is not worthy to be his disciple at all. It is true, also, that there are missionary stations of very great difficulty. But all are not equally so. Such is their diversity, that persons of nearly every variety of disposition, and every grade of intellect, may find stations suited to their capacities. In some places are required men, with all the piety, learning, and talents of Martyn;[2] while in others, men whose acquirements little exceed those of a common Sabbath school teacher, united with ardent piety and untiring zeal, would be eminently useful. Therefore, no man who may be desirous to obey the last command of his ascending Saviour, by lending his aid to this glorious cause, need object that his abilities are too small. "It is not by might, nor by power, but by my Spirit, saith the Lord."

[2] Henry Martyn, 1781-1812, famous chaplain of the East India Company, missionary, and Bible translator. —Ed.

A want of talent for acquiring languages, is a serious difficulty with many. But it is a fact worthy of notice, that however great this difficulty may have appeared in prospect, no one has ever complained of incompetency, after being awhile in the field. Among the Moravian missionaries there must be many of quite ordinary talents; yet they all easily acquire the language of the people among whom they labor. So it is with foreigners who come into our own country; though a vast majority of them are men of very inferior intellect, yet they soon acquire a tolerable acquaintance with our language, which is said to be peculiarly difficult to foreigners. These facts clearly demonstrate, that the difficulty so much dreaded in prospect, will be very much diminished in the experiment. It is no hard thing to acquire the language of those with whom we have daily and hourly intercourse on the ordinary business and interesting incidents of real life. And if men of the world encounter such difficulties when impelled by motives of worldly convenience or profit, shall Christians be appalled by them, when called to execute the Saviour's commission, and to save the souls of men from eternal death? Besides, many of the languages which our missionaries are required to learn, are exceedingly simple and easily acquired, as that of the Hawaiian Islands, and those spoken by the native tribes of Africa and our own country; and the facilities for learning these and other languages, are constantly increasing.

Some, however, throw this difficulty into a different form. They object to go abroad, because they would thereby require the funds which ought to support abler men. This would indeed be a real difficulty, were there a sufficient number of men better qualified for the work; or were the church's resources limited, and now nearly exhausted. But this is not — never will be the case. Should there ever be a temporary deficiency, let it be told the churches, that on them rests the responsibility of refusing to send men, who desire to go forth and join the few scattered soldiers of the Prince of life and glory, now grappling with the powers of darkness, and endeavoring to rescue from their grasp the souls of dying heathens; and they will rise in the majesty of the true missionary spirit, and pour of their substance into the treasury of the Lord, and dismiss with their benediction every one who is willing to go bearing the wide commission of the gospel,

"Signed by God's own signature."

We are not, then, to expect any extraordinary interposition of the Spirit of God, telling us, as by an audible voice, what duty is — we are not to wait for a strong desire for the work of missions to be implanted in our minds, before we think it worth while to investigate the claims of the heathen — we are not to expect any peculiar call, or possess any extraordinary qualifications, before we can determine to devote our lives to the work of foreign missions. Let each one, then, divested of all these feelings and expectations, having thoroughly investigated the subject, and remembering that "the field is the world," permit his judgment — feelings and taste and preference all aside for the present — calmly to decide what portion of this field opens the widest prospect of usefulness; or rather, where is the most urgent demand for his labors; and then determine to go there, if circumstances will at all permit. Thus may this important question, freed of all its embarrassing accompaniments, be reduced to a single point; and that too, in most cases, probably not very difficult of solution.

To those whose circumstances would permit, and who profess a willingness to go where duty calls, but object that the field is wide enough at home, and the prospect of superior usefulness abroad at least doubtful, — it might be answered, that since the way of salvation may be known to all, and mercy is within the reach of all in this country, so as to render them altogether inexcusable, it is extremely doubtful, whether — expediency aside — it is consistent with the duty imposed by our unconditional commission, for us to remain and urge upon our countrymen those offers, for which they manifest entire disregard, or obstinately refuse, while the hundreds of millions of heathen are perishing for *lack of vision,* to whom the offers of salvation have never been made. While this is the case, is it for us to sit down and coldly calculate whether we might not, probably, be the means of saving some souls at home; or does not the command of Christ bind us to go, if we can? This view receives additional sanction from the conduct of the Apostles. They were indeed required to *begin* at Jerusalem, but by the very terms of their commission they were forbidden to remain there, and when they were inclined to linger, a storm of persecution scattered them, and they then "went every where preaching the Word." In like manner Paul commenced his missionary labors among his own countrymen, but he was not permitted to tarry there till all were supplied with the gospel. But as he was pursuing his second missionary tour, in company with Timothy, "they were forbidden of the Holy Ghost to preach the Word in Asia," and when they would have turned homeward, "the Spirit suffered them not." They were instructed to pass over into Europe, and preach the gospel in Macedonia. Is not our duty the same? Many of our own countrymen, it is true, will perish; but, it is because they will not take the trouble to hear; or if they hear, they disregard the voice of mercy. The heathen must perish; but it is because they never heard the voice of mercy. Which of them should most awaken our sympathies, and call forth our efforts? Judge ye. Suppose, as a test of your views, you had been born and brought up among the idolatrous, degraded, and perishing population of the dark continent of Asia or Africa; but by some wonderful change of circumstances you had been brought to a knowledge of Jesus. With your present views, feelings and sympathies, could you ever have dreamed of coming to America to labor for Christ? And now is not your duty to preach to the heathen just as imperative as though this had been literally the case? A voyage of a few months will place you on those same benighted shores, and amidst that same degraded, dying population.

But to the objection stated above, it might be answered further, that, granting for a moment all it asks, that the need of laborers at home is as great as abroad, (and it surely is not greater; for what destitution can be greater than that which is total?) — then the utmost that can be fairly inferred is, that an equal number should be distributed to both fields. Now, until this be the case, on your own principles you are bound to go. You contend that the need at home is as great as abroad, and therefore one-half ought conscientiously to remain. It may be answered that the destitution abroad is at least as great as at home, and therefore one-half ought conscientiously to go. And this obligation obviously becomes the more pressing, since very far from the proportion of one-half usually go. Now it manifestly falls upon those whose circumstances will permit, and who profess a willingness to go wherever duty calls, to furnish this quota; since there are enough and, as yet, more than enough, to supply the other proportion, whose physical qualifications and domestic relations will compel them to remain. They ought, therefore, to feel themselves peculiarly called upon to examine their duty in this matter.

It is objected, however, that a man, by remaining at home, may awaken a missionary spirit in the churches, and may raise up several missionaries, who will do more good then he alone could have done, by going himself to the heathen. But how does any one know that he is to do this? The probability is against him, should it so happen, which is surely possible, that he has mistaken his duty. But granting this, and suppose every one of them to reason in the same manner, which they might do with equal justice, when would the heathen be converted? We must remember that it is the present generation alone with whom we have to do. The question is, Shall *they* have the gospel? Shall *they* be told of Jesus? Now it is manifest that such a system of means as that just mentioned, would, to say the least, suffer most of the present generation to perish without an effort for their rescue. This manifestly is not the spirit of the gospel. This is not — cannot be the true method of proceeding.

One grand end of the organization of the church is, that it may distribute to every kindred, and tongue, and people, and nation under the whole heavens, the bread of eternal life. Now suppose there was a famine in all Asia, and we wished to supply them with the means of sustaining natural life; should we send off immediately all we could for seed, and let them raise it for themselves, when in a fertile soil it would multiply fifty fold; or should we suffer many of them to starve, while we attempted to raise, in our limited territory, what we could with difficulty transport to them, but which would still be insufficient for their sustenance? So, to continue the figure, let us send seed to the heathen *immediately;* though it be but a handful now, it will soon increase, and let them raise, in their own soil, the bread of eternal life.

It is true, indeed, that the spirit of missions must be sustained at home. But this will be done by those who are compelled to remain, and it will be done much more *effectually* by those who go themselves. The pastor speaks only to a single congregation; the missionary, from the eminence of his missionary field, is heard throughout Christendom, and his words receive peculiar force from his own example of self-denial. The history of missions, we think, has clearly proved that the reflex influence of those who go to the foreign field, in awakening a missionary spirit, is ordinarily greater than the direct influence of the pastor at home. And what is the spirit of missions, but the spirit of Christ? Every increase of the one is an equal increase of the other. So far then from doing less for the cause of Christ at home, we may do more than by remaining; and this, so far from robbing the churches, awakens their zeal, elevates their piety, and multiplies ministers both for home and abroad.

Now, taking this in connection with the fact, that so large a proportion are absolutely prohibited by circumstances from going; and with our Savior's unconditional commission in our hand, and the number, condition, and destiny of the heathen before us, — let us, who are untrammeled by circumstances, feel that we are particularly called; and let us ponder it well, before we dismiss it with a negative.

There has been — *there is* guilt somewhere. Let *us* see to it, that it rest not on our heads. And let us do so immediately. We stop not now to point out the advantages — the immense advantages of an early decision, both as it regards our own enjoyment, and our preparation for the field of our future labors. We would urge it as a present, imperious duty; because delay, longer than is necessary to investigate the merits of the case, is not only useless, but positively unfriendly to the impartial decision of the question. It lulls the voice of conscience, and early impressions of duty are thus gradually erased.

Motives, when not yielded to, it is well known, lose their force; the mind only becomes more involved, and the judgment more liable to be warped by circumstances; and the Spirit of God may be pro-

voked, by simple delay, to withdraw his influences, and leave us to follow our own inclinations. Of this result, there are many mournful examples. There are many, who, if they would speak, would tell us,
that so far from gaining light, and removing difficulties by delay,
they are only involved in greater darkness, and are now further from a
decision than they were one year ago.

And as you value, therefore, the correct decision of this momentous
question, trifle not with the dictates of conscience and the Spirit of God.
Yield immediately to rational motives; and in proportion to their weight,
let them draw you just so much nearer to your decision. Carry with
you constantly, in devotion, in studying the word of God, in reading
missionary and domestic intelligence, a feeling that a most important
duty remains undischarged, until you have decided this question. And
let that decision be made as soon as practicable, subject of course
to revision, and even reversal, if circumstances seem to require it.

And never forget what interests are involved in your decision. It
involves your own comfort and peace of mind, for where else can you
expect to escape the lashing of conscience, when you discover your
mistake, as you one day must, especially if it has proceeded from care-
lessness on your part: where else than in that path, can you expect
that joy which sweetens every toil, flowing from the delightful consciousness of being in the discharge of duty: and above all, where
else can you expect the reward of an hundred fold in the present life
— the sustaining grace, and the approving smile of your Father in
Heaven? Your usefulness, and therefore the interests of Christ's kingdom, are involved. For where else can you expect to accomplish so
much for him and for your fellow men, as in that sphere for which
God has fitted and designed you? As, therefore, you value the testimony of a good conscience, and the approbation of God; as you love
the cause and kingdom of your Savior, and the souls for whom he died,
examine this question promptly, carefully, candidly, in the spirit and
with the prayer of the great Apostle, "Lord, what wilt thou have me
to do?"

Selection 12

ON DECIDING EARLY TO BECOME A MISSIONARY TO THE HEATHEN[1]

The object of this Tract is, to assign reasons in favor of the following proposition, viz.: *That every student, looking forward to the sacred ministry, should decide* EARLY, *in view of existing circumstances, whether duty requires him to become a missionary to the heathen.*

I have my mind upon a current maxim, which has deprived the heathen world, I fear, of many excellent missionaries. The maxim is this — "That it is better to delay deciding on our personal duty to the heathen, till near the close of our studies preparatory to the ministry." The reasons for such a delay are plausible. The student will be older — his judgment more matured — his mind better informed — the whole case more completely before him. My appeal, however, is to facts. For many years I have watched the operation of this maxim, and I am sure that its influence is, to prevent a thorough and impartial examination. The procrastination which it requires, becomes a habit, and is usually too long persisted in. The "more convenient season" for investigation, is generally allowed to pass by. Engagements are formed, rendering the case more complicated; solicitations and inducements to remain at home multiply; the natural love of one's own country grows stronger and stronger; the early predilection for the missionary life, if there had been one, wears away; the cries of the heathen, and their distress, move with less and less power; and the man remains at home: — not as the result of any vigorous exercise of the understanding upon the question of duty, but because he decided

[1] First published, Boston: The Board, 1834; republished as Missionary Tract No. 7, Boston: The Board, 1851.

to postpone consideration upon it till he was about to launch into the world, and then surrendered himself *passively* to the control of circumstances.

This is not the way to learn our duty on the momentous question, *Where is the field and the work, to which the Holy Ghost hath called me?* And what inquiry is there, which can be more important than this to our growth in grace, and to our happiness and usefulness in future life? And what more directly connected with the sentence to be passed upon us, at the great day, as the stewards of Christ? Next to the relation which we sustain to the Lord Jesus, there is nothing we are more interested to know, as his ministers, than where he would have us spend our lives; where the field is, which he commands us to cultivate; and where the Holy Ghost, the Comforter, will complacently regard our residence, and delight to bless our exertions and alleviate our trials. Is there not a foundation for solicitude on this point? Can it be a matter of perfect indifference to the Head of the church, *where* we preach, provided only we are diligent, and preach the truth? It was not so in respect to the Apostles;* nor is it so now. Mistakes on this subject, when committed needlessly, much more when committed because we *will* not consider, must have a very serious bearing upon us as ministers of the gospel.

The proposition is, that we should begin to look *early* at this question, with reference to the claims of the heathen world upon us, and that we should decide it *early,* in view of existing circumstances. An unconditional decision is not desired. Such an one is indeed forbidden by the word of God, in reference to *all* our future measures. We must say, "If the Lord will, we shall live, and do this or that." The decision should be in view of things as they now appear, and with an understanding that the grounds of it shall be occasionally revised — certainly as often as there is a manifest change in our circumstances. And is it not true, that however late the decision is made, it must still be conditional?

It is not necessary that the resolution to spend life among the heathen should be unconditional, in order to insure the advantages to be mentioned in the sequel, as resulting from its being made early. It is formed with reference to the Lord's will. As that will is now indicated, the determination is unreserved and decisive. No sooner is it formed, than a mission to the heathen world stands up before the mind as the great, paramount duty of life. The command to "preach the gospel to every creature," comes to us with a distinct specification of the unevangelized world as our field; and we rest in this decision, till

---

* Acts xiii. 2; xvi. 10.

unanticipated, unsought-for events change the grounds of our decision, and call for reconsideration, and perhaps a reversal.

Some may ask, 'Why decide early upon the claims of the heathen world, and not also decide early upon the relative claims of the different parts of our own country?' And truly I see no objection to deciding upon them, too, whenever the duty can be made clear. This latter question, however, is not one of so easy solution at an early period of our preparatory studies, as the other. The relative necessities, and of course the claims, of some parts of our country, are rapidly changing; and there is not such a broad distinction existing between any of them, as is found on comparing our own country with the heathen world. Moreover, the difference between parochial life in our northern and middle States, and that of a missionary in our western settlements, is not of so serious a nature, as that which distinguishes a foreign missionary, and his exposures and hardships, may not be greater than those of a missionary in our new settlements; and, in many instances, there may be less of travel, and more of the conveniences of life. But the sorest trials of a missionary, whether he be foreign or domestic, are those which chiefly concern the spirit; and this is pre-eminently true of him, whose dwelling and labors are in the midst of a heathen people. He is peculiarly insulated from the religious world — from society congenial to a man who has been nurtured in a civilized community — from that sympathetic, companionable intercourse, which ministers in this country may soon find almost every where. And even when God blesses the labors of a foreign missionary, and multiplies converts among the heathen around him, though this must be a source of unspeakable joy, those converts do not rise so high on the scale of intelligence, but that they are still far below him in almost all that constitutes a foundation for free and familiar intercourse between mind and mind. They are children — emphatically babes in Christ.

The limits of this article do not allow me to illustrate the numerous other points of difference. Some of them are sufficiently obvious. It is a serious matter to leave one's friends and country for life, and spend that life amid the darkness and pollution of heathenism. The question whether we shall remove far to the west, and preach the gospel there, and raise up families there, *where the wave of civilization will inevitably overtake us in a few years,* is nothing, in comparison with the other; — much less is that, whether we shall build up waste places surrounded by the institutions and privileges of our older States.

The way is now prepared for stating some of the principal reasons in favor of an early decision of the question, whether we ought to become missionaries to the heathen.

1. *In college, and sometimes in the academy, the student may en-joy nearly or quite all the helps in forming a decision, that he will find in the theological seminary.* With a little pains he may have access to all the important books, and to intelligent and discreet advisers, and may gain all the essential information respecting the moral condition of the world. There is not a principle, and there is scarcely a fact bearing on the case, of which he may not obtain as full possession before, as after he enters the theological seminary. What need, then, of delay? Is the student competent to decide the momentous question, whether he ought to be a minister of Christ, and yet, with the data all before him, can he not determine whether it be lawful for him to de-vote himself to the service of Christ in heathen lands?

Indeed, I believe the student may not only ascertain his personal duty to the heathen at an early period of his education, but that he may then ascertain it with comparative ease, — being, in some respects, more favorably situated for deciding correctly, than at the more advanced periods. The subject is really very simple; and it is most apt to appear so to the student while his position is remote from the world. He, too, is then more entirely uncommitted; and his views of the comparative claims of the heathen world upon himself, will be more likely to ac-cord with what is the actual fact, than in the later stages. Hence the reason why you find a greater proportion of pious students beginning to prepare for the ministry with some special reference to a mission in heathen lands, than you see entering the field of foreign missions.

2. *An early decision is desirable in reference to its bearing on the mind and conscience of the student.* Whether he desires to make ad-vances in learning, or grace, he should aim to preserve a tranquil mind. He should have as few unsettled and perplexing questions of duty as possible. He should endeavor always to preserve peace of conscience, that he may have joy in the Holy Ghost. When cases of conscience arise and demand a settlement, he should endeavor to settle them thoroughly and speedily. He must either do this, or else do violence to his moral nature; and if the case be one of importance and of fre-quent recurrence, he must either determine it, or submit to the alter-native of suffering much inquietude, and of weakening his conscience, if not all his mental powers. Now it is true of some institutions of learning, with which I am acquainted, that duty to the heathen early becomes in them a serious question of conscience. In several theologi-cal seminaries, it is among the first and most solemn inquiries, of a prospective nature, excited in the minds of students newly entered. And as the cause of missions advances, the members of all our semi-naries will find it more and more difficult to avoid coming to a speedy

decision; and their interest, as well as duty, in such cases, will obviously be to make up their minds with as little delay as possible. The only way in which they will be able to avoid meeting the subject, will be to place themselves in the attitude of resistance to the light, and to be less active in promoting the cause of Christ than they otherwise might be — and thus greatly retard their growth in grace, and their preparation for usefulness. The wisest course for them will be that described in the proposition I am endeavoring to establish. Let the inquiry come up early in the seminary, if it has not been settled before; or, what is better still, let it come up in the college; let it be met with a cheerful determination to examine into its merits; let the only question be, "Where will the Lord have me go, when my preparations for the ministry are completed?" and let the decision be formed in view of the existing indications of Providence. Whenever these indications materially change, or when the mind is led to regard them in new lights, then let the student inquire how his relations to the heathen world are affected by the change. Thus the mind will be preserved from useless and worse than useless agitation, and will always be cheerfully advancing with a definite object in view.

3. *A student, who decides early to devote himself to the cause of foreign missions, will be more useful to that cause during his studies preparatory to the ministry, than he otherwise would be.* Indeed, should he, after a conscientious examination of the subject, decide that it is his duty to go on a domestic mission, or to settle near his paternal home, I should expect him to be more active and efficient in the cause of foreign missions, than while he holds his mind in suspense. What I wish to see is, an early investigation and decision — no halting between two opinions — no shrinking from this great question of duty. But, if a man is led by his views of duty heartily to consecrate himself to the work of evangelizing the heathen, such a man begins immediately to think, with a special interest, how he may increase the number of missionaries, and the means of sending them forth, and how the deep intellectual and moral gloom resting upon the heathen world may be dispelled. There is no estimating how desirable it is that every college and seminary in the land have such men among its students. What may not a man devoted to missions do in the seven or eight years of his preparatory studies? The greater part of the influence, which Samuel J. Mills exerted directly upon foreign missions, and which has given him an imperishable name in our churches, he exerted while in the college and seminary. He decided on his duty to the heathen before entering college — imparted the noble design, which the Spirit of God had implanted in his own bosom, to the kindred minds of Hall and

Richards, whose dust now rests beneath the sods of India — and, after seeking divine direction many times on the banks of the Hoosack, formed a society, in which the members pledged themselves to effect, in their own persons, a mission among the heathen. Here was the germ of our foreign missions, and it was the fruit of an early decision. Had Mills, and Hall, and Richards, and Fisk, and others who might be named, deferred all consideration of the subject till they were on the point of entering the ministry, what a loss would the cause have sustained! And what good will be prevented, if the maxim, controverted in this Tract, becomes a common law of duty to our pious students! Every man has a circle of friends of greater or less extent, and an early decision to be a missionary gives him time and power to exert a salutary influence upon them. If he is a man of the right character and spirit, his influence will increase from year to year, and he may often effect as much for the cause, during the last two years of his residence in his own country, as in the first three or four of his labors among the heathen. Where we especially need the influence of such men, however, is in our public institutions of learning. Men in these institutions, who are not themselves decided to be missionaries, will rarely make vigorous attempts to persuade others to devote themselves to a foreign mission; and if they do make an effort, in public addresses to their fellow-students, while they are themselves generally supposed not to have given the subject a thorough investigation in regard to their own duty, (as I have sometimes known to be the case,) the effect is any thing but that which they aim to produce. But a man, who has given himself to this work, and is sincerely devoted, heartily interested, discreetly zealous, and properly qualified, may almost certainly increase the number of missionaries. And those, to whose direction missions among the heathen are especially committed, need such co-workers in all our colleges and religious seminaries.

4. *An early decision in favor of becoming a missionary to the heathen, makes a man more courageous and cheerful when in the field of missions.* I believe this is the general experience of those missionaries, who came to their decision early, of whom the number is considerable. By long anticipation, they had become in a manner familiarized with the missionary life before they entered upon it. Its peculiar trials were in some good degree understood, and the mind and heart acquires a sort of assimilation to the missionary work. This lightened the shock, which must always be felt on transferring our residence from a civilized and Christian land to one that is heathen and barbarous. The disgusting manners of the people, their sottish ignorance, their deep degradation, and their horrid rites, had been contemplated for years, and again and

again had the work been chosen with these things all in view. And when, after long and laborious toil, the obstinacy of the heathen still seemed unbroken, and success delayed, causing the spirits to flag, and faith sometimes to tremble; the mind was not invaded and harassed by misgivings on the subject of duty, as might have been the case had not the subject, for a course of years before entering the heathen world, often been carried to the throne of grace, and considered in all its bearings in the light of God's word. These seasons are recollected in days of adversity, and are as anchors to the soul. "It looks dark," the missionary says to himself, "but *here* is the field of my duty. I am where I ought to be, and God will not forsake me." He had long before taken time to lay a broad and deep foundation, and his superstructure stands. He went to the heathen from no sudden impulse of passion, but from a long resolved conviction of duty, to which the feelings of his heart and the habits of his mind gradually came into sweet subserviency. Till that conviction is destroyed, he will find delight in his work, and, on the whole, will be contented and happy. To have this conviction of duty well rooted in the mind, when the missionary is in the midst of disheartening trials with few outward supports, is of itself a sufficient reason for beginning early to look seriously at the subject, and, indeed, for looking at it with reference to a speedy decision; — for, whoever commences an inquiry with a determination to hold his mind in suspense whatever may be the merits of the case, will certainly be superficial in his examination.

5. *An early consecration to the missionary work will render a man more efficient and useful as a missionary.* It will do this for the reasons mentioned under the preceding head; and also, by the attainments it will lead him to make with particular reference to a mission, while acquiring his education, and by the effect it will be likely to exert on his intellectual and moral character. Whatever increases a man's courage and cheerfulness in the performance of the missionary work, increases his usefulness. The fact of having come to an early decision, and of having had the work long before the mind, may sometimes be the very thing which God employs to sustain a missionary under sharp adversity, and prevent his sinking in despondency and leaving the field. Besides, he who has had the missionary life in view through nearly the whole course of his education, will necessarily acquire a great number of principles and facts and considerations, which would probably be overlooked by scholars having in view only the common circumstances and duties of pastoral life, and which, in thousands of instances, will be of use to him. These peculiar acquisitions are such as may be made, and ought to be made, without neglecting any of the studies required in the collegiate and

theological course. So far as I have yet learned, all those studies are as important for the missionary, as they are for the minister at home; and there is this additional reason why the candidate for a mission should give them thorough attention, that it is almost certain he will have little opportunity to revise them after he has entered the field of his labors.

In addition to the peculiar acquisitions just now mentioned — which will bear some proportion to the length of time between the forming of the decision and the departure on a mission — there will be an important influence exerted upon all the other acquisitions, with direct reference to the missionary work. The degree of this influence must of course vary in different men. Where there is that intense interest in the cause of missions, which is desirable in all who aspire to a mission among the heathen, the mind will make all its acquisitions under the influence of this ruling passion. It is easy to find illustrations of this principle. The student who has given his soul to medicine, or the law, digests and secretes his learning (so to speak) according to the laws of the profession he has taken. The mere divine makes every thing bear upon natural and revealed religion. He who, like Payson, has consecrated every faculty to the high endeavor of drawing sinners to Christ, converts every thing into argument to flee from the wrath to come. So he, who has devoted himself to the enterprise of imparting the knowledge and blessings of the gospel to the heathen world, makes his acquisitions, and associates and stores them in the mind, with reference to that object. Ideas of all sorts, as they enter his mind, are marshalled and trained for the spiritual and holy wars of foreign conquest. I cannot conceive of a more desirable influence; nor can I help regretting that it cannot *always* be felt through the whole course of that man's education, who is destined to become a missionary in pagan lands.

I shall not do justice to this subject, unless I mention the influence, which an early decision to be a missionary may be expected to have upon the *heart*. Let it be remembered, that I am not speaking of a devotion to the cause in which the affections of the heart are imperfectly enlisted; but of a devotion in which they are all active. The decision, which is the ground of all my illustrations, is formed no less by the heart than by the judgment. The whole soul chooses, and chooses cordially and joyfully. I wish not to speak of this particular exercise of Christian duty so as to excite spiritual pride in those, who have determined to be missionaries. Let such as have been led to resolve on proclaiming their Savior's love to nations that never heard the glad tidings, give Him the glory, and wonder that *they* should be sent on an errand, which angels from heaven would rejoice to perform. It is obvious, however, that next to the determination which gave the soul to God, the decision to devote one's life to preaching the gospel to the heathen, must be the most important of those voluntary acts, which the grace of God employs to set the soul at liberty from the enchantments of the world. At God's command, the man resolves, like Abraham, to go out from his own country, probably without knowing where, and to become a stranger and pilgrim on the earth. He chooses a course of living for his whole earthly existence, which, if he has just notions of it, can appear desirable and tolerable only as the soul is animated and sustained by the faith that "overcometh the world." Such a choice, sincerely and understandingly made, must exert a great influence on the heart; for the influence of it must reach every earthly thing, and tend strongly to shut the world out from the affections, and to open the soul to the afflations of the Spirit. From the moment, too, in which a man forms this decision, he realizes, more affectingly than perhaps he otherwise could do, the relations he sustains as a disciple of Christ, to the world of souls in pagan darkness. They are brought nearer, and seem more like neighbors and kinsmen. The motives, which act on his benevolent regards, are increased prodigiously in magnitude and power. Numbers, extension, variety, all lay siege to his heart with mighty force. Six hundred millions of men, living in a moral gloom as dark as midnight; and this vast multitude spread over three-fourths of the world — found in all climes — exhibiting every painful variety of human condition and character — going from this state of probation at the rate of a million and a half a month, and in thirty years all gone! What affecting, what overwhelming objects of contemplation to any pious man; but peculiarly so to him, who has chosen his earthly home among those very millions. Let the decision, then, be formed early, that such contemplations may exert their influence on the heart for a longer time, rousing its sensibilities into habitual activity, and imparting comprehensiveness and efficiency to its desires. This will be a qualification of a high order for a mission to the unevangelized world.

6. *An early decision to be a missionary, will be no disadvantage to a man, who is providentially preverted from becoming one.* It will rather be an advantage. Some of the most devoted ministers in our churches, once had a foreign mission in view for a considerable period of time. They did not go, because unforseen and unavoidable occurrences prevented, making it necessary for them to remain in their own country. They lost no character by so doing, because it was manifestly their duty to relinquish their purpose. Neither did the "God of all grace" forsake them. They were enabled to carry their missionary fervor into their parishes. They remembered the heathen themselves, and suffered not their people to forget them. The acquisitions they had made in missionary history, while looking forward to a mission, and the habits they then acquired of reading, remembering, and communicating mis-

sionary intelligence, laid a foundation for their usefulness as pastors in a most important, but much neglected, department of ministerial duty. Their monthly concerts were not suffered to become lifeless and unedifying. Those occasions were embraced for opening *the volume of God's providence,* which is full of matter. At any rate, the habits acquired, and the attainments commonly made, by persons who, for several years, have a mission constantly in view, must be exceedingly favorable to the performance of this and other kindred duties of a parish minister.

Nor will it be any disadvantage to the parish minister to have cherished for years a spirit of self-denying enterprise, with reference to a mission in remote and barbarous countries. He will be none the less faithful as a preacher; none the less active and enterprising as a pastor; none the less alive to the calls of Christian charity; none the less "a workman that needeth not to be ashamed, rightly dividing" to every one, and to every object of pastoral duty, "the word of truth."

7. *An early and serious consideration of this subject, with a view to a speedy decision, either that it is or is not our duty to become missionaries, with an occasional reconsideration of the subject, is the most likely way of avoiding mistakes in regard to our proper sphere of labor.* I repeat what I have already said, that it is of the greatest importance to us to be in that field, in which God would have us be. And there will be many seasons, in the course of our lives, when it will support us exceedingly to be in possession of ample and clear evidence, that such is the fact. How, then, shall we avoid mistakes in the selection of this field, and how shall we acquire this evidence? Shall we do it, by delaying all serious thought on the subject, till we have so little time left us, and so many applications from different quarters, as to create a feverish anxiety in the mind? Shall we do it, when, immediately after our decision is made, we are under the necessity of *committing* ourselves, either by accepting or refusing an appointment from some church or benevolent society? And can we do it, if we postpone all thorough investigation till the close of our preparatory studies, and then, at the last, yield without much reflection, to the force of any current that happens to strike us? Certain it is, that not so many have gone to the heathen, as ought to have gone, and therefore *some* must have mistaken the field of their duty! How desirable that *they* had examined more thoroughly, and reflected more profoundly! Had they pursued the course recommended in this article, they could scarcely have fallen into such an error. And whoever comes to the question early, with a sincere desire to know and do his duty, and with fervent prayer for divine guidance; and decides early, with an humble reference to the divine will; and occasionally reconsiders the grounds of his decision; and habitually cherishes a

benevolent and obedient spirit — will be likely to understand where the Head of the church requires him to exercise his ministry.

In concluding this article, I ask, Whether there are not many, well qualified to be missionaries, who have more fear lest they should go without being sent, than they have lest they shall stay at home when they are commanded to go? To them I would put the question, Whether the greatest danger is not the other way? Does not the tide of feeling, in the great body of our pious students, set against the life of a foreign missionary? Far be it from me to intimate, that there is no danger of a man's mistaking the field of his duty when he decides to become a missionary. Such mistakes have been committed, and have had a most unhappy influence; and the inquiry should be approached with a godly jealousy of our motives, and with humble prayer for the illuminations of the Spirit. But I must insist that, taking into view the whole body of young men preparing for the ministry, the paramount danger is, that a man will give undue force to the reasons in favor of spending his life in his own country.

And now, what is it that I ask? Not that a man should become a foreign missionary; not that he should decide in favor of becoming one; but that he should look the question of his duty in the face, and look at it early in his education, and look at it with the determination to discover his duty if possible, and to do his duty. Is there any danger in this course? And is there any man, so destitute of *moral* courage and of the spirit of obedience to Christ, that he shrinks from this inquiry? Are you afraid that you shall be told to proclaim to the heathen the unsearchable riches of Christ? Consider well what you do. You have consecrated yourself to the Lord Jesus, and have solemnly engaged to do his will, and you will gain nothing by a neglect of your duty. No path will be so good for you as that — wherever it may lead — which your Divine Master shall prescribe. Nowhere else will you be so respectable, and happy, and useful; nowhere else will you find so much joy in God — a hope so full of immortality. Stray from that path, and you are on forbidden ground. You may avoid the wilderness and many a rugged steep, but must not expect God to accompany you, unless it be with the rod of rebuke.

You need have no fear whatever of this question. If it shall be your duty to leave your country and the charms of cultivated and Christian society, and you resolve to do so, you will have grace imparted to make the sacrifice with cheerfulness. He who commands you to go, engages to go with you; and he will go with you, and will give you "manifold more in this present time, and in the world to come life everlasting."

Should friends object to a man's devoting himself to a foreign mission, let him bring all their objections to the light of God's word, and if they will not bear that light, he must not allow them to have any weight in determining the merits of the case; but if they will bear the light, they are among the facts which he is seriously to consider.

The probability or improbability that the churches will furnish the requisite means of sending him forth, need not come into the inquiry. I am not aware that any man, well qualified for missionary service, has ever yet been rejected because there were not the pecuniary means for supporting him among the heathen. I trust this never will be necessary. The disposition of the churches to make pecuniary contributions to the missionary cause, will generally be greater or less, very much in proportion to the number of suitable men, who are pressing into the field.

When a decision is formed to become a missionary, the proper course to pursue in relation to it is, neither to take pains to conceal it, nor to make it known. If a man is under the guidance of humble benevolence, with his selfish desires subdued by love to Christ and to souls redeemed by the blood of Christ, he will be in little danger of ostentation, and need not fear the consequences of having it known, that he is aspiring to the missionary office, even should he afterwards find that his duty requires him to remain at home. A sincere regard for duty, and a resolute pursuit of it, are far less apt to be injurious to a man's usefulness, than is a timorous shrinking from responsibility, when duty calls.

Selection 13

MISSIONARY LIFE ILLUSTRATED[1]

I propose to illustrate the Missionary Life in some of its more important relations, as that life has fallen under my personal observation. Of course on such a topic I must draw my facts from the experience of that Board of Missions, with which I have been officially connected. There will be an advantage in presenting this particular aspect of the missionary life; and should secretaries of other societies do the same with theirs, it would doubtless be found, that there is no great diversity in its general aspects.

It is a fundamental principle, that the missionary goes on his mission in the discharge of his own personal duty; not as a servant of the churches, and not as a servant of the missionary society. The churches and the missionary society are his helpers, to carry out his own benevolent purpose. The missionary is indebted to the churches just as the churches are indebted to him; and he does their work in the same sense in which they do his by supporting him. This is the view that best comports with the prosecution of missions on an extended scale.

Moreover, the missionary and the pastor both derive their authority from the same commission. Both are alike "called of God" to the ministry of the gospel. The notion that "evangelists," in the Scripture sense of that term, were restricted, as an order of ministers, to the apostolic age, and that pastors are now the only Scriptural ministry, — which bears too great a resemblance to the old Popish notion, that ministers may not be ordained *sine titulo,* — though countenanced by some of the Puritan Fathers, was disowned by the Presbyterians in 1764, and is not in keeping with the command of our Lord, as it is now understood, to preach the gospel to every creature. If there be any class

[1] *Foreign Missions: Their Relations and Claims,* Ch. IX, pp. 145-168; 1869.

197

of gospel ministers, which is clearly recognized and enjoined in the New Testament, to endure until the world is converted, it is Christ's ambassadors to the benighted and the lost; it is those who devote their lives to the extension of his kingdom.

Should any one affirm, in opposition to this view, that we find directions in St. Paul's Epistles only for the office of presbyters, then what are the Epistles to Timothy and Titus?[2]

I now contemplate the missionary in some of his more important personal relations.

1. In his relations as a *son* and a *brother*. It is not uncommon for parents to make objections, at first, to the going of a son or daughter on a foreign mission. Often this is the result of mere natural instinct; as in the mother of Samuel J. Mills, though she had dedicated him from his birth to the work of missions, and when it is so, as in her case, the objection soon yields to reflection. Sometimes it is the result of ignorance concerning missions, or of a lack of pious reflection, or of deficient self-consecration. In such cases it is not common, I believe, for parents to yield, until they clearly see that the mind of their son or daughter is made up on conscientious grounds. Supposing the parent to be in the wrong, there is the more call for calm persistence in the child, because such a state of mind must be injurious to the parent, and because the parent will be almost sure to yield at last (if a true disciple), and to find the sacrifice conducive to his growth in grace and religious enjoyment.

---

[2] See Appendix V, "Preaching and Teaching."—Looking from the author's stand-point, it seems strange that the fathers of Congregationalism should have taken the limited view some of them did of the office and duties of the gospel ministry, and of the power and duty of the churches to provide a competent ministry for planting churches outside of Christendom, and supplying those churches with a competent pastorate. To instance only the excellent Dr. Owen, in his *Discourses of Spiritual Gifts.* [*Works,* iv. p. 275.] After declaring it to be the principal work of an evangelist, "to go up and down from one place and nation unto another, to preach the gospel unto the Jews and Gentiles as yet unconverted," he asks: "Who shall now empower any one hereunto? What church, what persons, have received authority to ordain any one to be such an evangelist? It cannot be proved," he adds, "that any church or person has power or authority to ordain a person into this office!" That the eminent divine was writing with no reference to the claims and exigencies of the heathen world of his times, with the restricted idea of the church as a self-preserving, self-governing, and not a self-propagating body, and mainly with his eye on hierarchal assumptions so rampant in those times, is obvious from the general tenor of his reasoning. Had he lived in our day, he would on no account have shut up the preaching ministry of the church to the pastoral office, nor to lands already Christianized. Nor will the evangelical churches and ministry of any denomination, in these days, allow themselves to be restricted in their labors for the kingdom of their blessed Lord and Saviour. [Appendix V not included here. —Ed.]

I recollect but one instance, and that many years since, in which a mother regarded the mission contemplated by her two sons with such nervous terror, as to threaten the overthrow of her reason. Both of the sons were members of the Andover Seminary, and the case was so marked, that I advised them, as a filial duty, to relinquish the idea of going abroad, and they are now highly useful pastors. Our Saviour's declaration, Mark vii. 11,[3] is obviously applicable to cases of this sort; as also, when the comfortable support of parents requires the young minister to remain near them. There is a tradition of Dr. Milné,[4] the celebrated associate of Dr. Morrison, in China, which probably has some foundation in fact; that before decidedly entering in his preparation for a foreign mission, he labored to secure a cottage, a cow, and a few other needful things for circumstances. In so doing, he complied with the spirit of our Lord's injunction. I recollect one instance, and but one, of a missionary actually coming home, which he did with the approval of his society, to look after an impoverished and dependent mother. Very few cases have been within my knowledge, however, where parents have actually suffered for want of support, as a consequence of giving up their children to the gospel ministry among the heathen. Questions of this sort have more frequently had weight when the theological student was deciding upon his duty prospectively, and generally because of younger brothers or sisters requiring protection and aid. It is my belief, that the claims of kindred have exerted very little more legitimate influence in relation to foreign missions, than they have when determining where to settle in pastoral life at home.

2. I contemplate the missionary in the relations of a *husband* and *father*. That he should generally go as a married man, is beyond all reasonable question. With an intelligent, pious, well-educated wife, having good health and a devoted spirit, his value as a missionary is greatly enhanced. She faces danger and endures hardship as well as he. Her courage, faith, and patience among barbarous heathens, fully equal her husband's, and her presence adds much to his safety, and the more if she have little children. When the wife proves unable to endure the exposures of the missionary life, if the medical opinion require a visit to this country, and the mission advise it, the executive committee seldom hesitates to afford the means for a return, and reasonable facilities, also, for a recovery of health. When a recovery is out of the question, such as

---

[3] "But ye say, If a man shall say to his father or mother, It is Corban, that is to say, a gift, by whatsoever thou mightest be profited by me, he shall go free," etc.

[4] William Milné joined Robert Morrison at Canton in 1813 and then transferred to Malacca to work among the Chinese there. —Ed.

would warrant a return to the mission, an honorable release is granted, and the missionary exercises his ministry in his native land. Some of the most esteemed of our home ministers have been of this class.

How is it with the children of missionaries? I am probably better informed on this subject than any other person, and I approach it with pleasure. I speak of the children after they have been separated from their parents, and brought to this country for education.

In continental tropical regions, there are reasons in the climate why children should be sent home; but in general they may be safely retained there until about the age of twelve years, in which time the very important result is secured, if it ever is, of impressing the parental relation strongly upon the mind and heart of the child. There are various reasons, besides climate, for sending the children home. By obtaining a part of their education here, they will be of far greater value as the probable successors of their parents in the missionary work. Indeed, a competent education for that service, or for any of the higher departments of a Christian life, cannot be well obtained either in India or China; and when the time comes for a transfer to the parental home, the parents, though weeping over the sacrifice, are ready, out of love to their offspring, to welcome it as a boon.

The time for sending the children home rests wholly with the parents, as also does the choice of a guardian; for it is expected that the parental authority will always be delegated by the parent to some one in this country. The expenses of the voyage are usually met by the missionary society, which also makes an annual grant to the child of about one hundred dollars until eighteen years of age, when applied for by the guardian. As the missionary society sustains an equal relation to all the returned children, and could not be at the expense of giving a liberal education to all, it is obviously precluded from making grants expressly for the education of any one at college. It aims to do just enough, as shown by experience, to secure a place for the returned children of missionaries in the great current of social life in this country, which bears along the children of Christian parents. It aims to do just enough to enable and induce relatives and friends to do the rest. More than this would tend to defeat the object of sending the children home. A permanent fund raised for this purpose, which some have urged, besides being unnecessary, would be detrimental in various respects to the best interests of the children. A separate school for them, which some have strongly recommended, would be a calamity, since they ought by all means to be educated along with other boys and girls, along with the young men and women of their generation. Missionaries would generally, and with good reason, oppose such a separation and isolation of their children.

I have made considerable progress in obtaining positive information as to the results of this system. Answers have been received to one hundred and eighty-four printed circulars sent to returned children above twelve years of age, or to their guardians. The age of the oldest of these is now almost fifty years, and their places of residence of course it is not always easy to ascertain. The number of males was ninety-five, and of females eighty-nine. Of the ninety-five males, seventy-one were reported to be members of churches; and of the eighty-nine females, seventy-eight were thus reported. That is to say, one hundred and forty-nine of the one hundred and eighty-four were church-members. Although the Board has never made a single grant, so far as I recollect, expressly for a college education, for the reason just stated, yet as many as fifty-one of the ninety-five males have received such an education, or are now receiving it; and thirty-one others are in academies, and believed to be generally preparing for college. That is to say, eighty-two of the ninety-five males are reported as having received, or as now receiving a liberal education; and thirteen of them have been or are now in the gospel ministry. Of the eighty-nine females, seventy-eight are reported as having received, or as now receiving, an education in academies or high schools; and thirteen of them are, or have been wives of missionaries. And I believe that responses from those not heard from, would vary but little from the reports already received.

These will probably be regarded as remarkable results, — superior, perhaps, to what we should find on a similar inquiry into the circumstances and history of any other class of children in our country; and they are directly referable to the providence and grace of God. How large a proportion of them we may number among the followers of the Lamb! How large a proportion receive the best education our country affords! And yet who is able to tell, in respect to most, in what manner all the expenses of their college or high school education have been met? We see clearly the hand of Him, who said, "Lo, I am with you always."

3. I next contemplate the missionary in his relations to his *Missionary Board*. The missionary has the same ecclesiastical liberty which pastors have at home; and he is, at the same time, as much under proper controlling influences. No body of ministers is more free, or under greater responsibility. I say this in view of the fundamental principle with which I started, that the missionary goes on his mission in the conscientious discharge of his personal duty of his Lord and Master. And I rejoice in being able to say, that, in this service, he is quite sure of what is or ought to be a comfortable support. The enterprise of the celebrated Müller, in England, is often spoken of as if it were peculiarly a work of faith. It does not seem to me to be so very peculiar in this

respect. That of the American Board, in appropriating half a million of dollars and more for an expenditure a year before it is received, is not less a work of faith. The trust in God is the same in nature, the same in degree; and so, substantially, is the use of means. This is true as to the support of every missionary. The pledge given by the missionary society of a support to its missionaries, is nothing more than the expression of an assured faith, that the means will be provided. The Board can give no more than it receives. There is no firm footing for the society, or for its missionaries, except in the promise of the great Lord of all. If the missionary feels sure of a support, it is for precisely the reason that is said to animate the celebrated philanthropist just named.

I believe there has been no case in the experience of the American Board, where the missionary has failed to receive his full salary, nor do I believe there ever will be. The ground of this confidence is in faith; strengthened indeed by a long experience, and by the well-known fact in missions to foreign heathen lands, that such a support is essential to their existence. Nor do I believe it will ever be found more difficult than it has been heretofore, to provide for the returned disabled missionary, and for the missionary widow. As for the returned children of missionaries, I cannot doubt that a way will ere long be devised, with but little actual increase of expense, to enable every missionary, acting through his relatives and friends, or in coöperation with them, to take the whole arrangement for the education of his children in this country into his own hands, just as ministers do who are in the pastoral office at home.

I next inquire, how it is with the missionary when no longer able to labor in his field. The case differs from that of the pastor at home chiefly in this, that the Executive Committee of the Board, perhaps without having greater power than parishes generally have to do what is equitable in the case, has yet a stronger disposition so to do. Each case is treated on its own individual merits, with the intention always to what is equitable. There is sometimes a difference of opinion between the missionary and his mission, and sometimes between the missionary and his committee; but in all cases, so far as I recollect, where an appeal was made to the public judgment, the final result has been, substantially, with the mission, and with the committee. I fear as much as this can hardly be said of parishes here at home as a general fact, nor even of churches, in relation to their dismissed pastors.

The case of returned widows is the most difficult to treat, because they so easily pass out from observation, and this is most true of the more meritorious among them. Nevertheless I believe, that as a class, they are, to say the least, as much favored as are the widows of pastors at home. Some persons have advocated the raising of a fund for their support; and such a fund could be raised. But it would injure the Board, without being of use to them. The possession, by the Missionary Board, of a greater amount of permanent funds than is actually needed for its credit in the world of commerce, would weaken that principle of faith, on which so much depends. And where it is a fact, that as much is allowed to widows, all things considered, as ought to be, to aid them in serving the Lord Jesus in their widowed state, then it would not be expected that they should receive a greater amount, were there a widow's fund. Nor would grants made to them from such a fund be any less a charity than they are under the present arrangement. Nor, in either case, would it be more a charity than our blessed Lord submitted to during his whole public ministry on earth. And the servant is not above his Lord.

After carefully examining the experience of the American Board from the commencement of its operations, I have no hesitation in affirming, that the widows of missionaries have been as kindly cared for, as a class, as are the widows of pastors in this country; and I could use even stronger language, were it needful.

The result of my observation on this whole subject, during the past five and forty years, is, that the relation between the missionary and his Board is one of great mutual satisfaction; though of course not without its share of the misapprehensions and trials which are incident to every sphere of human life.

4. We come next to the relations sustained by the missionary to his *mission*. In the mission he belongs to a self-governing republic, where every man has an equal vote, and where the majority rules; with the right, however (which is very rarely exercised), of an appeal to the Prudential Committee, and ultimately to the Board. Years ago, a certain mission was much afflicted by divided counsels among its members, and the cause was not apparent. It was at length ascertained, that this was the result of a want of a proper division of labor among the several missionaries. The missionaries had not a sufficient weight of responsibility resting upon them individually. This principle, in its relations to missions, was then somewhat of a discovery, and has since been acted on with the most happy results. When missionaries have been trained to feel fully the moral responsibility of a majority vote (as it has been found that Europeans, from a deficiency in their early education, seldom are), and when each has a sufficient pressure of duty, this method of organizing missions works exceedingly well.

The policy of the American Board is, to throw all possible responsibility upon the mission thus organized. The mission is not, however, in a technical sense, an ecclesiastical body. It is simply a mission acting under the commission of our blessed Lord, with liberty to do what is needful for its greatest success. Of course there is, as there ought to be, much room for the exercise of a wise discretion, and for the development of experience. We have been learning, during the fifty or sixty years past, in what manner a mission should be worked, but probably have yet more to learn. We have learned this: that particular forms of ecclesiastical machinery, because they work well at home, are not therefore to be regarded as exactly the thing to be set up in young Christian communities formed in heathen lands; and precisely what the modifications should be, is still an open question. We have learned, moreover, that matters of this sort should be mainly left to the discretion of missionaries in the field. They have liberty to form associations, or presbyteries, as they feel the need of them; yet since their financial questions all belong to the mission as such, and since most of the questions that arise have more or less connection with finance, their social life is very much in the meetings of the mission, or of its committees. Moreover, it is a fundamental principle, in the system of missions now under special contemplation, that ecclesiastical bodies for native churches and pastors, should be exclusively for them; the missionaries sustaining to them only the relation of advisors.

Of course the relations of missionaries to their missions in no degree affect their relations to their ecclesiastical bodies at home. The Board may dismiss a missionary for malpractice, but cannot depose him from the ministry; yet the ecclesiastical body at home may call upon the Board for the facts within its knowledge, when investigating the conduct of a missionary to learn whether he should be deposed from the ministry.

I should add, that missionary societies and the missions, though technically speaking not ecclesiastical bodies, have become (as has been elsewhere affirmed) a component part of the great modern structure of the Christian Church, as it is being organized under God's providence, for the conversion of the world; and they should be permitted to sustain the responsibilities and perform the duties, that are essential to the successful prosecution of the missionary work on the broad scale of the world.

5. We next contemplate the missionary in his relations to the *people for whom he labors*. He is an ambassador from the Sovereign Lord to benighted men in a state of rebellion, with a message of mercy. And it seems reasonable to suppose, after he has acquired the language of the people, that no elaborate process of education is needful to make the people understand his message. Many of the earlier missionaries thought otherwise; and it would be easy to find statements, by eminent men now in the "Better Land," showing how the heathen must be elaborately

educated into the Christian import of the words God, sin, holiness, and other similar terms, before they will be able to comprehend the gospel message. There is something in this, if the gospel message is to be conveyed to the heathen simply through a process of education. But the heathen *know* that they are sinners; they have a conscience; and if boldly and affectionately approached by one whose own heart is full of the subject, and solemnly assured of their lost condition as sinners, and of the free salvation offered them through the Lord Jesus Christ, experience has abundantly shown, that there is no way so effectual as this of securing the aid of the Holy Spirit for their conversion. The gospel may have direct access to the most debased heathen mind. Of this there is evidence in the abounding proofs of the success of missions. We see it in Sierra Leone, among the Karens and Shanars of India, in Madagascar, in South Africa, and on the Pacific Islands. The especial demand in missions for education and for books comes *after* the attention has been arrested, and more especially for converts, and for such as are being trained for the gospel ministry. Nothing precedes of necessity the simple declaration of salvation through the cross of Christ, when it comes from lips that have been touched with a coal from off the altar of God.

6. I now contemplate the missionary simply as a *man*. And, first, as to the influence of the missionary life on his mental development. I believe there is as much of this development in missionaries, as there is in the home ministry; and the question I raise is only how this is possible in circumstances apparently so unfavorable. I account for it by the fact, that, with the more intelligent missionaries, the pressure is not less upon the mental faculties, than it is in the pastoral office at home; and this is as true in the more barbarous heathen countries, as it is in the more civilized. I even think, that the mental pressure upon the intelligent and conscientious missionary is often greater than it is upon his brethren at home. For he finds that there is everything to be done, and that he is the only one to do it. He must be feet to the lame, eyes to the blind, ears to the deaf, and must almost reconstruct the intellect, and almost recreate the conscience. Did this responsibility come upon the missionary all at once, he could not bear it; but come it will, sooner or later, and the intelligent and faithful missionary need fear no loss of stimulus to his mind. It is the same that operated on the mind and heart of the apostle to the Gentiles; and it will increase with his years, especially in its demands upon the judging and administrative powers.

How is it with the influence of the missionary life upon the happiness of the missionary? Among the more than four hundred ordained missionaries, with whom I have sustained an intimate official relation, there have been cases of extreme sorrow; arising from early prostration of the health, from the predominance of morbid sensibilities, from failure to acquire the language, and other causes. But these have been the exceptions, not the rule. The missionaries as a body have been happy in the field and work of their choice. They have seemed to me, when among them at their several homes, both men and women, to be the happiest clerical families, as a whole, within my knowledge. There is no way of accounting for this, but in the fulfillment of the Saviour's promise. For it is a fact that missionaries, being far away from civilized Christian society, experience a certain degree of loss in the diminished pressure of a wholesome public opinion, which surrounds and sustains us in Christian lands like an atmosphere; thus creating a need of more grace to insure right feeling and living, than is required at home. Nor do I believe that any Protestant missionary, without this special grace, is likely to persevere in his mission. But the grace that is needed is usually imparted; and if sacrifices are demanded, there is a pleasure in making them for Christ which is proportioned to the sacrifice. That missionary mother, parting with her child on the Burman shore, when she raised her hand to heaven and exclaimed, "O Saviour, I do this for thee!" must have felt a joy at that moment, rising above her grief, akin to that of the martyr at the stake. And what joy had Sarah Lanman Smith, dying in Western Asia, when she declared that, for the world, she would not lay her remains anywhere but there on missionary ground.

And this leads me to speak, finally, of the influence of the missionary life on the piety of the missionary. For the reason just now stated, more strength of piety is required to be a good missionary among the heathen, than to be a good pastor at home. I do not claim for missionaries a more perfect exhibition of the Christian life, than is seen in the home ministry; but since, in their exposed circumstances, they need a higher and firmer tone of the inward Christian life, I think that, through divine grace, they have it. I believe that is the impression made by them, as a class, in their visits to this country. At any rate, that is the impression they have made upon me.

I have long been impressed with the general character of missionary death-beds. The love of native land and of the friends in that land, is not diminished by distance and the lapse of time, and death sometimes comes early to the missionary, and unexpectedly, and in circumstances of great discomfort; yet I recall no case of regret expressed at meeting it, by the missionary or his wife, under any circumstances on missionary ground. The sentiment expressed by Mrs. Smith, has been the common sentiment with missionaries; and the venerable Allen Graves, when he came from India, many years ago, for the benefit of his health, and found that he must die, proffered a request through me, that he might be allowed to return to India and die there, which request was granted.

Harriet Newell, when told, on the Isle of France, that she was soon to leave the world, exclaimed, "Joyful news! I long to depart." The last audible words of Levi Parsons, dying in Egypt, were, "The angel of the Lord encampeth round about them that fear him." Mrs. Poor's dying words in Ceylon were, "Glory to God the Father, to God the Son, to God the Holy Ghost" — words, it may be, among the first she uttered on reaching the heavenly world. And her venerated husband, dying many years after, whispered, as he closed his eyes on earth, "Joy! Joy! Hallelujah!" "If *this* be the *dark valley*," said the excellent Mrs. Hervey, dying soon after her arrival in India, "there is no darkness in it; all is light — light!"

And the cases might be easily multiplied of calm, peaceful trust in Christ in the dying hour, of a tranquil hope of immortality, and of gratitude for the privilege of living and dying in the work of missions.

I may not close without a few suggestions, which are needed to prevent misapprehension.

As I have stated the case, the support of the foreign missionary and his family is more nearly a uniform and adequate supply of their temporal wants, than is generally enjoyed by ministers and their families in this country. The final cause for this, in the ordering of Divine Providence, would seem to be, that the prosecution of missions among heathen nations by married missionaries, would not otherwise be a possibility. How could a missionary, with wife and children, as human nature is, possibly keep the field in a tropical region, surrounded by a half civilized, unsympathizing, heathen people, with only a partial or uncertain support? Very different would it be, were he anywhere within the bounds of his native land, in a community homogeneous with himself, where only a few years are needed for the incoming of civilization to develop a congenial home for his family; and still more, were he laboring in an already matured and well-organized Christian community. A mission composed of married missionaries does indeed cost considerably more than would a mission composed of unmarried missionaries; yet such a mission is so much more effective abroad, and so much more interesting at home, that it is easier, in point of fact, to obtain the means of supporting it from the churches, than it would be to support a mission of unmarried missionaries. An adequate support is believed to be an essential thing in foreign Protestant missions, since on no other supposition would such missions be possible on an extended scale.

Yet it is by no means true, as is often asserted, and as is perhaps generally believed, that the trials of the home missionary life are greater than those to which the foreign missionary is subjected. I do not undervalue the trials of the home missionary. My habit for many years has been carefully to note them, as set forth, monthly, by the Home

Missionary Society; and they are a noble testimony to the self-consecration and zeal of that enterprising, devoted, and most useful and essential body of Christian ministers. But the most painful trials of gospel ministers, whether pastors or missionaries, are those which appertain to their spiritual vocation; and here the foreign missionary must be the greater sufferer. I have long ceased to expect a foreign missionary to persevere in his work, who does not enter upon it as a life of faith, and with a certain amount of physical, mental, and moral adaptation. Mere philosophers will not go on such missions, and mere philanthropists would not remain long, should they happen to go. Impulsive, unreflecting piety will give out before the day of embarkation, or retire ere the language has been acquired, or the battle has fairly begun. Fine conceptions of the beautiful in social life, glowing apprehensions of pastoral duty, broad and elevated views of the nature and relations of theological truth, are not sufficient to give enduring life to the zeal of a missionary. Something more than all this is needed. There must be the grand aim, the living, undying purpose, of reconciling men to God, and thus extending the kingdom of the blessed Redeemer. There needs to be a real enthusiasm, sustained by a spiritualized doctrinal experience, and by the "powers of the world to come." Nothing short of this will keep the foreign missionary cheerfully and long in the field.

And even with such missionaries, — who are men after all, — it would be disastrous for a mission, should a well-founded apprehension come over it of failure in the temporal support of their families. And it is a great mercy to the heathen world, and to the churches as bound to publish the gospel through the whole extent of that world, that the providence and grace of God, in the experience of the past fifty years, afford a wonderful guarantee for the earthly support of the missionary and his wife and children. It is one of the significant facts of our times, for which we should ascribe glory to God.

Selection 14

THE MARRIAGE OF MISSIONARIES[1]

A more convenient opportunity than the present may not occur, for stating some of the grounds on which pious females are justified in going on foreign missions as the wives of missionaries.

The missionary, whose duty it is to explore a country, should in general remain unmarried till this service has been completed. "It is obvious too," to use the language of one of the older American missions in a recent communication, "that the cares and duties of married missionaries must interfere with journeys, the supervision of scattered schools, and the like, and that this interference will be much greater among a barbarous or semi-barbarous people than in christian lands. A class of laborers therefore is needed, who may find homes in the families of married missionaries and enjoy all their advantages, without being entangled with the cares which families necessarily produce. There might be one or two unmarried missionaries connected with every considerable station. These, without embarrassment of any kind, might take a wide range, visit schools wherever established, hold meetings wherever practicable, distribute books and tracts, collect information, watch for opening doors, and act the part of the vanguard and scouting parties of an army. Such men, when worn down with labors or attacked by diseases, will have comfortable homes to which they may retreat for assistance and refreshment. Missionaries of this class would have many

[1] *An Introductory Essay on the Marriage of Missionaries,* by Rev. R. Anderson; pp. vii-xx in *Memoir of Mrs. Mary Mercy Ellis, wife of Rev. William Ellis,* etc., by Rev. William Ellis; Boston: Crocker & Brewster, and N.Y.: Leavitt, Lord; 1836. See also "Marriage of Missionaries," in ABCFM, *Annual Report, 1842,* pp. 42-44. William Ellis was a noted missionary of the London Missionary Society in Tahiti and Madagascar and a secretary of the Society.

important opportunities for doing good denied to such as are confined at home by the cares of a family."

But generally, it is not good for the missionary to be alone. In most instances those who reside permanently in one place should be married men, and for the following reasons.

1. The reasons which make it proper and expedient for ministers at home to marry, all apply to the case of the missionary. As a man he possesses the same nature, and it is no better for him to be alone than it is for them. Nor are his circumstances better fitted to reconcile him to the monastic life. They will rather give strength to that powerful law of nature which is operative alike in all countries and classes of people, producing the family state. It might seem indeed, that the perpetual cheerlessness of his habitation would urge him, as a christian, to more frequent and intimate communion with his Savior, than is common with married men; but experience has long since demonstrated the cloister not to be the most favorable place for meditation, prayer, and a close walk with God. Indeed there are no reasons in favor of marriage in the minister who remains at home, which do not apply generally to the minister when sent abroad as a missionary. Regarding the wife as a friend, counsellor, companion, the repository of her husband's thoughts and feelings, the partaker of his joys, the sharer of his cares and sorrows, and one who is to lighten his toils, and become his nurse in sickness; the missionary needs such a helper far more than the minister. If he be going to reside among a savage people not migratory in their habits, he ought then always to be accompanied by a wife. The uncivilized character of the people, instead of being a reason why he should not be married, is in all ordinary cases a conclusive reason why he should be so. His wife if judiciously chosen, will endure privations and encounter dangers with as much cheerfulness and fortitude as he, and among savages woman is the best earthly protector. No weapon of war should ever be seen in the hands or about the person of the missionary, and no symbol of peace is so significant or so well understood and appreciated by savages, as the presence of wives and children. Female missionaries in considerable numbers have gone among untutored pagans within thirty years past, yet I recollect no case in which the hand of licentious violence has been laid upon them. Their persons have been inviolate, and they have often proved safe-guards to their husbands. Moreover, in a barbarous or semi-barbarous country it is impossible for the missionary to secure regularity and comfort in his establishment, and such food, clothing, and retirement as habit has made necessary, without female assistance. In supplying his personal wants, he will be subjected to great disadvantages and loss of precious time, and the loneliness and

vexations of his situation will waste his spirits, curtail his efforts, perhaps shorten his days.

In a word, woman was made for man, and as a general thing man cannot be placed where he can long do without her assistance. You cannot educate him so that it shall be natural for him to live alone. It is vain to say that a missionary ought to obtain a victory over his nature and rise above his circumstances. God never designed that any *class* of men should be able to obtain such a victory. The desire for the marriage state is a part of the original constitution of human nature, and not a perversion of it. The married state is the natural state of man, and the missionary, if a resident in one place and sustained by the presence of a suitable wife, will bear up better against adverse circumstances than one who is unmarried, will be more of a man, a better Christian, a more contented, zealous, faithful, useful missionary.

All this is generally true. It is important truth the force of which should be admitted, and no unreasonable objections should be made to the marriage of missionaries to heathen lands. The holy and blessed enterprise of protestant missions must not be spoiled by introducing into it the monastic principles of the Romish church. Yet it is important to repeat, that there are circumstances and parts of the service which render it good for missionaries to follow the example of the great apostle to the Gentiles; as, for instance, where they will be exposed to persecution as he was, as may be the case in China and Japan; where they will be perpetually traversing large countries; or even where itinerating on a more limited scale is to be their principal employment. In these circumstances a single life, if voluntarily assumed and with due reflection, may be greatly promotive of the cause.

The examples of merchants and other secular men, who go and reside abroad in great numbers unmarried for the sake of emolument or honor, will not be adduced in favor of unmarried life in missionaries by those, who know the lamentable extent to which this class of men violates the laws of purity; and besides, they generally go with the expectation of returning after a few years to their native lands. Missionaries should not ordinarily be led into such temptations; and experience has fully shown the inexpediency of sending them forth for a limited period of time. Few missionaries will bring all their powers into action, acquire the language thoroughly, feel as devoted to the cause, and labor as faithfully, on a limited term of service, as when they engage in it for life.

2. The heathen should have an opportunity of seeing christian families. The domestic constitution among them is dreadfully disordered, and yet it is as true there as every where else, that the character

of society is formed in the family. To rectify it requires example as well as precept. The missionary must be able to illustrate the duties of the family state by means of his own household. Where the wife is a degraded slave having no conception of a better destiny, she will need to be taught everything that goes to constitute the virtuous, useful, praiseworthy wife and mother. And who shall instruct her? In what manner shall the images of domestic order, neatness, comfort, and whatever else sheds beauty and sweetness over domestic life, be imparted to her mind? She must have female teachers, living illustrations. She must see these things exemplified in actual life. And the christian wife, mother, husband, father, family, must all be found in all our missions to pagan and Mohammedan countries.

3. The wife of the missionary may be expected to exert much influence in the department of education. The centre of her appropriate sphere is, indeed, within the domestic circle. The care of her household is the duty, to which all others must be subservient. This is the scriptural view of her peculiar responsibilities under all possible circumstances. And in countries, where are no faithful servants; no mother, aunt, sister, or female friend to reside in the family and assist in its duties; no village school to instruct her children and take the oversight of them during the greater portion of each day; her domestic cares will often make severe demands upon her time and strength. Yet, with a common measure of health and in ordinary circumstances, she may exert a propitious influence over the whole extent of infant and female education, especially if she made herself familiar with the subject before leaving her native land. An infant school may rise and flourish under her personal instruction. Schools of this description belong almost exclusively to the female, and perhaps they are the sphere in which mothers, having little children of their own, can operate to the best advantage. These schools have not yet been thoroughly tried in heathen lands, except in South Africa where they are said to have been signally successful. But there can be no doubt of the importance of commencing the religious education of heathen children everywhere at a very early age, before the mind is pre-occupied and perverse habits are formed. Could infant schools become general and successful among all heathen nations, they would shorten the work of missions by one or two generations. It is for the female missionary to search out and collect the young children for these schools, and to shed a softening, subduing influence over their dispositions and manners, and impress religious truth, with the aid of the blessed Spirit, upon their hearts and consciences. The whole business of female education, whatever be the nature of the schools or the ages of the pupils, should be to a consider-

able extent under the presiding influence of the female members of the mission. It has been urged upon missionary societies to send out unmarried females for this purpose; which of course would imply the existence of families where these could find a home. Few however appear to be aware of the difficulties in the way of placing the single female in circumstances to live and labor happily in pagan lands. The difficulties cannot be stated here. The result to which missionary societies and missionaries generally have been conducted is, that unmarried females should rarely be sent on missions, except in connection with families to which they are related by the ties of nature or of intimate and endeared friendship, and where it is known they would be received gladly as permanent members of the family. If this rule is departed from, it should only be in compliance with the wishes of some particular family or missionary station, and the person should be selected as far as may be in the manner they shall propose.

The result on the whole is, that while many unmarried women, as well as men, will find their way into the field and become useful members of missions, the great proportion of the laborers of both sexes will be married. Of course the married females will have the greater responsibility resting upon them, to see that the female portion of the heathen world receives proper attention. They must exert themselves to the utmost. More attention must be paid to their education before they enter upon their missions. Education is becoming a science, an art, a profession; and they must study the science, practise the art, and become interested in the profession. They should be familiar with the most approved modes of teaching, with the best books, the choicest apparatus. The more they know about school-teaching in its several varieties, and about the helps to instruction which modern science and ingenuity have devised, the easier will it be for them to labor effectively, and the stronger motive will they feel to make exertions in this department of usefulness, notwithstanding the pressure of domestic cares. The obstacles to such efforts are fewer in some countries, and the influence of female missionaries beyond the domestic circle has also been greater, than in others. At the Sandwich Islands more than a dozen of the married female missionaries are regular instructors of female schools, some of which are numerously attended and by women as well as children. In Ceylon the late Mrs. Winslow exerted an admirable influence over a charity boarding-school of native females. And Mrs. Thomson who died not long since in Jerusalem, having been a successful teacher of a female seminary in this country carried all her zeal in behalf of female education with her to Palestine, and no doubt would soon have presided over a flourishing school of females in that land, had not a mysterious Providence seen fit so early to remove her. There are now two female schools in Syria, one of Arab girls taught by a married female, the other of Druse girls on Mount Lebanon taught by the exemplary widow of a missionary not long since deceased. Making all due allowances for the circumstances of married females, it is unquestionably true that their influence on female education at the several missions would be far greater than it is, if as a body they had been better acquainted with the subject of education and more interested in it before leaving their native land. A similar remark might be made in respect to the lay teachers, who have been employed in American missions to the heathen. In this view the attempts which are now made to render school-teaching a profession in the same general sense that the preaching of the gospel is one, and to educate a numerous body of male and female teachers expressly for the instruction of schools, are full of promise for the heathen world. The knowledge thus diffused will in process of time develop a power to do good, which but few of the married females and few of the lay assistants now among the heathen have imagined that they possess.

4. The opinion of missionaries themselves on this subject is entitled to consideration. Melville Horne, in his eloquent letters on missions,[2] advocates a life of celibacy for missionaries, but on mistaken grounds. Swartz,[3] who was never married, was of opinion that missionaries would be most useful in the single state; yet the greater part of his associates, notwithstanding the force of his opinion, were married men. Swartz himself was probably more useful in the state of celibacy, than he would have been in the other. He was every way an extraordinary man; and so, it is needless to remark, was the apostle Paul. But even Paul claimed the right, although a missionary to the heathen, "to lead about a sister, a wife, as well as other apostles, and as the brethren of the Lord, and Cephas." The opinion of missionaries at the present day is, that the missionary ought generally to be a married man; and this opinion has been gaining strength, not only among them, but also among their directors, for the last five and twenty years.

The grand objection to the marriage of missionaries, is the necessity of sending so great a proportion of their children for education to this country. This was the subject of a lengthened and earnest correspondence with the American missionaries in Ceylon for six years, before the point was conceded to them by their society. It was yielded upon full

---

[2] *Letters on Missions Addressed to the Protestant Ministers of the British Churches,* by Melville Horne, Chaplain of Sierra Leone, was published in London in 1794 and powerfully stimulated interest in missions. —Ed.

[3] Christian Friedrich Schwartz "of Tanjore," Danish-Halle Mission pioneer in South India, from 1750 to death in 1798. —Ed.

conviction, that the views of the missionaries were substantially correct and their requests reasonable. The principal objections urged against the sending of children to this country were concisely these; — that one of the first principles of human society requires children to be generally educated near their parents and within reach of parental influence; that the children would not here find a competent guardianship; that the parents would be prone to leave their work and follow them; that what was done for the children of one mission must be done for all in similar circumstances; that the expenses would probably be greater than the churches would willingly sustain; and that the general return of the children of missionaries would create a prejudice in the public mind against the marriage of missionaries. The first proposal of the missionaries was, to have a seminary founded in this country expressly for the education of children thus returned. This they at length abandoned, as being evidently inexpedient and unwise. In reply to objections, they alleged, that their circumstances were extraordinary; that their children after having attained to a certain age would be better taken care of by friends, and even by strangers, in America, than they could be by their parents amid the appalling vices of Hindoo society; that missionaries would be more inclined to remain in the field, if their children were allowed to be sent home for education and if need be for settlement, than if such permission were withheld; that justice should at all events be done to all missionaries; that the liabilities of the Society for the expenses of the children would be less if they were sent home, than if they were to remain with the mission, and that this fact being known, the churches would not object on the ground of expense; and that if it were an evil to send out missionaries as married men, it would be a greater evil, as a general thing, to send them unmarried to such a country as India. They also urged, that there was no room for their children and their descendants to settle in India; that their children could not there find suitable employment; that they could not generally obtain the means of subsistence; that they could not be properly educated; that they could not form suitable connections in marriage; that they would not be prepared to continue the mission; and that their moral and religious character would be exposed to imminent danger.

The argument based on these propositions was deemed conclusive in respect to the Ceylon mission, and of course all other missions similarly situated; and the Board of Missions, after correspondence with English societies on the subject, adopted rules and regulations accordingly.

Granting that the children will generally return to this country for education and even for settlement, would the marriage of missionaries on that account be an evil? Those who have given most thought to the subject and are best acquainted with its nature and bearings, are by no means of this opinion. No evils in practice have yet resulted from missionaries having the right to send their children home. The parents labor as contentedly and faithfully after their children have left them, as they did before. There has been no increase of expense to the treasury, nor will there be any while the patrons of the cause continue to be disposed to befriend the children. And surely that must be a delightful and most useful charity which, by receiving and educating the child, leaves the devoted parents at greater liberty to spend and be spent in direct labors abroad for the conversion of the heathen to God. If the children are with their parents until they are ten or twelve years old, as most of them will be, the pagan world will not lose the christian examples of missionaries as parents. The children will remain long enough for this purpose, and missionaries will ordinarily have some of their children with them as long as they live. And will not many of the pious among the children of missionaries, after having completed their education, be powerfully drawn by the combined influence of love to Christ, the heathen, and their parents, to return as missionaries or assistant missionaries to the countries of their birth? Should they do this, the increased value of their services and influence above what it could have been had they remained with their parents, will be ample compensation for the cost of their visit to the land of their fathers.

Another objection to the marriage of missionaries is found in the supposed condition of their widows. The widow of the missionary is indeed entitled peculiarly to the sympathies, prayers, and if need be to the assistance, of the churches. These she will be as likely to have as the widows of ministers at home; and having them, the prospect of widowhood is but little more an objection in the one case, than in the other. There is this difference, however; the missionary has no opportunity to accumulate property, at least the American missionary has none; while the minister at home may have, to some extent, and of this his widow will enjoy the benefit. But if the Lord of missions, by means of his church, by blessing the personal efforts of the missionary's widow to be useful, or in any other way, provide for her necessary wants, will not his promises be fulfilled, and can anything more be demanded? There is no reason to apprehend that the widows of missionaries, who continue to act upon the principles of their high profession after their return and make no unreasonable demands on the churches, will suffer from want of friends to relieve their temporal necessities. With peculiar energy can they lay hold on the promises of God, and they shall find all his promises "yea and amen" in Him, in whose service their husbands were faithful unto death. Many of them, it should be remembered, will continue to reside and labor in connection with the mission, and will there be supported as are the other missionaries.

I close these general remarks with an extract from an unpublished letter of a married missionary who has been many years in the field. He describes what the wife of a missionary ought to be.

"It is not exegesis, it is not theology, it is not philosophy, it is not divinity, it is not law, it is not precept or command, which the people need; but it is the gospel, the pure gospel, which they want all day long. It is Christianity embodied, acted out, living, breathing. The missionary's wife, as well as himself, should be a sort of moving commentary on the Bible; every thing she says or does should remind the hearer or beholder of something in the Bible; her whole life should be altogether a New Testament life. The whole spirit of the New Testament should be inhaled, and the whole spirit of the New Testament should be breathed, in every breath."

INDEX

219

BIBLICAL REFERENCES

Date Due